Crossing the Road to Entrepreneurship

by Bert L. Wolstein

Written with Adam Snyder

LCCN: 2004096195

ISBN: 0-9760832-0-5

To Iris,
my partner, my guide, my love
since 1946

"This book provides an unusual look into the life and career of an entrepreneur who realizes that his success is due to factors beyond just his personal skills. Bart Wolstein explores a multifaceted life of fulfillment that can be achieved by a true entrepreneur. It is a must read for anyone trying to understand how and why some entrepreneurs are able to achieve success in both life and business."

—Joe Alutto, Dean,
The Fisher College of Business
at The Ohio State University

"Bart Wolstein knows the sacrifices required to achieve your dreams, to become your own man, and to create your own destiny. However, a truly successful man doesn't sacrifice one dream for the other, but manages to achieve success in both business and life and make it appear easy."

—David Simon, Chief Executive Officer,
Simon Property Group, Inc.

"There are lessons to be learned from reading this book. One of the greatest is that with wealth and power comes responsibility. Henry Ford once said, "The highest use of capital is not to make money, but to make money do more for the betterment of life." I admire Bart Wolstein as a businessman. I respect and admire him even more for his philanthropy. In this book you'll learn why, with the great entrepreneurs, the two go hand in hand."

—Fred C. Rothstein, MD, President and
Chief Executive Officer, University Hospitals of Cleveland

"Bart Wolstein is a master entrepreneur. He started with nothing and eventually amassed a real estate empire with his own, unique entrepreneurial approach. Learn how he did it and how you can apply his strategies to your own business and life. It is equally impressive to me that Bart and his wife, Iris, continue their success in the commitment to their philanthropic work as well."

—Michael Bolton, Singer and Entertainer

"Bart Wolstein thinks big and perseveres when others would falter. This book details how he built a successful business empire and a lifelong partnership with his wife, Iris."

—Susan Dean
Executive Director, United Cerbral Palsy

Dedication

I simply wish to thank the thousands from the Cleveland community, the country, and, yes, the world, for the outpouring of love and admiration bestowed upon my family and me after Bart's passing on May 17, 2004. I thank the bugle player who volunteered to play taps at the cemetery, the OSU football player who sent a fruit basket with kind words, and the many unknowns who sent cards, though they never met Bart. I thank those who worked with him and those against him. And I thank those who loved him near and far.

I am happy that Bart was able to read the final manuscript of his book before his passing, but remorseful that he never saw the final product you hold in your hands today. It memorializes what so many of you have recognized—the humanity, the greatness, the integrity, the generosity and the brilliance of this man, my husband, my hero, Bart Wolstein.

Iris Wolstein

Acknowledgments

I want to express my thanks to those core group of people who spent the time to review the many drafts of this manuscript. Their support and specific suggestions were invaluable. Our regular "readers" included my son, Scott; John McGill; Mohsen Anvari, the former Dean of the Weatherhead School of Management; Gary Previts, Weatherhead's Associate Dean for Undergraduate Studies; Tina Stephan, Jim Miller; and Jon L. Iveson PhD.

Also special thanks for those people who graciously agreed to be interviewed by Adam Snyder:

Al Adams	Bobby Goldberg	Frank Moss
Mohsen Anvari	Tim Grendell	George Nanchoff
Blake Baird	George Hasman	Scott Pember
Rob Benjamin	Jon Iveson	Dick Perlmuter
Hall Baetz	Jim Karabec	Tony Sasala, Jr.
Sonny Booth	Ali Kazemani	Tony Sasala, Sr.
Richard Bowen	George Kimson	Dr. Morton Sass
Ben Cappadora	Robert King	Jim Scarpone
Rabbi Armand Cohen	Brad Kowit	Jim Schoff
John Collier	Greg Levy	Roy Sea
Eddie Davis	Timo Liekoski	Bob Shemory
Susan Dean	Frank Mancine	Walter Teninga
Richard DeLatt	Steve Marton	Judy Thurber
Frank Doctor	John McGill	Jim Tressel
Paul Donahue	Joe Migliorini	Tina Stephan
William Dorsky	Jim Miller	Myron Vernis
Art Fitzmartin	Michael Miller	Larry Weiss
Don France	Jim Mirgliotta	Scott Wolstein
Jim Fritsch	Carlos Molina	Iris Wolstein
Paul Garofolo	Carlton Moody	Ken Young

And finally, particular thanks to Adam Snyder, who wrote this manuscript and sat with me for hundreds of hours listening to my tale.

Table of Contents

Foreword
by Scott A. Wolstein

 My father could sell ice to the Eskimos. How? First, the Eskimos would take a liking to him and they wouldn't want to disappoint him. Second, my father would convince them that the ice he was selling was something they couldn't live without. And, finally, he wouldn't take no for an answer.

After all, is selling ice to the Eskimos so hard when you have sold 1,000 homes in Twinsburg, Ohio twenty years before its time, or when you have sold thousands of season tickets and dozens of sponsorship packages to an indoor soccer team, or when you have sold sites for hundreds of luxury homes and country club memberships to a golf club on the site of an abandoned seminary in North Canton, Ohio? I could go on and on. Suffice it to say that my father is the most effective salesman I have ever witnessed.

What enables an individual from humble beginnings and no real advantages to become so effective? What are the ingredients that enable someone to fashion such a remarkable career as an entrepreneur? This book provides some insights and answers to these questions, but first, allow me to share my own views from my own very unique perspective.

First, what is an entrepreneur? According to the dictionary, an entrepreneur is "one who organizes and directs a business undertaking, assuming the risk for the sake of profit." My father is surely this, but he is also so much more.

On a lark, I also looked up the word "charisma" and I hit the nail more squarely on the head: "a special quality of leadership that captures the popular imagination and inspires unswerving allegiance and devotion." That is my father: a charismatic entrepreneur. It is this charismatic quality, combined with an incredibly intense passion to succeed, that has enabled my father to accomplish such great things. When he sits in a meeting, he controls the room. He commands respect and attention from everyone at the table. When he speaks, people listen.

My father has always been able to assemble a team with "unswerving allegiance and devotion." He builds a team, not based on their knowledge and experience, but rather on their desire to succeed and their willingness to learn. And many have blossomed under his tutelage, and have produced for him.

Many believe that the success of an entrepreneur is primarily derived from a unique "idea" or invention. To be sure, my father has had some innovative ideas in his career. Arguably, he is the brainchild behind the modern community shopping center anchored by a discount department store. After all, he was the first to convince Kmart (the Wal-Mart of the 1960s and 1970s) to locate within a multi-tenant shopping center, which was revolutionary at the time. But in my father's case, I don't think his success has derived from his ideas, but rather from his extraordinary execution of those ideas. He's never picked easy projects. Often, he embarks on new undertakings solely on instinct or a feeling in his gut that they can be successful, rather than on extensive research or analysis. In fact, in many ways I think the bigger the challenge, the more he enjoys it.

No, his success is a result of execution. He is quick to make decisions and he has the courage of his convictions. Once he has set his course, he will not be deterred. He pursues success with an unbridled passion and an absolute refusal to fail. Failure simply cannot be tolerated. To say he is relentless is an understatement. No task is beneath him. His business is his life. Whatever deal he is working on consumes him 24 hours a day, 7 days a week. His friendships nearly all come from his associations in business.

Even when he is on vacation on the other side of the world, my father demands that his employees track him down and keep him informed. Even that is not enough. After a week or so, he can't wait to get back to the office. And when he travels with my mother, he is never really away from the office, because my mother is intimately involved in every aspect of his undertakings. In fact, she is an integral part of his success. She brings a unique sense of style and an absolute demand for quality to everything they do together. It is this quality and her pursuit of perfection that combines with my father's unparalleled intensity that creates spectacular projects. Their relationship is truly extraordinary. They are soul mates in every way and they make a remarkable team.

What fuels my father's intense drive to succeed, this refusal to fail? I think it derives from his childhood, from growing up on the other side of the tracks. His entire career has been about proving to everyone, including himself, that he is just as good as the "other guys" who grew up on the right side of the tracks. The great irony is that he is not just "as good." He is better. Unlike them, he has done it the hard way. He started with nothing. He overcame great obstacles.

The further irony is that if he ever felt like he was truly accepted and appreciated by the "other guys," the establishment, he would probably lose his remarkable intensity. Like Samson after his famous haircut from Delilah, the power that drives him would be gone. While he claims to crave that acceptance and appreciation, deep down I think he really prefers the pursuit, and he revels in the opportunity to prove himself over and over again.

So his career is in many ways like Sisyphus, the character from Greek mythology who was condemned to pushing a rock uphill knowing that whenever he reaches the top of the hill, the rock will roll back down the other side and the pattern will repeat forever. But unlike Sisyphus, my father thrives on pushing the rock uphill. He takes great pride and derives great pleasure from tackling challenge after challenge after challenge. If he ever stopped at the top of the hill to take in the view, he'd be miserable.

This aspect of his personality is manifest in his hobbies: golf and Ohio State football. What sport could mirror poor Sisyphus more than golf? Year after year, round after round, you think you've found the secret to better scores, but over and over again you find yourself back at the bottom of the hill. My father loves golf and he plays often. His other great passion is Buckeye football. Week after week, when the Buckeyes take the field, they put everything on the line. My father is always there, living and dying with every play, sometimes even pacing up and down the sidelines himself, like a coach. He even once gave a locker room pep talk to the Ohio State team before a critical game. And, of course, they won!

He pursues each challenge in business like a football coach in a championship game. Just like the coach, for my father everything is black and white. You're either with him or against him. If you're with him, he is incredibly loyal and extremely supportive. If you're against him, he is a very tough adversary. He is perceived by many as very "tough." That is the great contradiction, because in fact, my father is very sensitive. While he thrives on challenges, he hates conflict and confrontation. He will not back down from a fight, but he really does not like to go to battle.

This sensitive side of my father is manifest in his extraordinary generosity and philanthropy. Many of my mother and father's major charitable gifts are well known and high profile: the research building at University Hospital, a magnificent facility to support undergraduate business education at Case Western Reserve, the headquarter facility for United Cerebral Palsy, the armored bus for children in Israel, the playground at Boulevard Elementary School where both my father and mother went to school, and many more. But what is less well known is the private gifts and loans to friends in need. It is these gestures that speak volumes about the type of person my father is.

This is the person I know so well. As a child, I didn't spend much time with my father on a daily basis. He often worked long hours and weekends. But we had great family vacations and my sister and I spent many weekends in the back seat of the car as he inspected his projects. During those weekend excursions, I observed his phenomenal work ethic up close. But as hard as he worked, he was always there in the bleachers at all my athletic events, cheering me on and insisting that I pursue success on the field with intensity and desire. When I graduated from law school, he was supportive of my decision to pursue an independent career, sharing the hope that we could someday work together. And we have worked together and have accomplished some great things. And while we haven't always seen eye to eye, I have great respect for him. He has been a wonderful role model for me throughout my life.

While it is difficult to capture the man and his remarkable career on paper, this book provides the reader with a glimpse of the "rags to riches" career of this extraordinary, charismatic entrepreneur, with insights into the ingredients behind his success. In so doing, I hope it provides an inspiration for those who choose to pursue the entrepreneurial path to success. In the words of that familiar Frank Sinatra tune, my father did it "his way." He has created a legacy of remarkable accomplishments, many very special projects, incredible gifts to his community and to the world, and a son who loves him very much.

Scott Wolstein has been Chief Executive Officer of Developers Diversified Realty, the company founded by his father in 1965, since it became a public company in 1993. He is a graduate of the Wharton School at the University of Pennsylvania and the University of Michigan Law School.

Introduction

Irecently read an article in *USA Today* about entrepreneurship. It addressed the debate of whether entrepreneurs are *born* with some kind of innate ability to start and grow a business, or whether they are *taught* how to transform good ideas into successful companies. This is a hot topic in today's business school and boardrooms because of the important role entrepreneurial firms play in creating jobs and boosting productivity. The result has been an onslaught of new courses on entrepreneurship, designed to teach students how to become something many experts believe is inborn and can't be taught.

I don't fit either of these definitions. I certainly wasn't *born* an entrepreneur. For many years my goal was to reach a weekly wage of $90 so I could support my family. But I also can't say I was *taught* how to be an entrepreneur. Although I did learn helpful skills and knowledge in law school and in my first two full-time jobs, I had never ever even heard the word, 'entrepreneur,' until after my schooling was finished.

I became an entrepreneur out of necessity. I wanted to "make it;" to cross over from the proverbial wrong side of the tracks. Out of necessity, I figured out how to do it. No college classes or personal traits could have prepared me for the situations I would face and decisions I would have to make in my career. Experience became my teacher, imparting lessons I could never have learned inside a classroom.

After more than 50 years in the business world, I am often asked to share my experiences with college and MBA students and explain how someone who started with nothing can build a successful business. Sometimes friends will ask me to speak to their sons or daughters. Other times, like at the 2003 commencement address at the

Weatherhead School of Management at Case Western Reserve University (CWRU), I address larger groups. The questions they pose are often the same:

- "How did you decide you wanted to start your own business?"
- "Who were the most influential people in your life and how did they influence your success?"
- "What advice would you give a student looking to start a new business?"
- And the most popular question, "To what do you attribute your success?"

The answer to the first question is that deciding to start my own business evolved out of my desire to cross over to the other side of the tracks, in my case Taylor Road. After years of working hard, I wanted to create something and have a personal stake in its financial success. For me, the entrepreneurial route was the way to achieve this. It put me in control of my own future.

Throughout my career, there were many times I wish I would have had a mentor, especially during my early years as an entrepreneur. Of course there were many people who would teach me valuable lessons, but there wasn't one person whose advice and guidance I could seek. I had to learn the hard way, by figuring it out for myself how to deal with the complex issues entrepreneurs face when building their companies. How can I get funding for a new business venture? How can I get an inside track into making an important sale? How can I balance work and family? These are the types of questions I might have asked a mentor. These are the questions I'm asked when I talk to student groups and try to answer in this book. No one took the time to offer me advice when I was just entering the workforce, so I feel a responsibility to take the time to help young people today.

I've found that young people seem to be most interested in learning about what makes an entrepreneur successful in the business world. I could cite hard work, persistence, patience, perseverance, and a roll-up-your-sleeves work ethic as significant factors. But my answer is simpler, more fatalistic than that. For me, the fear of failure was a great motivator. What was my alternative to success? The obvious answer is failure, which I never considered an acceptable option. It was a matter of survival, and I knew it. I'd better work harder than anyone else because if I didn't do it myself, who would help me? Nobody. It was strictly up to me.

My advice to students and would-be entrepreneurs is not rocket science. First, never lose your common sense—there is no substitute for it. Common sense and instinct play an important role in the decisions entrepreneurs need to make each day. Look within yourself for the answers. Listen to other people, but make your own decisions because you think it's right.

Second, if you want to be successful you have to work hard and do whatever it takes to get the job done. Don't let your title dictate which tasks you will and won't do. Life is a race to the finish line, walked very slowly by most people. To succeed, all you have to do is walk a little faster than everyone else.

Third, never give up or take no for an answer, even when others tell you something can't be done. There were many times when it seemed I was embarking on what everyone was telling me was an impossible task. In 1959, when I started developing houses in Twinsburg, Ohio, the local media and the real estate establishment pointed out that it was too far from Cleveland to draw a significant number of new home buyers, that the quality of the homes I was building was too high for the area, and that the water line didn't even go out that far. People laughed when I announced I would raise $1 million in one day for Cerebral Palsy by taking over Sea World for a charity fundraiser. In 1979, when I bought Cleveland's professional indoor soccer team, the sports pages called it possibly the worst sports franchise in professional sports. In 1992, when I decided to build a world-class country club and spa in Canton, Ohio, all the experts said the small town would never support such an ambitious venture.

But Twinsburg became my first real estate success, we raised the $1 million for Cerebral Palsy, we turned the Cleveland Force into the best soccer franchise in the league, and the Glenmoor Country Club in Canton is now a smashing success. In each of these cases, and many others, there was something inside me that told me I could succeed if I worked at it hard enough. Sometimes it was having a little more common sense than the next guy. Other times it's been a personal mission to prove the nay Sayers wrong. And still other times it's been a sense of urgency to prove to myself that anything is possible with a steadfast commitment to hard work and a vision of what is achievable.

I've made my share of mistakes in the past fifty years. I've been swindled by an art dealer, flummoxed by uncreative city governments, outmaneuvered by one of the largest real estate developers in Cleveland, and lost control of my life's work while I wasn't paying attention. But through it all I've tried to maintain my focus, deciding quickly on the best exit strategy when necessary, or just waiting out the bad times, taking my lumps.

Crossing The Road to Entrepreneurship is my life story. It chronicles the most important events I've experienced in both my business and personal lives. But I hope this book is more than an autobiographical timeline. Instead, I hope by relaying how I reacted to the pivotal moments in my life I am able to help would-be entrepreneurs who may be experiencing similar situations. I've tried to show how I've applied an entrepreneurial approach to all aspects of my life–not just business, but also to Iris and my charitable giving, our personal relationships, and our approach to our own healthcare. It also, on every page I hope, evokes my most significant relationship, my partnership with Iris, my wife of 55 years. Most entrepreneurs would agree that starting and then growing your own venture often creates tremendous pressures and stress, and sometimes loneliness. I've never experienced that last problem because I've been very fortunate to have Iris as my confidant, my friend, and my unwavering partner. Together we have weathered a few storms, lived many adventures, and shared a lifetime of happy occasions.

I really don't know if entrepreneurs are in fact *born* or *taught,* but I do know that I don't fit either of these molds. I also know that there isn't a magic formula of knowledge and personal characteristics that can insure success in the business world. That is the beauty of entrepreneurship. It doesn't close its doors to anyone. You don't have to have a certain grade point average, be of a certain religion, or come from a wealthy family. If you want to be an entrepreneur, you can try, regardless of race, gender, or I.Q. It most likely won't be an easy road, but it will be filled with lots of opportunities.

In the end, only you can determine your future. It is up to you, just as it was up to me many years ago. My solution was to be focused and to work hard every day. Every day I tried to cross the road to entrepreneurship.

Chapter One

Choosing Sides of Taylor Road

Somewhere, in the recesses of my mind, I had anticipated a welcoming committee. Okay, balloons and a brass band seemed farfetched, yet to me it seemed fitting that the Mayor, or at least someone from his office, would be there to greet Iris and me as we arrived on the island of Pohnpei. But rather than the beat of drums, marching feet, or crash of symbols, only the thump of the stamp on our passports marked the completion of our 8,000 mile journey from Cleveland, Ohio to the capital of the Federated States of Micronesia.

Courtesy of the U.S. Navy, I first landed on this tiny Pacific island shortly after the first of the year in 1946, six months after the dropping of the atomic bomb on Hiroshima and Nagasaki ended the war in the Pacific. I spent 4 long months on Pohnpei, learning about life and myself and dreaming about a future back in the States.

For at least twenty years, after reading that an airport had been built on the island, I had wanted to return to Pohnpei—this time with Iris. Yet something always prevented us from making the trip. It was too far, too inaccessible. A pending deal needed supervision. Ohio State was playing Michigan. I always had a ready excuse. Finally, Iris said, "we're going," and we bought the tickets. On September 28, 2002, after watching the Ohio State University (OSU) football team beat Indiana, our four-day journey began. We flew from The OSU airport in Columbus to St. Louis, where we spent the night, before flying

1

on to Honolulu the next day. The following morning a four-stop hop took us to Pohnpei.

Suddenly there I was, back in the place where my life took a pivotal turn; the place that gave me perspective on my future. I thought perhaps someone else would remember my time here. But only I remembered. Only I recalled that it was while in the Navy that I decided to become something, to become someone. At the time, I didn't use the word 'entrepreneur'. I don't think I had ever even heard that term before. It was here that I also realized that the military, at my level at least, was a meritocracy. I figured that working harder than everyone else was the way to get ahead—a lesson I followed throughout my life. I had always worked hard, don't get me wrong, just as many of us had, growing up on the lower east side of Cleveland during the Great Depression. Though I probably had two dozen different jobs by the time I graduated high school, life as a competition or a zero-sum game, with the winner making out better than the loser, was a new concept to me. It was during these years that it dawned on me that good things come to those who work a little harder than the next guy.

Hello, My Name is . . .

Before going any further, let me introduce myself. I was born Bertram Leonard Wolstein on February 23, 1927. In my twenties, I legally changed my name to Bert L. Wolstein. Frankly, I just never liked the name Bertram. To me, it conjured up an image of a guy who went to school in shorts and a bow tie, sporting the proverbial 'kick me' sign on his back.

To make matters more confusing, Bert is a name that today only appears on formal documents and nametags. Ever since my early teens I've gone by the nickname, Bart, remaining Bert only to my mother and my favorite aunt who never did get the hang of it.[1] The

---

[1] The genesis of the pronunciation is a trifle impolite, so I'll explain it in a riddle for those who really want to know. I was walking home one day with my friend, Richard, who went by that prename's common nickname. We were about 14 at the time, the perfect age for us to march down the street, loudly rhyming our names with the rudest words we could conjure. My friend's name was easy, as his nickname rhymed with all sorts of words more risqué than "trick" or "lick." But he had trouble thinking of anything sufficiently scatological to rhyme with B-e-r-t, and was much more successful with B-a-r-t. Think about it. The pronunciation, although fortunately not the rhyme, stuck.

multi-identity does sometimes come in handy, though. Anytime any-one gives me a big slap on the back and asks, "How ya doin', Bert?", I know that person is a stranger.

Mine was a typical second-generation Jewish upbringing. Both my parents emigrated as teenagers from Eastern Europe, near the Lithuanian border. Life was hard for poor Jews in 19th century Russia, and my grandparents and their children never expected anything more when they came to America—first New York and almost immediately to Cleveland.

My mother's parents died when I was very young, but until I was 12, I lived in walking distance of my paternal grandparents, who lived in the Glenville district on the east side of Cleveland. My father's mother was the typical Jewish grandmother— a short, plump woman who spent most of the day in the kitchen cooking. She was warm and loving. Every Sunday after religious school, she would stick a quarter in my ear when my grandfather wasn't looking. My grandfather was a religious man, spoke mostly Yiddish in the home, and walked back and forth to synagogue every day. He was a tailor by trade, but despite his hard work, he remained very poor. He saved his nickels until he could afford a small two-family house on the east side of Cleveland, where he opened up a small tailor shop in the attic.

My father followed in his father's footsteps, living a life filled with hard work and minimal financial gain. He worked primarily as a cloth-cutter in a series of sweatshops, first in New York and then in Cleveland. Work was sporadic during the Depression, and at least once a year he would come home early to announce he had been laid off. Although he was a union man, it wasn't unusual for him to be given a two-month seasonal furlough, without pay, of course. Like many people of his generation, he didn't trust banks. In fact, I don't think he ever had a checking account; he paid all his bills with cash. I can remember him hiding a twenty-dollar bill under the carpet, which represented his entire fortune at the time. I also remember him walking to the bank to pay his utility bill because he didn't trust the mail.

Ours was a frugal household. When I was very little, my father had saved enough each week to buy two two-family homes, proving that wealth is determined more by what you save than what you make. Receiving rent from tenants was the height of his entrepreneurial activity, and my first exposure to it. But after the stock market crashed, he lost both houses, as well as the few dollars my mother and he had managed to save. Iris and I supported them as soon as we had the means. After they retired, one of my great pleasures was sending them each year to Florida for the winter.

My father was not a warm, get-down-on-your-hands-and-knees kind of dad. There was love there, but we just led separate lives. I saw him crying in the kitchen when I left for the Navy, but we never spoke of it. I have only one memory of just the two of us taking an outing together. We went to the circus. Even when we ventured out as a family on summer weekends to the park, we would immediately split up, with my father playing nickel pinochle and my mother penny poker. I was left to fend for myself, which wasn't bad since it freed me to swim or play basketball. Many Sundays we were also part of an extended family convergence to my Uncle Dan's cottage on Lake Erie, where the garage served as home base for guests to take part in a day of swimming, boating, eating, and card playing.

The only overnight family excursion of my youth was when my parents, my sister and I took a room for two nights at the Cedar Point Amusement Park, 60 miles west of Cleveland. I laugh when I compare that single vacation with the experiences of my son's four children, who range in age from nine to fourteen and are already extensive world travelers. They've been to Africa, Antarctica, Central America, and England, and at least twenty states within the U.S. Today, that is not uncommon. For many Baby Boomers (and now their kids), the downside of being handed everything from cars to expensive educations is that they may lack something most people in my generation had—motivation. We were motivated to work from the time we could carry a newspaper or make change from a cash register because we had no choice. No one was going to give us anything.

My mother instilled in me a strong work ethic, which began with chores around the house, including adding coal to the furnace and what I considered woman's work—vacuuming or getting down on my hands and knees with a brush to sweep the dust from where the baseboards met the carpet. In those days you'd leave newspapers on the kitchen floor and stairway to protect them from people tracking in dirt from the outside. My mother worked hard every day and expected her house to be spotless. Yet for some reason, my parents were much easier on my sister Malvene, six years my senior. She had no regular chores. She was even given piano lessons.

My mother was more nurturing than my dad, showing her love more openly. She did, however, have a long memory if you crossed her, holding grudges against people for all sorts of petty offenses. We called her the elephant, because she never forgot.

Like so many others who came to the United States with very little, my parents understood that education was the way to success. After graduating high school, my parents sent my sister to Ohio State. When it was my time to go to college, I was expected to figure out how to pay for it myself. Treating one child differently from the other never made much sense to me. Maybe it was as simple as the old-world notion of doing everything they could to prepare their daughter for marriage. In fact, Iris and I waited until Malvene was married before we wed. I'm not sure what we would have done if she had ended up a spinster. Yes I do—we would have been married anyway.

My parents expected me to get a college education. I was, after all, first generation Jewish American, and the only son to boot. But I think my parents measured success by something less than my own view of what was possible. They would have been delighted if I had become any kind of professional. Their first choice was an accountant, which they figured was the most conservative, safest profession of all. I gave it my best shot during my first year in college, but I found accountancy courses particularly gruesome and I quickly switched to business administration.

Looking back, it's difficult to pinpoint exactly how my parents helped inspire me to reach beyond my modest upbringing. I loved my mom and dad, and I never had any doubt that they loved me back. I also respected them. But their unspoken mantra was that you struggled for a living, something I never adopted as my own. Rather, I focused on my entrepreneurial tendencies, harnessing an ambition that has served me well throughout my career. I really don't credit my parents for my entrepreneurial bent, unless my drive was in fact a rebellion against their old-world views, which I guess would be giving them credit in reverse.

Growing Up on the Wrong Side of Taylor Road

People have told me I have a chip on my shoulder about my modest roots. Maybe that's true. I certainly think I was motivated by growing up on the wrong side of the tracks, and even today I think I'm still trying to prove that I'm as worthy or as smart or as successful as my friends who grew up on the right side of the tracks.

In my case, it was actually the wrong side of Taylor Road. In 1939 my parents moved us from the lower east side of Cleveland to 1776 South Taylor Road in Cleveland Heights. Structurally, the difference between our new home and our previous one was that there was a shower in our new bathtub. Socially, the differences were much greater. My older sister, Malvene, and I were exposed to a higher socio-economic community and to one of the best public school systems in the area. At both Roosevelt Junior High School and Cleveland Heights High, I had wonderful teachers who told us that if we put our minds to it, we could do great things. Among other things, they drilled into us the importance of loyalty—to our homeroom, our Country, our parents, and to each other. But mostly to our homeroom, as I recall.

The affluent suburb of Cleveland Heights was unofficially divided by Taylor Road. To the east was street after street of two-story single-family homes, and to the west were more modest two-family homes. While most of my friends lived on the east side, we rented on the west. My friends would get picked up from school or social events in big cars. They drove their own cars once they turned 16. Most of them didn't have to work, and chose instead to spend their summer days playing football, baseball, basketball, and tennis in Cain Park. They tried to include me, but I was usually working one job or another while they were playing. The conversation usually went something like "Bart, are you coming?" "No thanks, I've got to work."

My father was a man of many routines, many of which I remember today. The first one up every morning, he would immediately march down to the basement to fire up the hot water heater and the coal furnace in the winter. He'd then leave for work before anyone else had risen. After returning home he'd often put a spoonful of jelly in a glass and pour whiskey over it—a tradition I haven't continued. Today, I prefer a Belvedere vodka martini on the rocks. After dinner he'd lie on the couch, smoke a cigar, and listen to opera or whatever else was playing on one of his favorite radio stations. Other evenings he'd play pinochle with his friends.

Before we moved to Cleveland Heights, my father would take two streetcars to the health club at the Jewish Center after work. Following his ritual of a steam, sauna, and swim, he'd walk the five miles home. Once we moved to Taylor Road, he only went to the health club on Sundays when he took me to Sunday school. Dad was a very good swimmer and tennis player, and I must have gotten my love of exercise from him. I'm still at the exercise machine every morning before six, lifting weights and speed-walking on the treadmill for an hour.

Upon reflection, I realized that my parents had inherited a strong work ethic, but also a vision of very limited horizons. My mother's total net worth when she died in 1988 was $4,000. She was as sharp at 92 as she had been at 50, driving a car until her final days. My father, who had died six years earlier, didn't even own a car until he was almost fifty—a 1935 Ford V8 he bought for $550. At 88 he entered the hospital with a kidney infection. He was improving until he got out of the hospital bed one day and slipped and fell on the wet floor. He was in a coma for five weeks. I was told his condition was hopeless, and I finally agreed to have the doctors remove his feeding tube. That decision was more difficult and more emotional than any business decision I ever made.

Growing up on my side of Taylor Road made me very cognizant of the difference between my life and that of most of my friends. It transcended the issue of wealth and just having the things money could buy. It was more intangible than that. My parents worked so hard, but it seemed that they were running in place. The American dream was passing them by. I refused to believe it had to be that way. I never intended to make that my reality.

A Glimpse of Life on the Other Side

I didn't have to look far to discover a variety of avenues, characteristics, and values that could help me cross over to the other side of Taylor Road. After all, most of my friends were from families who embraced the American dream I so wanted to live. Iris's parents and two of my uncles made huge impressions on me. They were the people who helped lay the foundation for many areas of my adult life.

The Shurs Iris would describe the atmosphere in my house growing up as "cold." I like to think that's a little harsh, but compared to the household in which she grew up, her description is fair. As soon as Iris and I were engaged, her parents and younger brother immediately embraced me as one of their own. Their household was a real eye opener to me. It wasn't only the warmth they showed me and each other. There was also a sophistication and connection to the bigger world that I immediately appreciated and wanted to be a part of. The contrast between our two families was so vast that Iris and I made a very conscious decision when we had children to emulate Iris's upbringing rather than my own.

Not unlike my parents, Iris's father, Harold Shur, emigrated from Lithuania when he was 11 or 12. However, as my parents retained their old-world sensibility, the Shurs were very modern. It wasn't just that they lived on the other side of Taylor Road, or that they had an appreciation of art or had doctors and lawyers in their extended family. The Shurs exuded a certain 'hipness' to their outlook on life. Even before we were married, Iris and I socialized with them, going out to dinner and nightclubs. We never could have done that with my folks. But Iris managed to bridge the gaps between our two families so that Thanksgiving and the Jewish holidays were celebrated with both sets of parents together.

Uncle Dan   The one role model I had growing up was my uncle, Daniel Wasserman, the husband of one of my mother's sisters. He was an influential lawyer, politician, and Appeals Court Judge in Cleveland. He was also the most learned person I knew, with a love for reading and exercising his mind. I was drawn to him, in part because he was the "player" in the family, hobnobbing with the mythical Cleveland "insiders," which represented a land as foreign to me as the eastern European shtetl (town) where my parents had grown up.

With Uncle Dan's help, my mother always had more dependable employment than my father, usually clerical jobs at either the Navy Department, or later at the Board of Elections. My father finally retired as a cloth cutter when he was 72, and Uncle Dan got him a job as a clerk for the county auditor. He set my sister up at the State Highway Department, where she worked for almost forty years. I also worked at the Highway Department one summer, cutting grass and doing other physical labor. I learned to operate a jackhammer. That was what I considered man's work—a far cry from the vacuuming my mother made me do. I enjoyed the challenge and hoped it would develop my muscles. I also remember the hope he instilled in me when I sat with him, in my mother's kitchen, and he told me that when I graduated college, he would have a job for me.

There was something magnetic about Uncle Dan that made me want to do things for him—anything, just to get him to notice me. If he asked for a cigar, I ran to the store to get one. If he supported a particular political candidate, I gladly passed out circulars. I have often thought about that quality and how I could replicate it in business. In my eyes, Uncle Dan had some sort of inside track to a better life, to getting to the other side of Taylor Road. From Uncle Dan I learned that you can't be knighted into business success, you have to earn it.

Uncle Samuel Berkman   Probably my fondest familial memories are of the times Samuel Berkman, another of my mother's brother-in-laws, would drive sixty miles up from Canton, Ohio to take me to a Cleveland Indians game. He was a tough little guy who had no children of his own. When I was 13, both uncles paid to have me go to Al Brown's Camp Caravan for two weeks. Ironically, the camp was in Twinsburg, Ohio, where I would have my first real entrepreneurial success, as I'll discuss in Chapter Three.

Family Influences   My mother and father, Iris's parents, and both of my uncles had a profound effect on me as a child and later as a husband, father, and entrepreneur. All of them believed in hard work. Some of them stretched beyond their current circumstances to push the envelope of the American dream. Others, like my parents, were content in making enough to live modestly.

I've tried to instill a feeling of family among the top people who work for me. I expect them to work hard and to stay focused; they'll certainly tell you that. I try to drill into my employees that they can be successful by making an effort to stay focused every day. Every day. Every day. In fact, I talk to all of my top people daily, often more than once. They give me a report on that day's events and I ask them, "What else?" "What else?" "What else?" until they run out of things to tell me.

I have a reputation as being a demanding boss, but I don't think anyone who works for me ever wakes up in the morning fearing for his or her job. If they make it six months with me, they tend to last a long time. Just go through the tenure of my top people—35 years in the case of John McGill, and virtually all their working lives in many other cases. You'll get to meet some of these extraordinary people in later chapters.

All Work and No Play . . .

Although this phrase is usually finished with the words "makes Jack a dull boy," I like to finish it with "helped make me what I am today." I worked hard as a kid—outside of school that is. In high school I never really cracked the books in a serious way. I was satisfied with B's and C's. I was a jock, interested in playing basketball and baseball and enjoying myself when I wasn't working. I took various jobs out of necessity, but in school I just wanted to get by, have fun, and not be that dull boy. Don't misunderstand. I didn't drink, smoke, or party hard.[2] What clicked even before high school was the entrepreneurial spirit to make money. I had all sorts of different jobs beginning at an early age. On August 15, 1935, I was only eight years old when Wiley Post and Will Rogers died in a plane crash in Alaska. I went up and down the street selling extra editions of the *Cleveland Press*. I wasn't much older when I went into the soft drink business. It seemed like summers were much hotter in those days, or maybe it was just that most people didn't have air conditioning. At any rate, fancy new homes were always going up on the other side of Taylor Road, and I came up with the idea of loading a red wagon with iced soda pop and selling them to the construction workers. In the evenings, a truck would deliver cases of pop to my house. Another delivered huge bags of ice. I'd carry them down to the basement and dump them into a washtub. In the afternoon heat, I began my daily trek, walking five miles, house to house, shouting "Cold soda! Ginger BEER!" (It was always more effective to make the workers think I had beer, although in fact I did not.)

From the time I was 12 until I graduated from high school, I worked Saturdays at my Aunt's fruit store. I got my first shot at management at age 16, when I began running the place on weekends, doing everything from stocking the shelves, arranging the items in the window, making deliveries, and taking care of over-the-counter sales. Without a calculator, I became very adept at adding numbers, which no doubt helped me later when it came to deciphering unnecessarily complicated balance sheets.

Every day after school and on weekends, when I wasn't working at the fruit store, I also worked at a succession of four different drugstores, mostly at the soda fountain. At 14, I was making 15 cents an hour, but when the opportunity arose, I switched to a drugstore two streetcars and fifty minutes away because it was owned by a family friend who was willing to pay me 20 cents an hour. Once I turned 16, I got a raise to 25 cents.

In addition to working in a bakery, I worked at a shoe store on the west side of Cleveland. I started as a stock boy, but on busy days I doubled as a salesman, specializing in working men shoes because I

---

[2] I had a puritan view of the value of working for a buck. When I won $70 from some friends playing craps I felt so guilty I couldn't sleep. My parents had drilled into me the evils of gambling, and I felt like a criminal. I gave most of the money to my big sister to keep for me. I quickly regretted that because I never did get it back.

had memorized each style and where they were stored. The highlight of each day was the short break I was given for lunch, when I would spend 35 cents for six White Castle hamburgers and a drink. I loved those tiny White Castle burgers.

I was almost always the youngest person at any of these jobs, and sometimes my co-workers couldn't resist having a little fun with me. At the shoe store one day I was told to walk down to the local hardware store to buy a left-handed box stretcher. I didn't quite make it out the door before I realized they were putting me on. There was, of course, no such thing as a box stretcher, much less a left handed one. This and similar experiences didn't hurt my feelings. In fact, they helped me feel like one of the 'guys'—a member of the team, if you will. They taught me that humor can bridge all sorts of gaps, but it has to be in good taste and shouldn't make anyone feel stupid.

By the age of 17, I had become a full-fledged working machine. I took a summer job in a factory making commercial displays, commuting to and from work with my parents every day. On Saturdays I worked at my aunt's store and at Cleveland Stadium, selling hot dogs, beer, and Coca Cola. This was the 'Cadillac of jobs' for any teenager, and with thanks to Uncle Dan it was mine. Just before the summer of 1941 Uncle Dan had a local politician walk me down to the stadium to introduce me to the right people and make sure I was hired. At 14 years old, I was the youngest "hustler," as we were called, a coveted job because if you worked hard and learned a few tricks you could make as much as $20 in one evening—a vast sum in those days.

Opened in 1932, the historic Cleveland Stadium was one of the first large stadiums to be built with lights, which made it possible for the Indians to play night games in front of as many as 80,000 fans. The stadium also hosted important college football matches, like Ohio State versus Illinois or Notre Dame versus Navy.

Cleveland Stadium became a fertile breeding ground for my entrepreneurial instincts. On my first night at an Indians game we were given our assignments. I was told to sell hot dogs—not the easiest task. Who eats a hot dog after dinner on a humid summer evening? I sold 80 hot dogs, for a total profit of 80 cents.

Before long, however, I came up with ways to increase my profitability. At the commissary, we didn't actually buy the hot dogs. We bought a bag of twenty buns for nine cents each, then they just estimated the number of dogs that were dumped into our hot boxes. Sometimes they put in as many as 30. I guess the meat was less expensive than the bread, or maybe they just figured you'd come back for more buns when you ran out of hot dogs. But I just offered people two dogs for 20 cents on the same bun, which meant that instead of a penny profit, I would make eleven cents, which had a huge impact on my bottom line, as you can imagine.

Sometimes I'd auction the dogs off to the highest bidder. "Six for a dollar; get your hot dogs," I'd cry out. On really cold days, football fans would pay almost anything for a cup of hot chocolate or a "hot" dog. It was supply and demand at its purest, and an early entrepreneurial lesson for me. A fair price was whatever the market would bear, or in this case what a cold football fan would pay. I finally worked my way up to manager of a concession stand by age 17 and was put on salary. I was running what was in effect a small business, with half a dozen people working for me.

My job as a hustler at Cleveland Stadium was my first official entrepreneurial venture, and from it, I took several lessons. Most theoretical definitions of entrepreneurship say that it entails risk, and there was *some* risk, I suppose. If the vending company had gotten wind of our hot dog selling tactics, it probably would not have looked very kindly on our ingenuity. But we never gave that a second thought. A penny profit on each hot dog sold just wasn't enough for me. I don't think it should have been enough for anyone.

These early experiences also played a foundational role in how I would conduct business throughout my career. In all my business deals my most important principle has always been that the transaction has to be good for both sides. I've made a good living by not stepping on the other guy to cut the best deal possible. When you win and I win, we create a winning partnership. Should either of us be on the losing end of a deal, the arrangement is going to turn sour sooner or later and we likely won't do business together again.

During the past fifty years I've developed more than 1,000 homes and 300 commercial properties representing more than 50 million square feet of retail space. Time and again I call on the relationships I've built and the reputation of being a straight shooter. If I had focused on getting the best deals possible for myself, I would have run out of people to do business with long ago.

Starting a Business with Al Ratner

I created another entrepreneurial venture with a high school friend of mine by the name of Al Ratner. Al was a good basketball player despite weighing no more than 125 pounds soaking wet. What he lacked in height and mass, he made up for with quickness. He later played for Case Western Reserve University. Coming from a privileged background, Al always had money in his pocket and often would buy us all milk shakes. He also invited us to his house to make our own shakes because he had an amazing device in his kitchen—a professional blender just like what you'd see at drugstore soda counters.

I recruited Al to go into business with me spinning records at high school fraternity and sorority dances. Together we put up $200 to buy used equipment—basically a couple of turntables, an amplifier and some speakers. Al's nickname was Eggy, so we called ourselves "Musical Art By Eggy and Bart," and before we knew it, we were working gigs on both Friday and Saturday nights.

We had the perfect partnership—part capital and assets, part sweat equity, and clear roles and responsibilities. Since Al owned a car, he drove me to the dances, where I stayed and played the records. Then he would pick me up afterwards. It might seem like Al had the better deal, but we each contributed in our own way to the partnership. With all that heavy equipment, I needed the transportation. Besides, I liked playing disc jockey. It made me feel like a big shot for a few hours, catching a glimpse of what it was like to be important. When I was a D.J., the other kids saw me in a different light, and it showed me that what I *had* wasn't as important than what I *was*. On a practical level, the job was quite lucrative. At $15 per gig, even split two ways, we were making what for me at the time was serious money. I had no expenses, so within a few months I had recouped my initial $100 investment. Everything else was pure profit.

In many ways, Al epitomized the division represented by Taylor Road. I was poor, and I knew it. Al was rich, and he knew it. While my family struggled, his parents went the entrepreneurial route, starting out in the creamery business and then branching out to develop the largest lumber supply company in Cleveland, and perhaps all of Ohio. After World War II, the Ratner family became very successful in real estate development, establishing Forest City Enterprises as a major player in Cleveland and, subsequently, nationally. As fate would have it, I would repeatedly run into his family in the business arena. In fact, Forest City maneuvered me out of my first big real estate deal, but that's a story for another chapter.

Despite the successful partnership with Al, I never stopped feeling like I was on the outside looking in. In fact, I still feel that way. I remain that kid from the west side of Taylor Road. No amount of financial success has ever really changed that. I've never been part of the Cleveland establishment, to say the least. I've never been invited to join the Union Club, Cleveland's elite social club for the business establishment. I've never been asked to sit on the board of a single public corporation. Even some of the Jewish establishment has seen fit not to include those of us born on the other side of Taylor Road in its inner circle, despite the fact that many of us have given a lot of money to various Jewish causes supported by the Federation.

What I Could Do for My Country

My entrepreneurial spirit would have to be put on hold. I enlisted in the Navy right out of high school, mainly because I didn't want to be drafted into the Army. I'd heard things about the Army, like having to march for miles up and down hills with a full pack. I expected Army recruits to have to sit night after night in a foxhole or be forced to jump off assault boats, with bullets whizzing over their heads (if they were lucky) as they ran onto a beach somewhere in Europe or the Pacific. For some reason, none of that appealed much to me. I figured that being on a ship would be safer and might even offer more opportunities for advancement. Besides, Army guys were called dogfaces, and being called a dogface didn't appeal to me much either.

The Germans surrendered while I was in boot camp at the Great Lakes Naval Academy, just outside of Chicago. I got a break on my first day there when I received a choice guard duty assignment—inside an office rather than outside somewhere. There were guards posted throughout the camp, and it was my job to make certain everyone was in their proper place and that no one was sleeping on duty. In reality, most of my four-hour shift was spent sitting in the office reading magazines and writing letters.

I don't know why out of 154 guys I was selected for special responsibility and avoided having to stand guard like everyone else. The officer in charge was tall, and so was I; maybe it was as simple as that. Regardless, I learned quickly that rewards were out there for the taking. This was reinforced when the aptitude test we all took directed me to go to hospital corpsman school in Farragut, Idaho. This kid who hated the sight of blood was selected to receive medical training in preparation for an assignment as a medic attached to the Marine Corps. But I had no complaints. As a medic, I wouldn't even carry a gun!

The benefits of working hard and being in the right place at the right time became crystal clear to me. All I had to do was look at the officers who had their own quarters and officer's club. Their work and leisure time were much more pleasant and enjoyable than those of the schleps like me who they ordered about. I found myself on yet another Taylor Road, and I knew exactly on which side of the street I wanted to be. So, in Idaho, I hit the books hard, finding an isolated spot in the woods every day after class to devour my medical texts. It paid off immediately. I graduated Farragut with a stripe, putting me ahead of most everyone else in my company.

As a First Class Petty Officer, I never saw the inside of a galley and never had to clean floors or the latrine. Once at sea, I was actually able to take fresh water showers by ingratiating myself with the corpsmen in charge of the sickbay. In Idaho, I had worked hard on my volleyball game. We played on teams in organized competition amongst the different companies, and each time we won a tournament, which was quite often, we were given extra liberties, usually a night on the town.

Things became more serious after I left Farragut for an assignment at the Naval hospital in Corvalis, Oregon. It was there that my friends and I started thinking about what it would mean to get shipped overseas. I had enlisted in the Navy in hopes of avoiding storming the beaches of Europe or Asia, but as medical corpsmen, we began to realize that our future was to join the Marines and do just that. I realized that you can't go to war much more defenseless than armed with a hypodermic needle as your most potent offensive weapon. I can't begin to describe the relief we all felt when the Japanese surrendered on September 2, 1945. Suddenly, my vague, suppressed fear that I might die for my country was replaced with the confidence that I would eventually return home in one piece after completing my tour of duty.

During my stint in Corvalis, I became head of the recreation department, which gave me a chance to relive my high school days as a jock. Since I had plenty of time to play on the basketball team, I was able to hone some of the talents I had developed playing pickup games in Cain Park. We matched up against the local university teams and more than held our own. Being young, energetic, and bored, I also decided to try boxing. One day my friend Sonny Booth from Tuscaloosa, Alabama and I slipped on some boxing gloves and got into the ring together. I saw an opening and landed a right hook to Sonny's nose, drawing blood. As I began to celebrate, he returned the favor with a left jab, and soon blood was spewing from my nose as well. That ended my boxing career, but solidified a connection with Sonny. We're still in touch today, without boxing gloves, of course.

Other recruits had more dangerous pursuits. Some of the guys got into the habit of putting half an ounce of clear white, denatured alcohol, which was kept under lock and key in the hospital, into a glass and filling it with grapefruit juice. The concoction must have been mighty potent because one day one of the recruits strolled down the glass-enclosed hallway connecting the buildings and smashed out every window on both sides with his fist. The next morning the commanding officer called a muster, lining everyone up with their palms outstretched. The guy with the bloody knuckles was figuratively wrapped on the knuckles. Typical Navy, his only punishment was being put in charge of the German prisoners.

In the hospital, I worked mostly in the allergy ward. In those days, we tested for allergies by making tiny slits on the patient's back with a sharp razor and putting drops of various foods, like cantaloupe or tomato, on the exposed area. If it turned red, it meant they were allergic to that particular food. It was very unscientific, and I'm not sure how much good we did. But many of the men were just slacking off anyway, looking for ways to be excused from particular assignments or even discharged.

After about eight months in Corvalis, I spent a few days in San Francisco in preparation for a sea voyage to the South Pacific. To me, being in California was like being on another planet or a different dimension. I found it mind-boggling that Bart Wolstein, who had never been outside of Ohio, was walking around the most beautiful city in the United States. Until I joined the Navy, the furthest I'd ever traveled from home was to a wedding in Columbus, Ohio, about 150 miles from Cleveland. This was before the interstate, so it was a five-hour drive, and I thought that was an adventure.

I was only in San Francisco a short time, but was fortunate enough to be there with my closest high school buddy, Mel Light. He was about six months younger than I was and started at the Great Lakes Naval Academy just after I came home on furlough for the first time. He went to the corpsmen school in Farragut after I had already left, and by mail I encouraged him to try to get to Corvalis, which he did.

Not only were Mel and I fortunate to share our time in the Navy, we also got lucky in San Francisco. A group of gypsies lured us into their house, asking us each for a quarter which they promised to bless for good luck. What did we know? We were just a couple of naïve, underage Buckeyes. It wasn't until they started grabbing for our wallets that we caught on to their scheme. We ran out of there as fast as we could, trailed by a large group of gypsies, mostly children as I recall.

Admittedly, we may not have been smarter than they were, but fortunately we were faster.

Anchors Away

From San Francisco we boarded a merchant vessel bound for Honolulu, where we transferred to another ship headed to Guam. I was at sea a total of thirty days, but I was fortunate because even before we left San Francisco Bay, virtually all of the other new recruits got seasick, lining up on the deck and throwing up in unison. Poor Mel. He was so sick he couldn't get out of the bottom bunk of the hammocks where we slept, which swung back and forth no more than six inches from the ground. He was hanging there like a dead man. No matter how much I pleaded with him to come out on deck or to get something to eat, he refused to move. It was at least a week before he finally got some fresh air and could hold down some food.

The sea voyage was incredibly boring. Day after day we either sat on the cold deck or lounged below on our hammocks, reading books and playing cards. It seemed to take forever. Sometimes we yearned for someone to get seasick just for a little excitement.

From Guam, I was assigned to a net tender, the smallest ocean-going Navy ship other than a PT boat. There were 15 of us, including a doctor and a dentist, who spent two weeks visiting the islands and checking the health of the native populations. Hundreds of tiny islands, almost all of which had been occupied by the Japanese, seemed just to float haphazardly in the ocean. The natives usually came out to greet us in small, remarkably well-made outriggers that had been crafted out of hollowed-out tree trunks.

There was a surprising abundance of U.S. currency on these islands. In fact, the natives seemed to have more than we did. We assumed that the Japanese had given it to them as bribes when they had occupied the islands, but we weren't really sure. Every day native islanders paddled out to us in their outriggers looking for cigarettes. After using a hand signal mimicking someone smoking and then waiving a handful of U.S. currency, the games would begin. We were continually negotiating over price, using just sign or body language to communicate. We would lean down and gesture that they should trade the currency for cigarettes. We would also try to grab the largest denomination they had, typically a $20 bill, as we offered them a package of cigarettes. But they knew what they were doing, and tried to place fives and tens in our snatching hands instead. The cigarettes only cost us 50 cents a carton, so either way we did pretty well. I used the profits as spending money, which meant I was able to save my entire Navy pay. That came in handy when I returned to Cleveland and started college. But at the time, selling cigarettes was just one more entrepreneurial teenage activity for me.

At one point near Okinawa we caught the outside of a tremendous storm, which tossed our little net tender around like a toy. All we could do was lie in our hammocks for ten hours feeling absolutely miserable. It didn't seem to bother the crew a bit. They were all seasoned sailors. When the seas finally calmed, we went out on deck, at which point I puked my guts out with all the others. It was the only time I got seasick in my life.

The men on these islands were always very friendly. They seemed to spend most of their time building boats. But more interesting were the beautiful Polynesian women, most of whom wore no clothes above their waists. The chiefs worried about us mingling with them, so whenever we were on land and would get close to a group of them the chief would clap his hands. Immediately a few of the younger natives would climb a palm tree to fetch us coconuts, and before we knew it we were all standing around drinking the milk. While we were distracted, the women mysteriously disappeared. It seems funny now to look back on this and admit that we were actually distracted by coconuts.

Throughout my tenure with the Navy I came to realize that the military had its own logic, which sometimes posed problems. Luckily, they were usually just harmless inefficiencies. Sometimes they could be dangerous. For example, since I was Navy, most of the officers assumed I had had some training at sea, which I had not. Sure, I had been at the helm of Uncle Dan's tiny outboard on Lake Erie a few times, but I certainly had never been instructed on how to steer a boat of this size. One day, however, while serving guard duty, I was suddenly told to take the wheel. The Captain was barking orders to turn the ship a certain number of degrees. Eighteen and inexperienced, I was quickly out of my league. I didn't realize that steering a ship is not like driving a car. When you turn the wheel of a ship there's a rather long delay before it responds. I kept turning the wheel, waiting for the compass to move, until I had turned the ship way too far. Fortunately an officer grabbed the wheel before I had a chance to run us aground.

As young managers and entrepreneurs, we are sometimes thrust into sink or swim situations that will not only determine the future of a particular deal but perhaps even that of the company. We have no choice but to step up to the wheel and steer. It can be dangerous and exhilarating at the same time. As a manager, you have to be willing to ask for help from advisors whose opinions and knowledge you trust. This is particularly true when you feel you might be in over your head. In the same way, as a company leader, you need to know when to step in and help your management team steer. Although at first they might resent too much input from the boss, they'll figure out that in the end, swimming together is much better than sinking alone.

A key strategy is to build a strong team that will work together to achieve a desired end result. An entrepreneur can't do everything by himself and, therefore, needs to rely on others to perform at least some of the things that are required to move the company ahead. But for a team to work well together, there needs to be an overriding sense of mutual respect and an opportunity for each person to play a role in attaining the end result.

Pohnpei, Then and Now

After accompanying the medical team to numerous islands in early 1946, I settled in on the small tropical island of Pohnpei, which became my home for five months. Located halfway between the Philippines and Hawaii, Pohnpei is slightly more than 400 miles north of the equator. It and the three adjacent islands were colonized by Spain in the 17th century and sold to Germany in 1898. In 1914, they were occupied by the Japanese, who turned them over to the United States in August, 1945 as part of their unconditional surrender. The islands continued to be administered by the U.S. until 1979, when the Federated States of Micronesia was granted full independence. Today there is still a U.S. army presence there, almost everyone speaks English, and the dollar is the currency of choice.

Most of Pohnpei's 200 square miles is rainforest, making it the rare Pacific island without a single sandy beach. The ever-present mist reinforces its isolation, but also creates a mysterious beauty as a sudden oasis in the deserted western Pacific. Tourists willing to forego lounging on a beach would find an island full of infinite views, spectacular waterfalls, and an indigenous people largely untouched by the outside world.

Life on Pohnpei was rustic to say the least. We showered with rainwater, and the latrine was a screened-in outhouse with four wooden seats cut out of a long board. We did have a dirt basketball court, and once in awhile a Navy ship would arrive for a short visit and we'd have a competitive game. We spent time practicing a few Pohnpeian words, particularly the lame pick-up line, "emen tong ook pongate," which supposedly meant, "I want to meet you tonight." All in all, my time there was incredibly boring.

To break up the monotony and also to become one of the guys, I learned to drink beer and smoke cigarettes and cigars. We received regular deliveries, via seaplane, of movies. Most of our nights were spent smoking cigars, drinking beer, and eating peanuts while sitting in our makeshift cinema. The night before Thanksgiving, a regular Navy man and I put a case of beer in front of us and started a drinking contest. He drank his entire twenty-four bottles; I drank fourteen. The next day we were served the best meal of my entire stay on Pohnpei—a genuine turkey, mashed potatoes, and cranberry sauce dinner. I was too sick to eat a single bite. It was the best meal I never had.

I spent my time on Pohnpei assigned to the hospital, with twenty-four other guys. We traveled to neighboring islands doing general health checks and took care of whatever ailments arose. One day before I was to go on an island visit I was in the delivery room, watching a husband help his wife with the final pushes of labor. Just before the baby arrived, the door swung open and someone shouted out the names of the people who had received orders to go home. "Wolstein!" he barked. And with that, I quickly wished the new Polynesian father the best of luck and bolted out of the hospital. I wasn't taking any chances, and I certainly wasn't about to give the Navy a chance to change its mind. This was well before the age of desktop computers, and those of us whose names had been called were happily amazed that the Navy was organized enough to know where we were, let alone that we were due to be discharged.

In minutes I was bouncing along in a jeep back to my quarters. It took me less than half an hour to shove everything I owned into my duffel bag, say a few quick goodbyes, and race the two miles back to the pier where I boarded a sea plane which would take us to the island of Truk (now called Chuuk), another of the four main islands that today make up the Federated States of Micronesia.

I was going home. I never did get to try out my one Pohnpeian phrase on any of the island girls, but I was going home.

Looking back on my experience in the Navy, not the rain, or the mosquitoes, or the bare breasted women, or the seasickness, or the cash I collected selling cigarettes to the natives, is what I remember with any real importance. This was the time in my life when it was almost like I had been touched by a magic wand. Maybe it was just because in the "hurry up and wait" atmosphere of the military I had a lot of time to think about my future. Regardless, the inner voice had been awakened and I could hear it taunt me, "Hey kid, you were born poor. You know what life is like on one side of Taylor Road, and you know what it's like on the other. Choose sides."

That is why it was so important for me to bring Iris to Pohnpei. I wanted her to experience the place that represented the beginning of the rest of my life, which fortunately for me I would end up spending with her.

Pohnpei Today

Fast-forward fifty-six years. Except for the indoor plumbing, the hotel where Iris and I stayed wasn't much different than the military barracks I had shared with two other corpsmen. Both buildings, then and now, were built on stilts, sunken into the ground next to the edge of a cliff. The modest all-wood building had no glass, only screens, which, along with the mesh netting that hung over our heads, thankfully kept out the mosquitoes. Iris pointed out that it was more like a screened in porch than a hotel. A new addition was the ceiling fan, which hung from the top of the thatched roof and served efficiently as an air conditioning. Although we found the island to have most modern conveniences, it still felt like something out of another era. Pig ownership remains a leading indicator of wealth, and the most important local decisions are still made over cups of a numbing local brew called "sakau."

The island itself, however, has changed dramatically. In 1946 the only motorized vehicles were the Jeeps brought in by the Navy, and the sole road was a two-mile stretch of dirt road that connected our barracks to the hospital and administration building. We used to circle the outside of the island by outrigger, but the only way to traverse it by land was on foot or by oxen-drawn carts. In addition to the airport, Iris and I were beneficiaries of new, paved roads and modern taxis. Getting around the island today is also aided by the fact that everyone on Pohnpei now speaks English. Lucky for us because the only Pohnpeian words I remembered were "emen tong ook pongate," which I was happy to have confirmed by our guide really does mean, "I want to meet you tonight."

But the biggest difference seemed to be in the level of activity on Pohnpei. The population grew from 5,000 to 35,000 people, who now have access to modern conveniences, retailers such as Ace Hardware and Napa Auto Supply, and job opportunities in manufacturing, education, and administration, to name just a few thriving industries. The island is also now home to concrete and asphalt plants, a college, government buildings, and a courthouse, since Pohnpei is the capital of the Federated States of Micronesia.

The first night Iris and I stayed in Pohnpei there was no wind; the silence broken only by the roosters crowing at 4:00 am. As usual, Iris was a good sport about it all. The next day we took a boat trip to the other side of the island, fortified by rusting Japanese gun placements pointed toward the harbor. We walked among the remnants of their military encampment, including their barracks and water supply infrastructure. Other, more interesting ruins date back to about 500 AD to a time when the island was ruled by a series of tyrant kings.

The food was certainly better than I remembered. In the Navy, I tried to fill up on breakfasts of rubbery pancakes and processed eggs because lunch and dinner of Spam or some other unidentifiable meat was generally awful. We would sometimes convince the cook to fry up some bananas or papayas, which in that tropical climate were plentiful. But without my own invention—a peanut butter, jelly, butter, and sliced banana sandwich—I don't think I would have survived. I must have eaten 400 of those sandwiches during my 140 or so days on Pohnpei, which ballooned my weight from 162 pounds to about 190. But 56 years later, Iris and I were ordering yellow tail sashimi followed by grilled tuna or crab. All were fresh and delicious. The cats, which seemed to swarm everywhere, were thankful when the portions were too much for us.

During our stay, Iris and I met very few people who had any memory of the U.S. military arriving on the island in 1945. I did speak briefly to a German woman who as a young girl had worked with us at the hospital. She was one of three daughters of a German couple who had been exiled on Pohnpei by the German government and later interned there by the Japanese for the better part of four years. Although Germany was their ally, any white face that far away from Europe was suspicious to the Japanese military.

I can hardly remember a day in 1946 when it didn't rain on the island, so I shouldn't have been surprised when during Iris' and my second night there a storm raged so intensely that we thought surely it would blow away our room and strand us in Pohnpei for weeks. The island is one of the wettest places in the world, with as much as 400 inches of rain per year. But when we arose in the morning, the sun was miraculously shining. We toured the new college, as well as the only two sites I remembered from my earlier stay—the dock where I had arrived more than half a century ago and the dirt road leading away from it.

Going Home Again

When I left Pohnpei in 1946 I was headed home to Cleveland to get started with the rest of my life. I had been totally isolated on the island; I hadn't spoken to my parents during my entire time overseas. Phones were much more exotic than they are today. Even mail was slow; it could take a month for a letter to arrive.

But not a day passed when I didn't think of home. I was proud of the stripe I had earned in the Navy and that I had elevated myself within its ranks. I was more bound and determined than ever to get serious and do whatever it took to cross to the other side of Taylor Road. I was ready to capture the American dream that had seemed to elude my parents, armed with the motivation that I'd better work harder than anyone else because if I didn't do it myself, nobody would help me. Nothing would be handed to me.. I was returning with 'fire in my belly.'

Since leaving Pohnpei fifty-eight years ago I've never been satisfied with standing still. Real estate developments, as well as most other business projects, are easily stalled. Often only a sense of urgency makes them progress rapidly and correctly. Every day I've tried to maintain that urgency. Everyday.

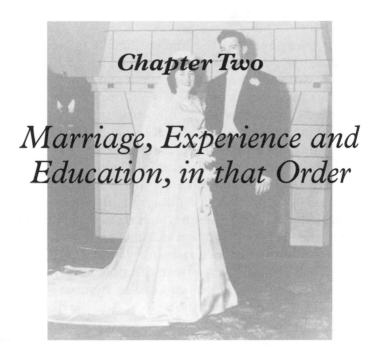

Chapter Two

Marriage, Experience and Education, in that Order

After living on an isolated island, in constant fear that the Navy would forget about us, I was going home. The seaplane to Truk[3] was the first time I had ever been on an airplane. I'm sure today a flight from Pohnpei takes less than an hour, but it took us three. There were no seats, so about a dozen of us sat on the hard floor, looking nervously at the emergency parachutes piled in the corner.

After a few days on Truk we embarked on a 30-day, 5,000-mile voyage back to San Francisco on a merchant marine troop ship. Just like our trip six months earlier, we idled away the time between meals, sitting on the hard deck, reading off-color books, playing cards, and gabbing with our buddies. It was about as boring as could be, but we didn't care. We were going home.

Our return to the United States was eye opening in many ways. We thought we were big-shot heroes as we stepped off our Naval ship,

---

[3]Prior to 1944, Truk had been considered the most formidable of all the Japanese strongholds in the Pacific. But in February, a U.S. attack, code named "Operation Hailstone," caught the Japanese by surprise and led to one of the most successful battles of the War. A follow-up assault in April 1944 completely destroyed the Japanese military presence on Truck. About twenty years later Jacques Cousteau explored the sunken Japanese fleet. Today the exotic fish floating through war machinery and soft coral reefs are the ghostly centerpiece of a thriving tourist industry. (Perhaps I should have taken Iris there instead of Pohnpei!)

dressed in our dress whites. But those on the home front were not nearly as impressed with us as we were with ourselves. The war had been over for more than a year, and the marching bands and keys to the city had been given way to a postwar boom that saw returning servicemen merely as inexperienced consumers waiting to be exploited. Even the barbershops in San Francisco took advantage of us, charging us $3.00 for a 50-cent haircut. We had been away from civilization for 18 months—how were we supposed to know the going rate for a haircut and a shave?

We spent two days in San Francisco, in the barracks on Treasure Island. I was still so naïve. While on liberty in downtown San Francisco, I realized for the first time that there was such a thing as homosexuality, when a young man, not much older than I, suggested I come up to his room so he could take my picture. I was naive, but I wasn't stupid, and I walked away as fast as I could, remembering how Mel and I had fled the gypsies on our last San Francisco visit.

From San Francisco, we took the train back to the discharge center at the Great Lakes Naval Academy. Before receiving a train ticket home, one by one we were brought into a small room where a group of regular Navy men made a pitch to try to get us to reenlist. "There is nothing better than the life of a Navy man," we were told. "Great adventures. Great opportunities. Great pay." I wasn't buying what they were selling. Granted, I didn't have a clue as to what my future held, but I knew it wouldn't be spent in the U.S. military.

Home at Last

On July 6, 1946, I headed to the Chicago railroad station with an honorable discharge hastily sewed onto my uniform. The next thing I knew, I was in Cleveland hugging my parents and sister. We headed downtown to celebrate. I was so excited and proud; I wanted everyone to see me in my uniform. It didn't take me long realize that tens of thousands of service men had arrived before me, with much more exciting war stories. What a schmo I was. I still remember taking the streetcar back home to change into jeans and a t-shirt before setting out for Cain Park to see which of my buddies were home.

I spent a month or so taking it easy, playing pickup basketball, softball, and tennis, trying to show off for the girls who were watching. (That particular activity wouldn't pay off for another few months). But when September rolled around my buddy Eddie Davis and I were the first two in line outside a dim six-story building on the downtown campus of

Cleveland College to apply for a college grant under the GI bill. One thing the Navy taught me was that good things happen to those who are First, and I certainly wasn't taking any chances. Cleveland College was at that time a kind of stepchild to Case Western Reserve University, but it was the school I could afford. But I counted myself lucky. The Navy was paying the tuition, plus a $65.00 per month stipend while I was in college.

When it came time to choose a major, I could hear my parents voices guiding me toward one of their three "professions" of choice—doctor, lawyer, or accountant. Since I had no inclination toward medicine, and I assumed law would take too many years of schooling, accountancy seemed to be the reasonable choice. I figured that as a certified public accountant, I could pretty much do anything I wanted in business.

I found accounting to be torturous. Every time I was off a penny or two on a homework assignment I'd stay awake, sometimes until four in the morning, until I got it just right. Years later, I would appreciate the foundation these courses gave me when reading a balance sheet or deciphering an amortization table. But for now, accounting wasn't for me.

That left the looming question, "What *was* for me?" I was good at math, but those classes were all tied in some way to my accountancy major. I wanted more action. I took a couple of marketing courses, but they didn't excite me either. My favorite class was geology. I got an A, but what was I going to do with a major in geology? (Little did I know that my "nose for dirt" would serve me well in later years.) I couldn't get enthused about anything.

Finding Iris

I did get enthused one day in early October, however, when a ball finally bounced my way. I was playing touch football with my buddies in Cain Park, when an overthrow landed at the feet of Iris Shur. She was standing with a group of her friends, watching the guys perform, but I noticed her right away. When she called me that evening I pretended I knew who she was, although I actually thought she was another girl, who was not nearly as pretty. I learned later this was the first time Iris had ever called a boy, and she was shaking as she dialed. She told me her best friend's boyfriend was a friend of mine, and she wanted to know if I was interested in double dating with them to a sorority dance the following month. I readily accepted her invitation, but called her a few days later to ask her out so I could test the waters. We went to dinner and a movie at the Hippodrome Theatre in downtown Cleveland.

She was very shy. I was very interested. But I was not the smoothest of Casanovas. As we were crossing the street near the restaurant, Iris caught her heel on the streetcar tracks. "First pair of heels?" I asked her smartly. What a jerk I was. I thought I was pretty hot stuff, a 19-year-old Navy veteran taking out a 16-year-old high school junior.

I remember that first date like it was yesterday. Iris ordered a pink lady and I ordered a beer. I had another date for the following week, and so did she. Mine was miserable; so was hers. Neither of us dated anyone else ever again.

In the fall of 1947 Iris started at The Ohio State University, and we resolved to see each other every weekend, either in Columbus or Cleveland. We were both so miserable being apart that after two months she dropped out of school and came back to Cleveland, getting a job at the fine jewelry counter in Halles department store. We were engaged on Valentine's Day the following year.

I was very fortunate that Iris's parents embraced me the way they did. It wasn't like I was such a great catch. I had no money, no connections, no prospects, really. But Harold and Ceil Shur didn't seem to mind, or perhaps they just kept any reservations they may have had to themselves. At least I was Jewish; that was something. I think Harold and Ceil did see that I was serious, and a seriously hard worker. But most importantly, it was obvious to them that their daughter and I were head over heals in love with each other.

The summer before we were married I regularly hitchhiked to visit Iris at the Shurs' modest summer cottage on Mentor on the Lake. I slept inside, on the bottom bunk below Iris' brother, but at night I would sneak out to visit Iris on the screened-in porch where she slept. All we did was kiss and hug. I'm not embarrassed to say that Iris and I waited to do anything more than that until we were married. It was a different era, and as square as it may sound now, we thought it was the right thing to do. We expected to be married a long time, and we looked forward to cherishing the moment together.

On September 11, 1948, having completed only two years of college, I married the love of my life. That day, 9/11, remained all our own for another 53 years until a handful of idiots gave it another meaning.

Working for Harold

Harold Shur, Iris's father, was a sweetheart of a man, which is a great characteristic for a father-in-law, but not necessarily for a businessman.

Like most everyone else, he had gone through some tough times during the Depression, but he was very talented with his hands, and that got him through. Iris's house always had the neighborhood's nicest swing set, sliding board, and doll house, all of which Harold made by hand. His skills transferred well to pretty much any kind of plumbing, electrical, or carpentry repair that was needed. He made a living during the Depression by going door to door, asking for any kind of work. He had no trouble finding it. Everyone liked Harold.

Harold emerged from the Depression with a business that installed heating and air conditioning systems in new homes. The Harold I. Shur Sheet Metal Company did quite well for a time, particularly as the end of the War prompted a national housing boom. But people tended to take advantage of him. While he was always busy, his customers often didn't pay on time, or at all, and consequently often short of cash. Iris's mother used to say that the wives of his customers were wearing mink, while she could barely pay their bills. A few years after we were married, Iris and I helped keep the company out of bankruptcy by handing over our savings, $1,700.

But Harold was always looking out for Iris and me. Shortly after we were engaged, he came up with a scheme for the three of us to open an appliance store together. He felt there was an opportunity to undercut the prices of most of the stores in the area by selling an off-brand line of appliances manufactured by the Kalamazoo Stove and Furnace Company. So in early 1948 Harold, Ceil, Iris, and I drove up to Kalamazoo, Michigan to inspect the manufacturing plant and to arrange for the franchise. It was an ugly, rainy night, and the sole hotel in town was under renovation. There was only one vacancy, and it wasn't until the four of us were settled in that we realized water was leaking at all four corners of the room. Iris and I didn't care. We slept on cots side by side, a couple of feet from her parents, guiltily holding hands all night.

The sleepover turned out to be the highlight of our retail experience. In June we opened Kalamazoo Sales and Service on Coventry Road, an area which today is filled with trendy galleries and restaurants. But in 1948 this was a decidedly blue-collar neighborhood. I worked the counter between classes and after school. Iris ran the store during the day, or sat in the window demonstrating a mangle–an old-fashioned machine used for ironing laundry by passing it between two heated rollers.

From day one, we had very few customers. We tried everything, from leaflets, to free laundry service, to pleading with our friends. It was pathetic. No one wanted to buy an off-brand appliance when Maytag and General Electric were selling more modern units for almost the same price. Kalamazoo may have been revered on the farm for making a reliable coal stove, but people wanted the very latest modern appliance in their postwar suburban homes.

Instead of sitting in the store with nothing to do, Harold and I came up with a way to generate some quick income. We purchased a commercial vacuum cleaner suitable for cleaning the ashes and soot out of coal furnaces. I went door to door, and since most people had coal furnaces, business was plentiful. I put the vacuum cleaner on the back of one of Harold's trucks and stopped at every house within entire neighborhoods to ask if they wanted their furnace cleaned. I charged $15 to go into the basement, take apart the area of the furnace where the soot collected, and vacuum it all up. I'd get home looking like a chimneysweep.

This is one of those entrepreneurial ventures that can't miss because it offers a product or performs a service that virtually everyone within the market needs. In this case, it was easy to walk downstairs at potential customers' homes and show them that they needed to have their furnace cleaned. It wasn't the cleanest of jobs, and not many people were willing to do it. There are these kinds of niches all over the place; you just have to open your eyes to see them. Just recently I hired a company to remove the barnacles from the bottom of my boat. They specialize in diving and scraping them away. Who would have thought there's a business just for that? It isn't the most glamorous of jobs, but it provides a good, steady income for those willing to do it.

We closed Kalamazoo Sales and Service after about eight months. Its failure was a smack in the face to us all, but at least we knew when to get out. One common denominator of all the business mistakes I've made is that even the refusal to fail has its limits. Sometimes you have to recognize that you've made a mistake and walk away with the marbles you have left. The trick is to find the best exit strategy possible and to obey the *First Law of Holes:* When you are in one, stop digging.

The Honeymooners

Iris and I had a simple wedding ceremony at Heights Temple, just a few miles from where each of us lived with our parents. After spending our wedding night at the Cleveland Hotel, now the Renaissance, we took off for Florida in Harold's 1940 Chevy Business Coupe, a two-seater in which he had put a reconditioned engine just for us. We were so excited. Keep in mind, I was 21 and Iris was only 19. We had never been away overnight on our own before.

Armed with a box of leftover hors d'oeuvres, we enjoyed the first forty miles of our trip until steam started to billow from the radiator. At a gas station in Salem, Ohio the attendant poured something into our radiator, which was supposed to eliminate the blockage. But a half hour later, as soon as we entered the Pennsylvania Turnpike, steam again spouted from below the hood. It was a terrifically hot day, and ours wasn't the only car to break down. We followed others down a hill to a small creek where we filled a container we had found on the side of the road with water. It took several trips to refill the radiator. We returned to the turnpike, coasting down hills whenever possible, until fortunately, just off the next exit, we found a service station open on Sunday evening. They back-flushed the radiator, finally fixing the problem, and we continued on our way.

Four days later we arrived in Miami in the midst of a rainstorm and without a hotel reservation. I didn't want to be embarrassed at the front desk of a hotel we couldn't afford, so we drove by some likely candidates, then stopped at a pay phone to call ahead. The Versailles Hotel quoted prices of $10, $8, and $6, depending on the view. We took a $6 room.

By the time we awoke the next morning the rain had intensified, and we heard hurricane warnings on the radio. As Iris pointed out, the pool was being sand blasted anyway, so what did we care? From our hotel, we watched merchants board up their windows. At one point we lost electricity and had to walk up and down the seven flights of stairs. We spent three days never leaving our hotel. We spent a lot of time at the restaurant bar, even though neither of us were drinkers.

The first day the sun did poke through the clouds we quickly headed to the beach. I immediately jumped into the ocean, showing off for my new bride. When I emerged from the water, Iris was horrified to see blood dripping from my chest and arms. I had become slashed by the barnacles attached to the ropes that divided the hotel properties. We returned to our room and called the house doctor, who couldn't do much except charge us $25 to prescribe some ointment to ease the discomfort. Iris insisted on sleeping on the floor that night so she wouldn't disturb me. What a honeymoon!

A few days later, waterlogged, sore, yet still deeply in love, Iris and I began our trek back to Cleveland at 5 am. It was pitch dark, and I wasn't accustomed to driving a car, so neither of us thought to check the gas gauge, which we suddenly realized was in the red. We had decided to take the back way to Cypress Gardens, a 350-acre theme park in Silver Springs, Florida, about four hours north of Miami. Once we noticed the gauge, we started searching desperately for an open gas station. Scary-looking turkey vultures flew overhead, spooking us a bit, but we finally came upon a gas pump in front of an old house. When we knocked on the door at six in the morning a man screamed at us, "Get the Hell out of here," and threatened to get his shotgun. We got out of there fast.

We were getting desperate when we noticed a long driveway that led to a farmhouse, where we could see a group of men milling about. We were young and naïve and nervous as we drove up to them and asked if they had any gas to sell. It turned out they had their own pump for their farm equipment. They gladly sold us three dollars worth, which in those days got you a full tank. Finally, we were on our way.

Married Life: Setting Our Personal Foundation

Soon after Iris and I were engaged, Harold had told me that there was no way we were going to live in an apartment after we were married. I agreed with him that the difference between living in an apartment and owning a house was the difference between moving up in the world and taking a step backward.

The three of us went looking for a site on which we could build a house. I still had the $3,300 I had saved by never taking a paycheck while in the Navy, so we did have some resources. We found a lot in South Euclid on Verona Road for $1,200. We made a deal with one of Harold's contractors, Stein Home Builders, which was in the midst of constructing hundreds of bungalows in several Cleveland suburbs. For $10,200 they built us a two bedroom, one bath 800-square-foot house with no garage. Since we didn't have a car, we didn't need a garage. I bought my first car, a Plymouth, two years later and then, with the help of Harold and a few friends, we built a garage for $400 in material costs.

Our first home showcased what would turn out to be one of Iris's real talents and one which she would utilize in many of our real estate developments. She took a house and made it a home—making all our drapes, bedspreads, and curtains herself. She furnished our house in terrific taste, which was made more challenging by our budget. I look back on it now and realize that we recently paid more for a dining room set than we did for our entire house in 1948.

During construction there was a small fire upstairs, which burned some insulation and wires and charred some of the wood. Harold confirmed that there wasn't any serious damage. We had an electrician fix the wires, and we added more insulation ourselves. Then we covered the rest of the damage with a piece of plywood. We weren't planning to finish that floor anyway, so we used the $1,800 insurance settlement to furnish the house. Harold finished the basement for us, turning it into a wonderful recreation room. I can still see Iris, extremely pregnant, painting the walls in a zebra pattern to make it look like a nightclub.

Our mortgage payments came to a manageable $84 per month, still a major commitment for a young married college student. I now had the responsibility of supporting a family, so once again I was on the lookout for any kind of moneymaking venture. Although the Kalamazoo store had been a disaster, some of our other, more modest activities were more successful. For several months in 1947 I worked at a florist shop, ironically called "Flowers by Bart" owned by a man named Bart Holdstein. Then a friend of mine, Art Fitzmartin, and I got the idea of selling used clothing. We collected old clothes from our family and friends and rented a store for a few days in the lower east side of Cleveland. Iris pitched in, and we made upwards of $200. We did it again a few months later with similar success.

Law School

Just after we returned from our honeymoon, I made a decision that not only prolonged my schooling but also delayed any thoughts of making serious money. A cousin of mine mentioned that he had been accepted to Cleveland Marshall Law School after having gone to Cleveland College for only two and a half years. He also told me that my eighteen months in the Navy counted toward a half-year undergraduate credit.

I was frustrated with my college studies. I couldn't see where a four-year degree from Cleveland College was going to lead me, and I liked the idea of being a lawyer. Visions of becoming Uncle Dan's right hand man danced in my head. After all, he had always told me to come see him when I finished school. With his reputation as being a real mover and shaker in the community, I thought my future was secure.

Iris, conversely, wasn't too pleased about my decision. We were newlyweds, and she was naturally looking forward to me finishing college so we could start a normal family life. The idea of me spending the next four years going to night school didn't exactly thrill her. But she didn't fight me. She had faith that I knew what I was doing. That's love. I didn't at all know what I was doing, but her faith gave me confidence.

Working for Harold

The next four years were a frenzy of school and work, as just before beginning law school I started working five days a week for Harold. The Harold I. Shur Sheet Metal Company was housed in an old building on 105th Street and St. Clair in the lower east side of Cleveland. It wasn't much of an office—a large dusty room with a concrete floor and a small coal furnace to keep us (and the rats) warm. Three, sometimes four, days a week I would stop work at five, wash off the soot and grime the best I could, change my clothes, and take a streetcar to school. Classes typically started at 6:00 p.m. and ended at 9:00 p.m., and I usually was able to bum a ride part of the way home. I walked the rest of the way, which put me home around 10:30 pm.

My first task after starting to work for Harold was to put his books in order in an attempt to get the business on a more professional footing. I learned how important it was to be organized—to send out invoices promptly and follow up on them for payment, and to maintain an inventory of the material we had both in the shop and at the various construction sites we were servicing. I quickly realized we were leaving behind hundreds of dollars of material on each job site.

Like most problems I'd face in the business world, common sense played an important role in making the operation more efficient. It didn't take a genius to realize that our equipment and materials should be picked up, catalogued, and stored at the completion of each job. Although a bit more difficult to implement, it also seemed logical to design heating systems so that the efficiency of the ductwork was maximized. Keeping in mind that the shortest distance between two points is a straight line saved us money *and* made for a more efficient heating system.

At the time, people were converting to gas-fired furnaces, phasing out the demand for coal. Coal furnaces had typically used gravity to send the hot air through big round pipes, but most houses began adding blowers, which meant that we needed to design a system to connect square ducts through the basement and up into the house. I had no engineering ability (I still have trouble using a simple screwdriver), but I learned, out of necessity, how to measure all the connections, decide what kind of fittings were needed, and draw a plan of how it should snake through the house. I'd give the design to the shop foreman and together we'd figure out how to create the various fittings and piping that were needed. I'd then take it to the job and show the union guys how the system should be installed.

I learned a valuable lesson during my early years with Harold Shur Sheet Metal. I realized that taking college courses in certain subjects might help me feel prepared to tackle certain business tasks, and in fact, they gave me a good, solid foundation. But while school may have taught me how to think, my work experience taught me how to solve problems, make decisions, and implement them. Both the ability to conceive a solution and implement it are needed to succeed. It's therefore important to be flexible and be willing to learn from others around you who may have experience that you lack. In business, you never know what skills will be required to solve the problems thrown your way. It's also important to take on challenges for which you might not think you are fully prepared.

Iris Takes Care of the Home Front

Iris was incredible during these years. Both our children were born while I was in law school—Cheryl on June 19, 1950 and Scott on June 24, 1952. Iris' only relief was on Saturday afternoons when her mother would take her shopping and I'd stay home with Cheryl and have some friends over to play cards. Since I was the only one of my friends with a child, they enjoyed passing her around the table and playing with her. Soon Scott joined the poker game as well.

At that point in my life I was making $75 a week. Iris always said if we ever got to $90 per week, we'd have it made. But she always had confidence in me, in this case that these difficult years would eventually pay off for us both. I just took each week, each month, each semester at a time, working every day as hard as I could toward a goal I still could not define. It would be many years before I gave any thought to the idea of earning more than a middle class wage. Frankly, my ambitions were still fairly limited. I wanted to graduate, move into a slightly larger home, put a car in the garage, and support my family. That was about it. That to me was making it to the other side of Taylor Road.

Needless to say, I largely missed watching my kids grow up, particularly during these early years. I have Iris to thank for keeping our family thriving. But I did manage to spend some time with Cheryl and Scott. As they got older, Iris would take them to wherever I was selling homes. They'd sit in the car, and as soon as a customer left they'd come running out and I'd play with them until the next customer arrived. Then they'd return to the car to wait for another opening.

Bert L. Wolstein, Attorney at Law

The stimulation and excitement that eluded me in most of the college courses found me in law school, and I threw myself into my studies. I took concise notes and really applied myself. During my fourth year I attended class five nights a week, adding a refresher course to my full load in order to prepare for the bar exam. I finished seventh in a class that had started with 350 students. I graduated cum laude and received a scholarship to finish my undergraduate studies at Fenn College, a local business school. I actually attended three classes, but there I sat, a twenty-six-year-old Navy veteran, with a law degree, a wife, and two children in a classroom full of eighteen-year-olds. It was time to support my family.

Finally, in the summer of 1953 I took six weeks off to study for the State of Ohio bar exam. I studied as hard as I ever studied for anything, and was the first one finished out of 500 candidates. I was embarrassed to get up and leave early, so I just sat there until a few others started to exit. A few months later I was a lawyer! Finally I was somebody. Now I was certain that when I walked down the street everyone would point to me and say, "That's Bart Wolstein, the lawyer."

I should have known better. It was just like when I had arrived home in my Navy uniform five years earlier. People could have cared less that I was a lawyer, except maybe my mother, who was very proud, and Iris, who was happy that night school was finally a thing of the past.

While it seemed like we had much to celebrate, I couldn't find a job. I called everyone I knew and probably had about two dozen job interviews. But no one was hiring, particularly night school graduates.

My biggest disappointment was that my two uncles whom had been so supportive of me in the past turned me down. After promising me employment once I had finished my schooling, they now had nothing to offer. Although I wasn't really interested in insurance, I was hurt when Uncle Sam (Berkman), didn't give me a break when

I really needed one. But my real heartbreak was the rejection from my Uncle Dan. I remembered the day we sat at my mother's kitchen, before I enlisted in the Navy, and he told me to come see him for a job as soon as I graduated. I can still remember how elated I'd been, now matched by my disappointment when his son-in-law, Adrian Fink, joined his small firm instead of me. I'm not sure my mother ever forgave Dan or Sam—remember we called her the elephant. Adrian later became a State Court Judge. Could that have been me? Judge Wolstein. Perhaps, but I doubt it.

Getting a Real Education from Uncle Sol

The only job offer I received after passing the bar was from Sol Nadler, a well-known bankruptcy attorney in Cleveland. He offered me $50 a week, which was less than what Harold was paying me and hardly enough to support a family of four. Fortunately, another Sol, Harold's half brother, offered me a job, although not as a lawyer.

Sol Shur couldn't have been more different from his brother. Harold never had a negative word to say about anyone, and I never heard anyone say anything bad about him. I always got along great with Sol, but he was tough. Like Harold, he was born in Europe and had never been to college. With two of his other brothers, he had built a multimillion-dollar business that manufactured heating and air-conditioning registers. After reaping the rewards of the postwar building boom, he began to contemplate branching out into real estate development. I had met him at various family functions and began to see him more frequently once I started working for Harold because we bought the registers we installed in new homes from him. Sol also stopped by our office occasionally to take us to lunch. He knew me well enough to know I was young, aggressive, educated, and eager to succeed.

Sol had no interest in wasting time. He and I had that trait in common. Seemingly overnight he created the L & J Development Company, named after his and his brother's daughters, Leslie and Joyce, and planted me in a small cubicle at his midtown manufacturing facility. The first day on the job he told me to find some land on which we could begin building houses. We started small, with 26 lots on State Route 8 (Northfield Road) in the town of Bedford, about nine miles from where Iris and I lived. Sol bought all twenty-six sites for about $40,000. I was impressed when he wrote a check for the full amount.

In these early days I just took orders from Sol. I knew a little bit about the real estate business from spending six years installing heating systems with Harold, but what I didn't know far outweighed what I did know, that's for sure. Sol decided that the first time out in the world of real estate, he would build very modest homes, which fit with the land that I had found on a rather busy section of Northfield Road. We decided to construct slab houses—homes without basements— because they were coming into vogue. With no basement, the heating ducts, plumbing, and electrical wire all had to be housed inside the concrete, which was a relatively new technique. I took price quotes from all the contractors, everyone from roofers, to plumbers, to electricians, to kitchen cabinet makers. Harold, of course, installed the heating systems using Sol's registers. These home designs allowed us to offer more living space to buyers, as well as eliminate the costs associated with constructing a basement. That enabled us to keep our prices competitive. We marketed the homes by offering customers what they wanted—good quality, affordable housing.

Suddenly, at twenty-seven I was in the development business, in charge of every aspect of a small subdivision. I threw myself into the work, learning everything I could, as quickly as I could. I learned, for example, when building houses without basements you need to dig a trench below the frost line. (Three feet is usually sufficient, but if the ground is not firm you have to dig deeper to reach solid ground.) Then concrete is poured, just below grade so it doesn't show. The consistency has to be just right–thick enough so that it adheres quickly, yet wet enough to flow easily. Next, cinder blocks are laid up to the first floor and bolts are inserted so that the wood can be laid on top and the house construction begun. After the walls are insulated and the plumbing, heating ducts and electrical wires put in place, the excavation is filled with gravel and covered by a moisture barrier before concrete is poured over steel mesh.

This venture with Sol represented my first break, and I wasn't about to blow it. I arrived at the building site in Bedford at 6:30 every morning, six days a week, to walk through each house, making notes for myself about every little task that had to be done, who I needed to call, and when I needed to follow up. Many of the jobs I did myself—everything from sweeping the floors, to insulating the windows, to cleaning the construction site.

So many lessons that I learned during these years have stuck with me throughout my career. Although it sounds simple, I write things down, and I expect others to do the same. It's the best way to remember everything that needs to be done and track when things have been completed satisfactorily. Even today, when new employees walk into my office for the first time, I invariably have to point out that they've forgotten something. "Don't come to me without a pen and paper because I'm going to give you more to do than you'll ever be able to remember," I tell them. They quickly realize I'm right. Even when I drive around with Iris, she's always prepared to jot down a "to do" list.

My years with Sol represented on-the-job-training at its finest. I learned how houses were built, from the excavation of the site, through the building of the house itself, to every detail of its completion. I even interviewed banks to determine which would offer our customers the best mortgage rates and financing options.

When it came time to sell the homes we contracted with a real estate agency to initiate sales, but we also placed our own newspaper ads. Initial sales were slow. A building boom was still underway in 1953, and the market was full of homes that were much nicer than our basement-less houses and situated on less-traveled roads than our busy highway. We could, however, compete on price, and our units were solidly built, roomy, and offered an attached garage. I felt confident we had built respectable starter homes, and lo and behold one Sunday we sold six houses. After that, sales picked up, and within eighteen months of breaking ground on the first house, all 26 were occupied. My final task was to respond to every homeowner complaint, which ranged from a electrical problems to a missing heating register.

Another important lesson I learned from Uncle Sol was that you should never think of yourself as so important that you're above getting your hands dirty. One of the contractors I hired was responsible for insulating the walls, but Sol never liked to pay him to insulate around the windows because it was so labor intensive and extremely expensive. On Saturdays, Sol and I would move from window to window, tucking the insulation inside, making it ready for the drywall contractor to finish the wall the following week. We'd also pick up the debris from the yards to keep the sites looking clean and neat. I still smile thinking back on the image of a millionaire spending his weekends down on his hands and knees with me, Bart Wolstein, plucking woodcuttings, broken bricks, and other debris from the grounds. To Sol, keeping a clean site was an important part of building a reputation as a real estate developer who cared about his work. I honestly believe the weekends on site with me were Sol's favorite part of his week.

I also learned a lot about inspections, compliance, and filing appropriate paperwork, since we had Federal Housing Administration

(FHA) and GI financing for the consumer loans. I had to keep the inspectors satisfied that everything, from the thickness of the insulation to the quality of the electrical wiring, complied with their various, sometimes conflicting, regulations. Their nature was to constantly look for problems. I concentrated on developing relationships with the inspectors, as well as their supervisors downtown. It was important to convey to them that I wanted to do what was right and that I had no interest in taking shortcuts. It wasn't long before they got to like and trust me and that I felt I could go to them with a problem and resolve it together. I did the same with the many contractors we were hiring. I consciously made an effort to develop a reputation for honesty and integrity and to make them feel we were operating as a team to accomplish a job well done.

I don't remember learning in any of my business classes about the importance of relationships. Uncle Sol and I worked hard on developing close relationships with our contractors and developing a solid reputation within the industry. As a builder, no doubt the most important part of the developer-contractor relationship is the reputation the builder has for paying bills on time. I've taken this to heart throughout my career. Money is the fuel for the construction engine. If you want a contractor to be motivated to perform in a timely fashion, he needs to be paid promptly. Only then can he in turn pay his workers and fulfill his obligations.

I learned that personal relationships played in business. They are as much a part of the real estate business as bricks and mortar. I discovered that almost everyone in real estate hung out at Lefton's Delicatessen, the Tasty Shop, or Mawby's, all of which were just a mile from my house, near the corner of Cedar and Warrensville. I made it a habit to frequent all of them. They were veritable melting pots of the ethnic trades—Jews, Irish, Italians—all bragging about their latest real estate venture or the biggest deal that got away. These were the perfect places to befriend bankers, contractors, and developers and obtain information on current construction trends and costs. It was also the place to get the inside scoop on what was happening in town, or more importantly, what was about to happen.

These years constituted my *real* education, providing me with knowledge and experience that I think were much more important than what I learned in college or law school. I'm known for being decisive, for making instant decisions and not wasting any time carrying them out. But from Sol I also learned never to force a decision if it gives you discomfort. In those cases, often by waiting an hour or a day or a week or a month, the situation will evolve in some way and the solution will become clear. Sometimes simply not making a decision becomes a solution in itself.

Every principle I tried to follow, once I branched out on my own, was laid out during the six years I worked for L & J Development, summarized in the following chart.

Early Entrepreneurial Lessons

- Don't put off until tomorrow anything you can do today.
- Learn to hire the highest quality professionals you can find (lawyer or accountant or bricklayer or electrician).
- Have some understanding of what those professionals are doing so that with a little common sense you can tell if they are doing their jobs correctly.
- Learn to be flexible and do what it takes to get things done whether it is in your job description or not.
- Build a reputation for honesty and integrity.
- Respect your customers and vendors and don't hide problems that might arise.
- Customers are the lifeline of the business—treat them fairly and honestly so you can use them as a reference.
- If you're having a difficult time making a decision and find yourself really torn over what to do, just walk away.

Learning From a Tough Boss

I will always be indebted to Sol for the education he gave me. I don't think I could have received it anywhere else, certainly not in school. He taught me everything I know about business. But, as I mentioned earlier, he was tough. He was a relentless boss, always pounding me with questions until he found one I couldn't answer. I hated getting caught, so I tried always to be prepared for his questions. But he was a pro at that particular game, and I had to learn to swallow hard and admit when I didn't know an answer. That was a lot better than making something up because Sol could see right through those feeble attempts. But you better believe I'd have the answer for him ten minutes later. Uncle Sol always kept me on my toes.

Sol was all about work, something we seemed to have in common. I was always on the lookout for moneymaking ventures, including at one point partnering with a contractor we were using on the Bedford development to plow snow from people's driveways. Cleveland experienced some tremendous blizzards during those years. Businesses would shut down, but this contractor would pick me up in his front-end loader tractor and we'd go door to door. He'd plow the driveways and I'd shovel the walks. We covered entire neighborhoods in a single day.

Sol and I may have shared a commitment to hard work, but we had different styles. He didn't place much importance on people skills or personal relationships. He was always telling me I was wasting my time eating at Mawby's or one of the other local real estate hangouts. But I refused to stop going. I felt it was time well spent, even if almost everything I heard was someone's exaggerated version of his latest deal or project. I think it helped me learn to separate fact from fiction.

Sol also showed me a unique combination of micromanagement and delegation. On the one hand, he gave me a lot of leeway, expecting me to take responsibility for making certain construction was completed on time, on budget, and at a specified level of quality so we wouldn't be spending money fixing problems after the houses were occupied. But Sol also kept me on a tight leash. Sometimes it felt like I couldn't go to the bathroom without him wondering why I wasn't working. One morning I was driving to get a haircut and I saw in my rear view mirror that he was following me. But I stood my ground. If he expected me to work what seemed like 24/7, he'd have to have confidence that I would find the time to take care of personal business when it didn't affect my work responsibilities.

Garfield Heights: Surviving Business Lows

Even before the Bedford homes were completely sold, I had already begun to look for other opportunities for L & J Development. I found one in the more upscale suburb of Garfield Heights. This was my first introduction to taking a raw piece of land and turning it into a residential street. I hired an engineer to design the water and sewer lines, as well as the paved roads, and a contractor to handle the construction. We constructed thirty-nine homes, this time more substantial split level houses, which we began selling for $16,000 each. But it wasn't all clear sailing. We had just started the development when a rainstorm flooded the basements of some of the occupied houses, as well as some of the others under construction. Sol came up with the idea of installing sump pumps, which temporarily solved the problem. Eventually, we successfully petitioned the city to install storm sewers.

I blame myself for the mess. The engineering company we had hired had assured us that the basements wouldn't flood. I learned that it's not good enough to accept what your consultants put in a report or tell you at a meeting. It is your responsibility to probe and assure yourself that their answers are thorough and accurate. To do that, you have to have enough knowledge yourself about the subject at hand to ask tough questions.

Any free time I had was spent helping Uncle Sol with his manufacturing business. I'd often drive him to his large clients in Detroit and Pittsburgh, and made the deliveries myself to his smaller clients in Youngstown and Pittsburgh. I learned that a good developer has to be willing to do whatever is required to operate the business. In another suburb on the east side of Cleveland we chose a quieter, more desirable area and bought 40 lots. Now I learned how basements were built. In this case the developer had filled the low areas with dirt when he mass graded the site. That meant we had to dig twice as deep as normal to get through the fill and reach solid ground so that we could install footings. We could have filled the deep space with sand, but that would have been too costly. Sol came up with the idea of constructing a concrete bridge, really a reinforced floor fastened with steel rods to the basement walls. This became the basement floor and supported the weight of the walls.

Every problem had a solution, some more costly than others. Late in 1955 a 100-year storm introduced us to the fact that another piece of land we had purchased wasn't draining properly. I rushed out to the site only to watch helplessly as water swirled around some of our partially-built basements, causing them to cave. One of the houses under construction totally collapsed. We had a full-fledged disaster on our hands. Sol told me to call Mural House Movers to jack up the house to save it, but it was too late. For weeks Sol and I spent every day taking the house apart nail by nail, shingle by shingle, board by board, to salvage whatever materials we could.

After that disaster, Sol decided that homebuilding carried with it too many headaches and that we should pursue commercial projects. We built a 7,000-square-foot industrial building on Harvard Road in the City of Cleveland and a Fazio Supermarket in University Heights, within walking distance of my house. By this time Iris and I and our two young children had moved to a four bedroom home in Beachwood, a more fashionable suburb on the east side of Cleveland.

Sol decided to move his factory to a new state-of-the-art facility in Garfield Heights, and I helped coordinate the construction details. We didn't abandon homebuilding altogether, as we built six two-family homes in Garfield Heights to utilize the land Sol didn't need for the new factory.

The largest and last project I worked on for Uncle Sol came after Saul Biskind brought us a large piece of property in North Olmsted, an affluent suburb on the west side of Cleveland. He had plans to build a shopping center and already had lease agreements with several large retailers, including a supermarket and a JC Penney. But he needed a partner. I was at the meeting when Biskind announced that the deal was contingent upon Sol coming up with the down payment, at which point Sol blithely told him that *the partnership* would pay the down payment. Biskind, who didn't immediately realize that meant he would be paying fifty percent of the down payment himself, agreed. He compounded his mistake by blurting out what he had paid for the property. As a result, he ended up selling half ownership to Sol for half his original purchase price rather than half its value at the time. That taught me yet another valuable lesson—sell interest in a piece of land based on its current value rather than what you paid for it.

I was excited about supervising one of the most ambitious retail projects ever to be built in Cleveland. The projects we had developed thus far had given me some minor standing in the real estate community, and I thought that this significant shopping center in North Olmsted was my big chance to shine. Even after four years of building homes, then moving up to a few modest commercial development projects, Taylor Road still haunted me. I couldn't shake the feeling that I didn't measure up to those from the other side. I felt a strong need to prove myself.

I was ready to take this project by the horns and make an even bigger name for myself, but immediately I was chopped down to size. I came into the office one morning shortly after Sol made the deal with Biskind to learn that Sol had hired Skillken Contractors to construct the project. I was crushed that I wouldn't have the chance to put all of the skills I had learned to the test. But I really couldn't blame Sol. This was by far the largest venture we had taken on and I was a little out of my league. It was also more than 30 miles from my home, and it would have been difficult to maintain the same round-the-clock, onsite supervision I had maintained with our other projects.

Instead, I was given the task of signing up the smaller tenants, everyone except the anchor stores that had already been leased. This included finding interested tenants and negotiating and drafting the leases. I threw myself into the challenge, visiting most of the shopping centers in the greater Cleveland area. I went door to door, presenting the case why they should expand or move to the Great Northern Shopping Center. My legal experience finally came in handy, as I drafted lease agreements with more than two-dozen stores.

We marked the opening of Great Northern Shopping Center in October 1958 with a parade down Lorain Avenue. Iris and I rode in an open convertible with the local TV celebrity, Captain Penny.

Still Not Satisfied

Life was pretty good. I had a car in the garage and a savings account; we had even joined Lake Shore Country Club, a small country club where Iris could take the kids swimming in the summer. I was gaining confidence in my abilities, that I might just make something of myself, and that hard work really was rewarded. I was earning $18,000 a year, and I calculated that the following year I could earn $20,000 and perhaps $22,000 a few years after that.

Still, I was dissatisfied. Part of it was that when I looked around at my high school friends, most of them didn't have just paid employment. They were building something with their labor. Many of them had equity in a family business. One was a manufacturer of small electronics parts, one was in the tobacco and candy business, and another had joined his father's printing company. It wasn't so much that their annual salaries were higher than mine (although they probably were). They were all growing businesses and creating something with a potential limited only by their own hard work. In my case, it seemed to me that I was working ten- to twelve-hour days, six days a week, with very little financial upside.

Given the success Sol and I had made of the L & J Development Company and the fact that I was working such long hours, I thought I deserved a small piece of the action. For Christmas, Sol and his partner, Saul Biskind, had given me a bottle of Chivas Regal. It was a nice gesture, but I didn't think it was enough. Today, as the boss, I prefer to reward my employees with bonuses, which serve as much a better motivator than a short ride down a parade route or a bottle of booze. I built up the courage to ask Sol for a one percent stake in L&J Development. I figured that if you don't ask, you don't get. In this case, I didn't get.

When Sol turned me down flat, he had made my decision for me. His denial signaled to me that I was expendable, and if he thought I was expendable at age thirty-two, I'd be even more expendable at forty. It was time to do more than just carry a lunch pail. It was time to find out what I was really made of.

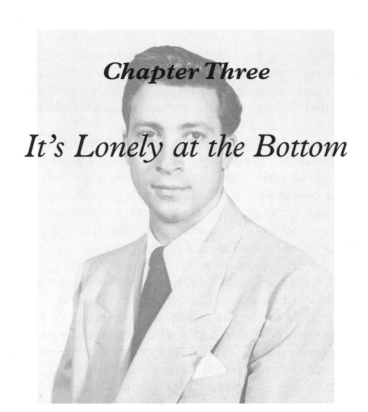

Chapter Three

It's Lonely at the Bottom

Forty-five years later it's difficult to remember precisely what possessed me to leave Uncle Sol and start up on my own. By 1958 I was supporting my family as well as I could have hoped, and I was comfortable in my job. I was even making a modest name for myself in the real estate business, and certainly my learning curve remained high. Even though not receiving a bonus was disappointing, it was more than money that was driving me to leave. Having a bigger house or better car was never really 'a goal' on which I focused. Much more important to me was to make something of myself in the eyes of my family and peers. I wanted to make it damn clear to everyone that I had crossed over to the other side of Taylor Road and that I was there to stay. When it became clear that Sol was never going to give me an equity position in the company, leaving Sol seemed inevitable.

Making the break from Sol was easier said than done, however. As soon as he so cavalierly dismissed my request for a meager one percent interest in L&J, I told him I'd be leaving after spending a few days completing some unfinished business. But I soon began to have second thoughts. I can still remember walking upstairs to our bedroom

47

late one night with my knees shaking with the sudden realization that I had a problem. I was totally unprepared for life after Sol. I hadn't a clue how I was going to make a living. Sheepishly, with tears in my eyes, I returned the next morning cut down to size and asked Sol for my job back.

Sol was nice about it, readily agreeing to have me stay on. Why not? I was building a business for him—he had a good thing going. But even after this little personal trauma, I knew my days were numbered. Most people in this situation would have taken the time to write down lists of the pros and cons associated with staying or leaving. I made no such lists. I just felt it in my gut. The question wasn't *if* I should go, it was *when* I should go.

I spent the next couple of weeks setting my mind upon the idea that I could make the break. I did make lists of the dozens of small tasks I would need to accomplish during the first few weeks on my own. I was buoyed by the fact that it was always clear that Iris and I were in this together. We reviewed our budget carefully and identified ways to cut back once my income had been slashed. That wasn't so easy, since we lived very frugally during these years.

I knew there were two possibilities for my life after Sol. I could be in the home building business, or I could be a lawyer. I particularly wanted to give practicing law a try. I had a law degree. I still wasn't comfortable calling myself a builder. Yet that was what I knew, so the answer seemed obvious. I'd do both simultaneously.

Fortunately, I could buy myself a little time before having to produce serious income. Iris and I had managed to save $14,000 during the six years I worked for Sol. I thought that was pretty good, considering the first couple of years I worked for him I was making only $12,000, and only the last year had I worked my way up to $18,000. My savings method was pretty simple. During the six years I spent with L&J, I continued to draw only $1,000 each month, taking the balance at the end of the year and banking most of it. Saving money, especially when you don't make that much, isn't an easy task. It takes discipline from the married partnership. Iris and I were on the same page when it came to saving. Having even a small nest egg to fall back on gives an entrepreneur options. For me, our savings mentality gave me the freedom to invest in myself. That's why I counsel students to learn to save during their early years because of the doors it may help open later. Without our savings, my transition from Uncle Sol toward becoming an entrepreneur would have been much more difficult, perhaps impossible.

Attorney at Law Again

Since my first choice, hands down, was to be an attorney, the first item on my "to do" list was to interview with law firms. I called everyone I had met during the years I had worked for Sol, but six years after graduating night law school and having never actually practiced law except for writing very simple lease agreements didn't exactly add up to a resume that knocked the socks off anyone at the top firms in town. So I did the only thing I could think of—I opened my own office on Chester Avenue in downtown Cleveland, sharing a secretary and a conference room with a few other lawyers. Suddenly I was in private practice! One of the proudest moments of my professional life up to that point was when the printer delivered my letterhead, which Iris had designed: "Bert L. Wolstein, Attorney at Law."

Unfortunately, it was one thing to have handsome stationery and finally to be able to tell everyone I was practicing law at my own firm. It was quite another to generate business and know what to do even if I did land a client or two. I knew I had a problem, but I was experienced and confident enough to also know that there were solutions. Hard work and focus every day had gotten me out of jams in the past, and they would come through for me again, I was certain. Hard work and focus. Every day. Every day. Those words became my mantra.

Each day I arrived at my office before 7:00 a.m. to spend a few hours in the law library reading about the practice of law. I studied mostly bankruptcy and divorce law and the various procedures necessary to draft lawsuit petitions. Slowly I began to get a few divorce, bankruptcy, and eminent domain cases.

But *slowly* was the operative word during these months, which pushed me to look for other ways to generate income. One of the lawyers with whom I had interviewed shortly after I left Sol was Edward Schweid, a brilliant attorney who had represented Sol when he bought a half interest in the Great Northern Shopping Center He was a partner in the prestigious law firm Bulkley, Butler, Rini and Schweid. The former U.S. Senator from Ohio, Robert Bulkley, was one of the other partners. Edward Schweid took a liking to me and offered me space in his firm. Except for the fact that I had to throw away the stationery Iris had just designed for me, I thought this was a good move. Although I wasn't part of Schweid's firm in any way, I figured I could go to some of his experienced lawyers for advice when I needed it, and the firm might occasionally throw some work my way.

One client I got on my own was the Great Northern Shopping Center, which was in dispute with a tenant over some extra costs incurred during construction. The Center had accepted partial payment from a vendor even though the check was clearly marked "paid in full." Our legal argument was that cashing the check did not eliminate any further financial obligation, as long as the party had scratched out the "paid in full" written on the check. The total amount in dispute was only $2,500, and the most I could have earned was one third of that. But I didn't take the case for the money. I had never been in court before, and Lord knows I needed the experience. We hadn't even had moot court in law school.

The case proved to be a tremendous learning experience for me even though I lost in State Court and then again in a split decision in the State Court of Appeals. I had a minor victory when a leading jurist at the time, Judge Lee Skeel, ruled in my favor in a descenting opinion. I appealed the decision to the Ohio Supreme Court, which ultimately ruled against us, stating that "Where a debtor, in a bona fide dispute over an unliquidated demand, tenders the creditor an amount less than the amount in dispute, under the express condition that it shall be in full of the disputed claim, the creditor has the alternative of accepting the amount tendered upon the terms of the contract or rejecting it entirely." The case can still be found in the law books and is cited as the definitive decision on the issue. It also represented the zenith of my legal career.

Developing a New Market in Twinsburg

At the same time that I was struggling to patch together a legal career, I was also pursuing several real estate opportunities. Shortly after I left Sol I went to see the top people at Forest City Enterprises—the large development company owned by the family of my high-school friend Albert Ratner. My mission was to convince them to give me a few lots on which to build houses. I knew they had made arrangements with local builders whereby Forest City provided the land and lumber and the developer built the homes. The partnership would then split the profits. Hat in hand, I didn't feel like the big shot attorney/businessman I wanted to be when I called on Albert. I tried to catch the ear of his father and uncle as they feverishly went about their business on what I assumed was a typically busy day. The flurry of activity excited me, and I wished I were that busy and that important. But even more, I wished they would give me the opportunity to prove myself.

After hanging around their offices for half the morning, I finally met with Al's brother-in-law, Sam Miller, who was in charge of developing partnerships with builders. He agreed to give me two lots in Twinsburg, Ohio with the promise of thirty more once the first two were started. I was ecstatic, until I drove out to Twinsburg and immediately decided that these lots must be the worst in Forest City's portfolio.

Twinsburg was not even considered a Cleveland suburb in 1959. Although it was only 25 miles away, it was isolated from Cleveland both geographically and psychologically. Even a telephone call between the two cities was a long distance call, and this area of Twinsburg didn't even have a reliable water supply. Twinsburg was also considered a "mixed" community, which in those days meant that the public school system was considered suspect. To make matters worse, the first two lots I was asked to develop were not exactly in the best location in town. They sat directly on State Route 91, Twinsburg's busiest highway. No wonder the first builder Forest City had sent there had gone bankrupt, a little fact I didn't hear about until after I started working there.

But looking past the obvious limitations, I saw potential. As Cleveland grew, its suburbs were expanding. It had already been announced that the Interstate would be going right through Twinsburg, so it wasn't a great leap in logic to think that twenty-five miles would soon be an easy commute. I also thought that growth could become self-fulfilling. A larger tax base would improve the schools, which in turn would raise housing prices. And I couldn't believe it would be that difficult to establish a municipal water system.

At any rate, I was determined to make a go of it. I incorporated Scott Construction, named after our son, and brought in Emil Hach, a carpenter/contractor and builder of specialty homes, as a partner. Hach had built the six homes on Sol's new plant site in Garfield Heights. He was a big, burly eastern European with a heavy accent, who could lean back his head and pour a bottle of beer down his throat without pause. He was a hard worker, talented, and honest–not a combination easy to find in the construction business. He brought in two carpenters, his nephews Jim and George Karabec, and they did most of the work in putting up two basement-less houses on Route 91. Iris added her talents to the project by decorated them beautifully, choosing all the paint colors, kitchen cabinets, and appliances. We priced each unit reasonably, at $14,000.

While these two houses were waiting to be sold, I began construction of five additional houses in a development named Summit

Hills, a subdivision just behind the two model homes we had built. These next five houses were in a better location because they were off the main road. My costs were low, and I was convinced I would easily be able to sell these more substantial, split level homes more readily if I priced them below $15,000.

As the five houses were nearing completion, Emil Hach suddenly decided he wasn't cut out for this kind of mass production work or the insecurity of our startup company. He gave me two weeks notice and was gone. Immediately I hired the Karabec brothers to handle construction. What other choice did I have?

Fortunately my law practice, if you could call it that, was starting to generate a little bit of revenue, much of it from Twinsburg. Once the electric utility company announced it was going to run the power lines right through Twinsburg, and the Ohio Department of Transportation decided that the highway would be going through as well, I began to take on a number of eminent domain cases. I hired two lawyers, Ken Zeisler and Jim Poland, to help me, and we moved into a top floor office overlooking the Public Square in downtown Cleveland. Iris decorated it in blue and beige, and furnished it beautifully, making it look like a professional legal office. Poland had worked for the electric company, and I thought the law practice was going to become my cash cow.

Things had begun to stabilize on the real estate front as well. The Karabec brothers were successfully putting up houses, and I finally sold both the homes we had built on Route 91. But as usual, there were problems. One day picketers started marching back and forth in front of my five new houses. It turned out that the wells providing water to the existing subdivision had run dry, which meant that twice a week huge milk trucks had to dump fresh water into the well. I had all the proper permits to build on the land and tap into the well, and the community didn't have the legal right to stop me. But an alarm had been sounded and I needed to do damage control. Any public concern that there was even a remote possibility that my new homeowners in Twinsburg would have no water would have doomed the project. I had little choice but to hire a contractor to build private wells for each lot, which solved the immediate problem with the picketers and assured my buyers of a continuous, uninterrupted flow of water.

In the long run, the picketers did me a favor because they energized me to take the steps necessary to bring public water to the area. I knew that individual wells were not a long-term solution. I had a few meetings with Cleveland's water department and arranged a series of meetings between them and city officials in Twinsburg. Fortunately, it didn't take much to convince them that it was in both their interests to extend the water line. Twinsburg agreed to build a huge new water tower and contracted with Cleveland to keep it filled.

Still, sales continued to be slow and I knew I had to do something to encourage potential buyers. We ran large newspaper ads throughout Cleveland, partnering with other advertisers, such as GE when possible, which allowed us to split the cost and get a little more bang for our advertising dollar. Even more effective was when I started accepting houses in trade. Just after World War II a developer had built hundreds of tiny bungalows in Twinsburg. They were barely more than garages really, but he had successfully sold them for $9,900 apiece. Now these homeowners were ready to move into something a little more substantial. About 75 people took me up on the offer to take their houses in trade, which allowed them to move up to much more spacious, more modern homes, with little or no cash. I also began taking second mortgages, which was another way buyers could buy one of our homes with a very small down payment.

I learned a valuable business lesson during this time, although it really was just simple common sense. People are more likely to buy your product if you make it easy for them. Consumers often abandon a purchase because of its complexity or if they feel intimidated. By showing potential buyers how they could easily afford a home with our trade-in and second mortgage options, sales began to increase substantially. That allowed me to persuade Forest City to develop the adjacent parcel of land into 95 additional building lots and sell them to our partnership. It wasn't like anyone else was clamoring to develop homes in Twinsburg, so I had no trouble convincing Forest City I was the right person for the job.

By this time my father-in-law's business was not doing well, so I brought him out to Summit Hills and trained him to sell houses. He was in his mid-sixties at the time, but he had the perfect personality for the job. He also knew the Karabec brothers, and it was a good fit. Now I had a salesperson on site every day whom I could trust, as I ran back and forth between the law office in Cleveland and the various construction sites in Twinsburg.

When the model homes were completed, we staged a grand opening under a huge tent, with musicians, food, and drink. We invited the Mayor and other City officials and it became a real 'happening' in town. After that, sales at Summit Hills really picked up.

Delegating Responsibility

It still seemed that I was dealing with one crisis after another. I discovered that sometimes delegating authority didn't work. Sometimes you have to take control of a situation yourself.

As sales increased, so did the number of complaints from new homeowners. A light switch didn't work; a shower was leaking; the garage floor cracked. It was always something, but no different than it had been building houses with Sol. Without close supervision, contractors sometimes became sloppy, or don't complete the job in a timely fashion. The difference was that when I was with Sol, I would pay daily visits to each house as it was being built, making a list of everything that needed to be done. I then immediately followed up with the contractor. I made it clear to them that if they didn't take care of their responsibilities and resolve each and every complaint, they wouldn't be paid promptly.

No one was paying that kind of attention at Summit Hills. Even my calls to the contractors or my pleas to Harold, Jim, or George to take care of the situations as they arose didn't stop the continuous complaints. Finally the situation became so bad that early one morning a homeowner came to see me at home. He was representing the other homeowners, and demanded that I immediately fix the problems in the subdivision.

My goal was to build a reputation for building quality homes. Instead, I had a homeowner revolt on my hands, which wasn't exactly a recipe for brisk new sales. My solution was to ask all the homeowners to write down a list of all the repairs they felt were needed. Then I scheduled a meeting with them early one evening in a garage at one of the homes under construction. I collected everyone's list, promising that I would personally see that every problem was taken care of. I also made it clear that I was prepared to make only those repairs to which they were entitled.

Back at my office I divided the complaints by contractor–electrical problems in one pile, plumbing in another, and so forth. I then called each contractor and gave them their assignments, and a few days later followed up myself with the homeowners to make certain each repair had been made.

I like to remind students who attend my lectures that just because you tell someone to do something, doesn't mean it will get done to your satisfaction. It also doesn't mean that you aren't responsible for the outcome. You're the guy with no back-up. You are responsible for following up on the progress of each task you've delegated. Staying personally involved in the process often means rolling up your selves and pitching in. Ultimately, it is my name on the door and reputation and resources at risk. That's why I spend so much time making sure the people who work for me understand my expectations.

Rules For Delegating Authority

- Be prepared to take full responsibility for the outcome of any project or decision you delegate.
- Delegate to those you feel represent your work ethic and attention to detail.
- Ask a lot of questions. Follow up with phone calls and personal visits to assure projects are completed on schedule, on budget, and at the expected quality level.
- Explain your standards for quality and other expectations to those completing the work.
- Be prepared to identify and fix problems as they occur even though you've delegated the work to someone else.

More Rain

Just after the homeowners' revolt was quelled, a heavy rain flooded the basements of the first five houses at Summit Hills. After my experiences with Sol I knew just what to do. I hired an excavation company to regrade all the backyards in order to direct the water away from the houses and into a storm water drainage area. Every day was a learning process that better prepared me for the next project or crisis.

While the houses in Summit Hills were selling well, my cash flow continued to lag behind expenses. Suddenly it was the middle of 1962 and after three years building homes in Twinsburg, I couldn't pay my bills. Turns out that taking your profit in second mortgages and plowing whatever revenue you do generate into new construction does not exactly leave you flush with cash.

Fortunately, my creditors trusted me, I think primarily because I was always forthright about my situation and alerted them if there was going to be a problem. These relationships now allowed me to convert my largest bills into bank debt. I sat down with the plumber, for example, to whom I owed maybe $40,000 and proposed that he borrow the $40,000 from a bank. He could keep the cash and I would sign a note taking on responsibility for paying off the loan. With some of the smaller contractors, I simply drew up a schedule that stretched out my payments over an extended period of time.

Forest City was my largest creditor, but it was also my partner, so I knew we had to come up with a solution. I convinced it to borrow $100,000 from the bank and give me $20,000 of it for operating expenses. I paid the entire note off in fifty-two weekly payments, with a balloon at the end. Looking back, it sounds a bit crazy to have been so forthright in my dealings with contractors and other creditors. I opened my books to them. They must have believed my business was legitimate and would continue to grow.

Diversifying

I was always on the lookout for additional ways to generate income, and even some early failures didn't dissuade me. I took lessons from each of them. I learned to:

- Think twice before jumping into a business I knew nothing about.
- Be careful whom I trust, and
- Be wary about hiring or doing business with friends or relatives.

One very early real estate venture was with Ralph Seidman, a former high school classmate, who showed me a four-family house on Quincy Avenue on the east side of Cleveland in one of the roughest parts of the City. The purchase price was $5,500, and the four rents totaled almost $250 per month. We figured we could own the building free and clear within four years. I couldn't argue with my friend's math, so together we co-signed a mortgage. It worked well until Ralph disappeared and left me to collect the rents myself. At least once a month for two years I would drive to the house to collect the rents. Armed with a puny pocketknife for protection, I'd extricate my 6'3" body from my tiny Mercury Comet and approach the house. There was always a different reason why it was impossible to collect rent—the tenant wasn't home, couldn't pay, wouldn't pay, or had moved out the week before. Although I was never in real physical danger, the situation was a nightmare.

Over time I paid off the mortgage. My reward? A notice from the city ordering me to either make a series of specified repairs on the building or tear it down. Demolition would have cost $2,500, and repairing it would have cost more. I couldn't afford either.

Again, I had to come up with a solution to avoid disaster. My overriding feeling during these years was that I was in this alone. Iris was my constant companion and advisor, but other than her, there was no one I could rely on to diffuse a crisis, solve a problem, or help me make the daily decisions that either create or destroy a business. It was like the old Three Stooges routine, as Mo hands a hot potato to Curly, who immediately hands it to Larry, who starts to hand it off to the person next to him, only to realize he is the end of the line. There's no one to hand it to; he's left holding the potato. I was Larry, poised at the end of the line, constantly reminded of the rhetorical question, "If not me, then who?"

Fortunately, in the case of the four-family house I found someone to hand the hot potato to, and it worked out for us both. One of the tenants had lived in the building since before I owned it. He always paid on time, and we had become friendly. I convinced him to buy the building from me for $800. More importantly to me, I would be rid of what had become a liability. I knew the City would never make the same demand of this African American tenant. It was a good deal for him because he now had the opportunity to both generate income and own the building where he lived. I probably made a $1,500 profit for all the many nights I slinked around the east side of Cleveland trying to collect $50 rents.

Another venture that fell into the wild and wacky category sprang from my revelation that second mortgages could be a profitable business in and of themselves. I subsequently got the bright idea that there was an opportunity in developing a business that made even smaller loans. Two wealthy friends of mine, Andrew Rosenthal and Archie Drosdt, and I kicked in $25,000 each to start a small-loan business. Rosenthal and Drosdt were both successful businessmen with the ability to arrange for significant lines of bank credit. The idea was to make small loans for televisions, furniture, or even vacuum cleaners, and charge people high, although perfectly legal, interest rates. We hired someone to run the business and soon incorporated the Twinsburg Loan Company, the Chardon Loan Company, and the Stow Loan Company. It seemed like we couldn't miss.

Sadly, we missed by a mile. For months our accountant had been assuring us that everything was fine, that the business was profitable. But none of the three investors had ever seen any cash. I finally insisted on looking at the books myself. It turned out that on paper we were doing wonderfully, but in practice more than half our portfolio should have been declared in default. I should have learned my lesson from the building on Quincy Avenue. How were we supposed to collect payments on a $300 loan without spending more money on collection than the value of the loan itself? The collateral for many of the loans was inexpensive furniture or television sets, hardly anything of value to repossess. We were relying on the integrity of the borrowers rather than on the value of the collateral—not exactly the wisest banking strategy. The problems were exacerbated by the fact that our manager had become friendly with a number of furniture companies, which were giving him gifts in return for making loans to people with little chance of repayment. It was a scam, and all of us, including our accountant, had fallen for it.

I felt responsible for the disaster. I finally found someone to buy the business, although all three of us lost most of our initial investment. This was another lesson in delegation. I learned that while having an accountant handle the books and take care of everyday financial matters makes sense, understanding the financial health of the business yourself makes even more sense. You, as the entrepreneur, are ultimately responsible. It was an expensive but valuable lesson.

By now, perhaps I should have been saying to myself, "Bart, you should stick to what you knew—homebuilding." But even some of my ventures that were directly related to selling homes in Twinsburg didn't work out as well as I had hoped. One idea I was certain would work was when I teamed up with a friend of mine in the insurance business. I set him up in an office in Twinsburg to manage home sales. About the same time I also hired a real estate agent to open an office in Warrensville Heights just a few miles away, which we called Space Realty. He was a sharp cookie, always with a cigarette hanging out of his mouth. He was also a terrific salesman. In fact, in 1968 he talked me into buying a piece of land in Strongsville, on the other side of Cleveland.[4]

By 1963 we were selling 50-60 new homes each year, worth a total of more than $1 million. We were also reselling at least half as many homes we had received in trade. My Hillbrook Building Company built the houses, Space Realty sold those that we took in trade, and my financing arm (me) made sure almost anyone could afford the homes.

---

[4]To date, I've never been able to sell or develop this piece of land. If you're interested in this prime property, call my office.

In theory, it seemed so logical. In practice, it was flawed. Although the building company thrived, Space Realty and the insurance agency did not. Each party seemed to have its own agenda. The insurance agent spent his time selling insurance in which I had no interest, and sold very few homes. The manager of Space Realty also had his own agenda, and I had to close that business as well. In fact, this was the first time I fired anyone, much less a friend, and it was no fun. Unfortunately, it would not be the last time. But the discomfort I felt from severing these relationships was nothing compared to the difficulties I had with Iris's brother, Lee. He had been working for his father, Harold, until that business closed and had taken on some roofing jobs. I offered him a position selling houses and allowed him and his wife to live in one of the new homes in Summit Hills until it sold. But things were not going so well for me that I could afford to have him occupy a new house indefinitely. I had to ask him to find another place to live so I could sell it. This put me in a very uncomfortable situation. One of the dangers of trying to help family is that if it doesn't work out, there are always bad feelings. It is natural for people to take things more personally the better they know you. Fortunately, in this case any ill will has dissipated over the years.

By mid 1963, traveling back and forth between Twinsburg and the downtown law office had become ridiculously time consuming, particularly since most of the legal work was being generated from Twinsburg anyway. Jim Poland had moved on to another firm, so I decided to close the downtown office and move Ken Zeisler into a new law office in Twinsburg. I also hired the elderly Mrs. Fashionpauer as my bookkeeper. That turned out to be a terrific move. Because I had so many financial transactions going on simultaneously—paying contractors, collecting and making loan payments, sending out invoices— I was waking up at 5:00 a.m. to write checks and address payment envelopes. Mrs. Fashionpauer took on those responsibilities and I was grateful.

A Handshake is Fine, But Get It in Writing

Despite some setbacks, the Summit Hills development was finally proceeding smoothly. I continued to scout out additional land in Twinsburg and other suburbs, convinced that the thousands of acres of undeveloped land in the area represented a gold mine of potential—despite the nay sayers. Twinsburg was still not exactly considered an upscale suburb, but

I could see its perception changing before my eyes. I don't know from where my confidence in Twinsburg came from, but I couldn't shake it. I knew that I had to somehow figure out a way to purchase and develop more land than I could possibly afford on my own.

Sometimes it seemed that all roads led through Forest City. Back in November Al Ratner had already offered me a full time job, which at the time seemed like it might just solve all my problems. As I mentioned earlier, I had $14,000 in the bank when I left Sol, but I was down to $2,000 ten months later. That's when I got a call from Al's right hand man, Paul Lipman. He told me Forest City was just getting involved in the shopping center business, and because of my experience with Great Northern, they wondered if I would be interested in coming to work for them. I was intrigued. At the time, this entrepreneurial thing wasn't going too well, and Forest City might just be the brass ring I was seeking. Al and I took a DC 3 to Utica, rented a car, and visited various possible sites in upstate New York, discussing the possibilities of building a series of shopping centers. It had started snowing, so we took the train home. Al told me to come into his office the following Saturday.

I was full of anticipation, but when I met with him he offered me a job at $12,000 a year. I was devastated and not a little insulted. I had just left a job with Sol that paid $18,000 per year. I was 33 years old with two kids, trying to make ends meet. I told Al I wanted $25,000 and stock options. I didn't really know what stock options were, but I thought I was supposed to ask for them. His answer was a resounding 'no', marking the end of our job discussions. I had no choice but to return to Twinsburg to tough it out on my own.

Now, just a few years later, I approached Forest City, telling them I was confident that I could option hundreds of additional acres of land in Twinsburg. Al Ratner and Sam Miller agreed that if I could deliver signed purchase agreements for between $1,000 to $1,200 per acre, they would provide the cash, and we would be partners in developing the land.

I spent countless hours driving from farm to farm, persuading the owners to sell to me by convincing them they could still keep enough acreage to maintain their homes and the peace and quiet to which they had become accustomed. Sometimes it took hours sitting in living rooms, talking to entire families, to gain their trust and come to an agreement. In some cases I returned to the same home two dozen times over a period of many months.

Iris would accompany me just so we could spend time together, which meant that either the kids were in the car with us or that one of our parents was watching them. I found the land, wrote the contracts, and handled all the property transfers. I also branched out into the communities of Macedonia and Northfield. Altogether, during 1960 and 1961 I signed options on 800 contiguous acres in Twinsburg, and in total purchased 2,500 acres in Forest City's name on which it ultimately built more than 2,500 homes and numerous commercial and industrial properties.

Unfortunately for me, they did it without my involvement. I didn't have the smarts to put our deal in writing, and as per our agreement I had purchased all the land on behalf of Forest City, in their name. Shortly after I presented Forest City the agreements signed, sealed, and delivered, I was told to take a hike, almost in those words. They had changed their minds and decided to develop the land themselves. I was flabbergasted, to say the least, but I had no recourse. I wasn't about to sue the great giant, Forest City, and I probably would have lost anyway. It was my word against theirs. Forest City did pay me $140,000 to disappear, which sounds like and was indeed a lot of money. But the thousands of hours of legal work alone would have totaled more than that, not to mention the fact that they had not paid me any real estate commissions.

The Vision of a Blind Banker

All was not lost, however. It seemed like Twinsburg had an almost limitless supply of undeveloped land. Just as I began seeing a positive cash flow from Summit Hills, the Suburban Building Supply Company approached me with an offer. Suburban owned 350 lots on 175 acres, which coincidentally at one time was the site of Al Brown's Camp Caravan, my old summer camp. By now I was the largest (and one of the only) builders in Twinsburg. Suburban offered me 100 of the developed lots for $3,500 each, plus an option on another 250. I was chomping at the bit. Somehow I had to find the cash, but I was stretched so thin. I knew I needed to find additional financing. I wasn't about to let this deal slip through my fingers.

Now came one of these turning points which doesn't seem as logical in its retelling as it did during its occurrence. I had been working in Twinsburg now for five years, and many of the buyers of my new homes had opened accounts at the Twinsburg Bank. I had built a name for myself locally, so when I asked for a meeting with the chairman of the bank, Lester Roxbury, and its president, George Hasman, they knew who I was and agreed to see me. I proceeded to tell them my life story, about how I had started with nothing and how I was bound and determined to make something of myself. I told them how much I had learned about the development business during my time with Uncle Sol and my first few years in Twinsburg, and about the tremendous potential I saw in their town.

Mr. Roxbury, who happened to be blind, had a reputation for picking out people with sound business ideas. For some reason, he took a liking to me. I know he liked that I spelled out for him precisely how his money would be used. Perhaps that's why when I asked him for $350,000, he gave me $375,000 so I'd have a little operating money. That was a tremendous amount of money in 1964, and while I did have a solid track record in Twinsburg, I was still just a 37-year-old kid with more moxie that moola. A year later he loaned me another $350,000, allowing me to continue the new development that by then Iris had named Heritage Hills. Although Mr. Roxbury never saw me, he took a chance on me, and to this day I can't really explain why. What I can explain is the effect his decision had on my life. To Mr. Roxbury, I will always be grateful.

The Birth of Heritage Hills

By 1965 we were really rocking. Iris, while keeping everything running smoothly at home, was also making significant contributions by making most of the interior design decisions. She was a natural. She had grown up visiting construction sites with her father, accompanying him when he bought supplies, and at his sheet metal shop. She became quite adept at cutting out pieces of metal shaped as small dolls. I always thought Iris's talents came from her father's side of the family.

Her flair for design was put to the test at Heritage Hills. We built an office and eight model homes, which Iris named after presidential estates, like Greenway, Lawnfield, Monticello, and Gettysburg. She chose the furnishings and made a myriad of other decisions about wall coverings, flooring materials, and appliances. She also worked closely with the architect to make certain each model was unique. Her contributions made Heritage Hills into a first class development in a suburb that suddenly didn't seem so isolated from the rest of the Cleveland metropolitan area. We featured General Electric appliances in all our homes, hoping that the quality most consumers associated with GE would position our development similarly in the eyes of potential buyers. Together with GE, we bought a six-page supplement in the *Cleveland Plain Dealer* which showcased the various models and the GE appliances. During one three-week stretch we must have had 10,000 people walk through the model homes. Iris had become an invaluable member of the team, and we'd eventually put her talents to work in a much bigger way at our shopping centers, hotels, and country clubs.

Even amidst the flurry of activity surrounding the Heritage Hills project, I couldn't keep the serial entrepreneur in me at bay. During the early stages of Heritage Hills, for example, I built the first condominium project in Summit County on a piece of property at the front of the development that backed up to some office buildings. I went through the laborious process of educating county officials about the state law concerning condominiums. But it was worth it, as the attached townhouses sold quickly.

While business was good, I was constantly strapped for cash during these years, choosing to plow everything I earned right back into the business. I couldn't afford to keep empty the model homes Iris had developed as showcases, so we began to sell them. Unfortunately, that meant we no longer had models to show would-be buyers. Feeling the pressures that go along with being stretched so thin, my solution was to bring in a financial partner, a furrier who with a nephew had entered the homebuilding business and had become quite successful.

At first I was delighted when he pretty much took over the Heritage Hills development. Although Iris and I had worked hard on this project, I try never to get emotionally attached to a business asset. I stepped back, content to spend my time on the law firm, accumulating more land and jumpstarting a number of other developments. But I paid dearly for passing the buck. The new model homes this man's wife designed were so poorly constructed, particularly compared to those we had already sold, that not only couldn't I use them as models to attract buyers, it took years for me to sell them all. Something didn't seem right to me. It was almost as if they had purposely done a poor job and I began to wonder if my friend's ulterior motive was to force me out of Heritage Hills altogether. I confronted him and insisted we part ways, with me retaining full ownership of the development I had created. He was older than I was and much more established in business, but I refused to be intimidated. I sensed this was a turning point for me personally. I grew up quickly and pushed back hard.

I was still financially strapped, so this same friend, perhaps feeling some remorse, offered to lend me $40,000 to tide me over while I figured out how to get Heritage Hills rolling again. Barely a month later, he wanted the $40,000 repaid in full, which once again made me wonder about his motives. But there was no way I was going to allow him to move me out of Heritage Hills and take over the 300 lots. With considerable difficulty, I scraped together the money to repay him.

Despite the fact that my association with him almost put me under, we stayed friendly. I try never to allow social and business relationships to affect each other. There are some people I don't necessarily like or even trust, but that doesn't mean I won't go into another venture with them. It does mean that the second time around I make sure I'm in total control of the venture. Many years ago I started putting a covenant in my partnership agreements that we can't sue each other and that the other party is a passive partner.

Looking back, I'm not really sure how Iris and I survived this period. By 1967 the homes in Twinsburg were selling almost as fast as I could build them, but cash-flow problems continued to hound us. It seemed like we went from setback to setback, with a few successes in between. I had so many ventures going on simultaneously that at least life was never boring. But Iris and I never lost our optimism. I was confident that once we reached a critical mass in Heritage Hills things would get easier. I was a builder, and slowly I began to accept the label without apology. It wasn't so bad. Soon I would close my law practice altogether and commit myself to becoming one of the largest commercial developers in Ohio.

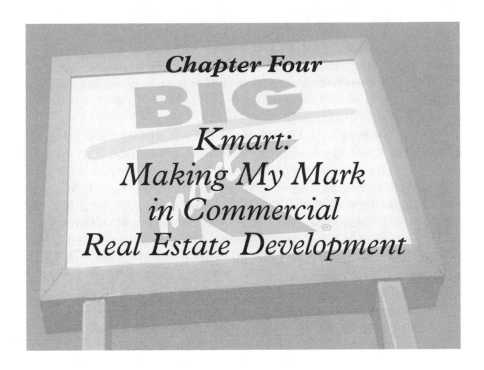

Chapter Four

Kmart: Making My Mark in Commercial Real Estate Development

After six years of working with my Uncle Sol and another six wheeling and dealing on my own, I had come to accept that I was, indeed, a real estate developer. The optimism Iris and I felt about our future began to manifest itself into real success by 1965, once sales at Hillbrook Development Company began to rise. Heritage Hills had just opened, the homes were selling reasonably well, and I had recently expanded into the nearby communities of Streetsboro, Stow, and Kent. I realized that I wasn't going to make it by focusing on my career as an attorney, and I spent less and less time at the firm.

My question now was, "How could I make my mark as a real estate developer?" Concentrating solely on residential development had proven problematic. Although I had built a lot of houses during the past few years, all the projects were long-term plays from which I didn't expect to generate positive cash flow for several years. Building and maintaining a steady cash flow remained difficult.

It Didn't Take a Genius

I was having more short-term success by buying land cheaply and quickly selling it at a profit. It was a matter of public record when and where the rapidly expanding Interstate highway system would be passing through the greater Cleveland area. It didn't take a genius to figure out that the value of the land would increase, either because the federal government would have to buy it or because gas stations and other service providers would desire properties in easy proximity to a highway interchange.

To me it was common sense that there was money to be made by investing in these kinds of properties. My problem once again was cash. My solution was to pull together groups of investors to create different partnerships. Many of them included my friend, Michael Miller. I had met Michael a few years earlier when we both had offices at the 75 Public Square building in downtown Cleveland. Our first venture together was in 1962, when I brought him in on a deal to purchase a 60-acre parcel (a former turkey farm) on the south side of Route 82 in Macedonia, just east of Route 8, halfway between Akron and Cleveland. It had already been announced that I-271 would be constructed right through the property. We created a complicated plan to come up with the $120,000 we needed. Michael Miller was responsible for half, and I and my other investors for the second half. We soon sold half the acreage to the Ohio Department of Transportation for $129,000, leaving us with 30 acres fronting Route 82. By 1965 the investors I had put together had become impatient, and I was more than happy to buy them out. I knew it was just a matter of time before we'd have the opportunity to sell or develop the rest of the land.

In the late 1970s I attempted to buy from Edward DeBartolo Sr. a 75-acre parcel adjacent to the old turkey farm, with frontage along State Route 8. We couldn't reach an agreement, but I persuaded DeBartolo's group to partner with me so I could build a Kmart and a Kroger supermarket on the site. DeBartolo was one of the largest shopping center developers in the country, and I considered it quite a coup to be going into business with someone of his stature. Finally in 1990 I bought out both DeBartolo's and Michael Miller's interests, and by joining the properties together I was able to build a large and very successful shopping center, called Macedonia Commons, the dominant center in the area.

I've learned that in real estate, usually it just takes patience to eventually see a profit. In 1970 Michael Miller and I paid $24,000 for a sixty-foot wide, .2-acre parcel on Route 82 in Macedonia, Ohio. Over the years, we went through numerous aborted attempts to sell or develop it. Finally in 2003 we sold it for $260,000 to a developer to build a Walgreen drugstore. It didn't hurt that the land was located directly across the street from our Macedonia Center, anchored by Wal-Mart, Kohl's and Home Depot.

During the next twenty years, Michael Miller and I collaborated on more than a dozen deals together. We even struck oil on an 80-acre parcel in Milton Township near Youngstown. The gas and oil leases more than repaid our purchase price, while the value of the land increased substantially. Of course, not every deal has been so successful. We've never been able to sell or develop a 20-acre parcel in Strongsville, which we bought together more than 30 years ago on the advice of my former manager of Space Realty.

My ventures with Michael Miller and others, while speculative, showed me that there was more than one way–hey, there were more than a hundred ways—to be successful in real estate. It doesn't take a genius, but it does take persistence and patience. All I had to do was keep my eyes open and use a little common sense and hard work.

The Big Opportunities Inside New Big Box Stores

In February 1965 I was still on the lookout for new ventures, although little did I know that I was about to have a conversation that would change my life. While at my parents' 50th wedding anniversary, I talked with Howard Young, a cousin by marriage whom I had seen at various family functions. I knew he was in the construction business, but I had never spoken with him at length about his business. It turned out that Howard, with his brother Ken, owned and operated a company called Hannan Construction. They were having considerable success as one of the first companies to build what became commonly known as "Big Box" stores.[5] They began working with Zayre, the department store chain, and soon thereafter for Kmart, the new chain of discount department stores being opened by the S.S. Kresge Company.

I'll never forget the day Howard, hunched over a cup of coffee, explained to me in my mother's kitchen that Hannan Construction had no direct relationship with Kmart. Howard and his brother built the buildings for developers, who leased the stores back to Kmart. Hannan was just the general contractor; it retained no ownership. I immediately understood that Howard and Ken were doing everything a

---

[5]A "Big Box" is just what the name implies - one large single-story store, in the case of Kmart about 100,000 square feet, that doesn't have the traditional walled-off areas of a department store.

developer did, but without the accumulation of real estate assets—a negative twist on the traditional real estate development business model. It made no sense to me. While I was no expert on retail construction, I had learned enough from the shopping center I had built with Sol and from my experiences during the past six years in Twinsburg to know how difficult it was to develop a site, whether it was to build 30 homes or a single big box store. Howard possessed a unique ability to conduct due diligence on a parcel of land and estimate the site improvement costs, including constructing sewer and water lines, installing electric power, and paving and lighting parking lots.

The Young brothers were doing the heavy lifting of designing and preparing the site, getting the various building permits, and constructing the building on time and on budget. After all this work they were left with what was surely a decent profit, but no ownership. I said to Howard, "If you're going to go through the brain damage anyway, why not develop the site yourself and end up with ownership?"

Howard understood the logic in my question, but explained that the developers who hired them to build stores for Kmart were providing him and his brother with a good living. They didn't want to jeopardize those relationships. If they suddenly established Hannan Construction as its own developer, they would essentially eliminate the need for the middleman and risk alienating their relationships with longstanding clients, who, they figured, would not exactly appreciate the added competition.

Over the next several weeks, Howard, Ken and I tackled the issue of how to keep Hannan's current customers happy *and* at the same time create a bigger upside for themselves. Our answer was to become equal partners in a new company, which I would operate. My responsibilities would include finding the sites, making the deals with Kmart, and obtaining zoning approvals. Ken would help me obtain financing, and Howard, through the Hannan Construction, would contract to construct the big box buildings. Iris, taking into account all the different activities I tended to get involved with simultaneously, came up with the name, Developers Diversified.

Partnering with the Big Boys

My first task as the sole employee of the new Developers Diversified Company was to approach Kmart about finding suitable sites for them in the Cleveland area. At Howard's suggestion, I tried to get in touch with Paul Harn, the Kmart executive in charge of the region of the country that included Ohio. I must have called him twenty times before he agreed to see me. As intimidating as it was then to approach the big boys, it's even more difficult today. You can no longer just phone the corporate headquarters of a Kmart or Wal-Mart and ask for an opportunity. You could call the real estate department until you're blue in the face and probably no one would pay attention to you. Today you often have to go through an agent to make yourself heard. Yet the way to get their attention hasn't really changed that much. First you have to tie up a piece of land by 'optioning' it for a specified amount of time at a specified price. It has to be a site that one of the big retailers wants, and you have to convince them that they want it. That usually means sending them a site plan with marketing and demographic information and making a case that there is a gap in the market which a new store on your site could successfully fill. Only then might you get someone to listen to you, but only if you're extremely persistent. Once you get your foot in the door, and if you perform well, you may get future opportunities.

The problem today is that many of the largest retail chains try to acquire their sites through brokers, thereby eliminating the need for a developer altogether. We've found ways to circumvent this strategy by being more strategic about the sites we option. We try to think like the retailer, examining markets where it has location voids and a high concentration of its target customers. We focus on sites that we know, through research, meet the marketing objectives of these retailers. The more desirable the site is to the retailer, the more likely it will be to make a deal because losing the site to a competitor will carry a high lost opportunity cost for them.

To become a successful company in this business, you need a lot of irons in the fire at the same time. Zoning complications and decision-making delays by the retailer will continually throw roadblocks in your path. Once a client gives us the green light, we act quickly to take advantage of the opportunity. The largest stores, like a Wal-Mart or a Home Depot, are now insisting on deals with very low, if any, profit margins for the developer. We succeed in this environment by using the anchor store to attract other tenants. We'll bombard these smaller retailers with demographic, market, and other information in the same way we did the anchor. Our ability to secure smaller tenants and to provide out-lots—the land on the periphery of the development, usually with its own parking—is imperative to generating profits. For the developer, these independent parcels are often the most lucrative part of any development.

During the first weeks after starting Developers Diversified I just clobbered the one name I was given, Paul Harn, with phone calls until he agreed to see me. I went to Kmart's corporate headquarters in Detroit and pitched myself and Developers Diversified hard, explaining that I knew the Cleveland market like no one else, having been developing properties there since 1953. I told Paul about Heritage Hills and the Great Northern Shopping Center, and I quickly listed other real estate ventures I had initiated and concluded successfully by sheer force of will. But most of all I assured him that with Developers Diversified, backed by Hannan Construction, he'd get a quality site, a quality building, and on-time delivery.

I was fortunate to get involved with the Young brothers just as Kmart was peppering the country with a new concept—a national chain of huge, stand-alone discount stores. Kmart's parent company was S.S. Kresge, named after Sebastian Kresge who in 1899 opened his first five-and-dime store in downtown Detroit. By 1912, he had 85 stores, on his way to more than 700. Now, decades later, the company had embarked on an even more aggressive expansion. Under a new president, Harry B. Cunningham, in 1962 the company had opened eighteen Kmart discount department stores, and a new retail giant was born. By 1965, just as I was getting started with Howard and Ken, Kresge had already opened more than 150 Kmarts. At its height, it would have more than 2,000.

Building Cash, Creditability, and Kmarts

When Developers Diversified was in its infancy, I remember Iris saying, "if only we could build five Kmarts we'd have it made." Well, in the next ten years, I built almost one hundred, possibly more than any other single developer.

At the beginning, the key to our success was that Paul Harn agreed to consider any site I brought him. I could hardly ask for anything more than that. At our first meeting, however, Harn told me that Kresge wasn't yet ready to enter the Cleveland market, not until it could create a critical mass in order to spread advertising costs over the simultaneous opening of four or five stores. In his eyes, Cleveland was a "no," and he suggested I look in Akron instead.

I spent a few days calling brokers and driving around Akron, but I couldn't find a site that excited me. I kept thinking that the Cleveland suburbs were the region I knew best and that there were several sites there that I was certain would be perfect for Kmart. By now I also knew that in the real estate business, "no" wasn't so much an answer as it was an option that could be changed. Just because Harn had said to avoid Cleveland for the time being, that didn't mean I couldn't convince him otherwise. If you listen to everything people tell you, how can you possibly expect to be ahead of the crowd? You'll be doing only what the crowd is doing.

I invited Harn to Cleveland to show him several sites, along with detailed demographic information on each of them. We spent two full days together, visiting a number of potential sites, as well as the nearby competition. Harn agreed that the Cleveland suburbs had immense potential.

The first site Harn approved was on Vine Street in Eastlake, Ohio, just outside of Cleveland proper. It turned out to be the easiest project I would develop in a half century in the real estate business. It certainly got Developers Diversified off to a flying start. Everything proceeded seamlessly, primarily because the Mayor of Eastlake was such an enthusiastic supporter of the project. He shepherded all the permits and zoning approvals through the City Council and Planning Board. This wasn't the way a real estate project was supposed to work, but I wasn't arguing. The paperwork seemed to just appear on my desk without me doing much of anything, and before I knew it, Howard had begun construction. The town gave me a plaque at the ribbon cutting ceremonies in early 1968.

With the Vine Street project under my belt, I thought I had hit on the easiest job known to man. It seemed I would just point my finger and a big box store would materialize on our land.

Almost immediately it was time for a reality check. At the next site Harn approved, in Brooklyn, Ohio I had to clear out a trailer park and help relocate more than 100 people. In Stow, Ohio, I had a tremendous battle trying to get the needed permits and zoning variances after a nearby discount grocer with local political clout put all sorts of obstacles in my way. It took almost a year for us to begin construction, although by then I had many more stores in the pipeline, including Kmarts in Florida and throughout the northeast.

With a little experience, we developed a formula. We paid between $200,000 and $400,000 for the 12-14 acres we needed to build the specified 116,000-square-foot big box store. Kmart would then lease it from us for between $2 and $3 per square foot. We were satisfied if we ended up with a small positive cash flow because we were content to build equity.[6]

In these early years, Kmart usually signed gross leases, which meant we were responsible not only for insurance and taxes, but also for maintenance of the roof and parking lot, snow removal, and all the landscaping. In order to account for inflation, most leases had a percentage rent clause, whereby we received a rent increase of one percent of the excess sales volume if sales at the store reached a certain annual volume. I gradually tried to persuade Kmart to move to a semi-gross lease, in which our responsibilities were limited to roof and parking lot repairs. In these cases, Kmart tried to eliminate the percentage rent increase. It seemed like every time we'd build a store there would be another kind of lease to negotiate. We were always trying to encourage Kmart and other tenants to enter into a net lease with either a percentage rent clause or rental bumps every 3-5 years. Under this option, the tenant would be responsible for all maintenance except for the structural soundness of the building. (There are so many fluctuations in insurance, taxes, and maintenance costs that it can quickly become impossible to keep up with these costs with percentage rent increase clauses alone.) If you keep the buildings long enough, of course, you will eventually be rewarded because cash flow jumps substantially once the mortgage is paid and the lease is extended.

Today's Retail Environment

In recent years chains like Wal-Mart and Home Depot have started developing sites themselves and retaining ownership. It's gotten to the point where the big retailers either lease the land from us or buy it and then build their own buildings. I'm not sure how well this has worked out for the retailer. I do know that Wal-Mart, as it continues its strategy of opening larger stores, has a huge inventory of older stores it no longer wants. This leaves big retailers with a dilemma. Just as I'm never thrilled about getting involved in a business I know little about, I've always thought retailers should be wary about entering the real estate business, but should instead rely on the developer's ex-

---

[6]Today all these numbers are inflated, of course. We can now pay several million dollars just for the land. But the principle remains the same.

pertise. If we make a fair profit, we'll take all the risk. 'Sticking with what you know' makes sense to me, although I haven't always followed that wisdom myself.

The major tenants we work with today, like Kohl's, Home Depot, Wal-Mart, Lowe's, and Target, are very sophisticated and keenly aware of the leverage they possess. Without at least one of them as a major tenant, you generally can't build a shopping center. That sometimes allows them to be unreasonable in negotiations, especially if they feel they can get away with it. For the most part, they don't care if your side of the business is profitable or not. You particularly have to be wary of low-level employees who are only interested in showing their superiors what tough negotiators they are.

Negotiating With the Big Boys

It used to be that there were five or six major brands in each retail category, but the retail environment has changed over the years. In the long-run, most industries evolve and succumb to the "Rule of Three," in which three dominant firms within a market survive while the other competitors consolidate under the leadership of the dominant firms or simply die.[7] In fact, in many areas of the retail sector the Rule of Three often becomes the Rule of Two, as with Wal-Mart and Target, Home Depot and Lowes, Barnes and Noble and Border's.

While developers may not have the competition they once did, they still do have a certain amount of leverage. We try to option land we believe will be desirable to more than one tenant. We then set a price from which we won't budge. We advise respective tenants that if their sales estimates don't warrant paying the rent we need, they should pass on this particular project. We're usually willing to show them the numbers we've used to calculate the price based on a reasonable return on our investment. If they then decline to do business with us, we make it clear that we'll find other tenants to lease the space, but that we look forward to continuing to do business with them in the future on other sites that better meet their criteria.

One advantage the developer has in this situation is that today's large retailers are on a fast track, having announced to Wall Street that

---

[7]Professors Jagdish Sheth and Rajendra Sisodia wrote a book on this subject, *Rule of Three* (Free Press, 2002).

they'll open a certain number of stores per year. They don't have time for long negotiations; they need to get stores built. Once they realize you are financially capable of standing toe to toe with them, they more often than not will agree to a fair deal. But crumble once by settling below the line you've drawn and you'll likely not survive in this business. It's no different than negotiating for a piece of jewelry as a tourist in Greece or the Caribbean. If the merchant doesn't have a bottom line, he'll never make a sale because you'll always think you can make the purchase for less.

Closing the Sale: The Personality Factor

By the end of 1969 I was visiting Kmart headquarters about twice a month. I'd take a Tag Airline commuter jet from the Burke Airport on the lake in Cleveland to City Airport in downtown Detroit. I would often catch the first morning flight and be at Kmart's Detroit headquarters before the executives arrived at their desks. We'd meet all morning, negotiating leases and discussing sites, and then a number of us would go down the street for a meal, which often turned into a two-martini lunch. I didn't think people really had two-martini lunches, but the Kmart "organizational man," clad in suit, white shirt and tie, proved these lunches were not mythical at all. I've never been a big drinker, but I tried to keep up with them because these lunches were a great way to get to know the other Kmart real estate executives to whom Harn was introducing me. In fact, the relationships I made in Detroit restaurants were critical to Developer Diversified's ultimate success.

I can't stress enough that in addition to working hard and staying focused 365 days a year, the other important ingredient for business success is relationships. Trying to do business with a mega-retailer can seem like an impersonal task. The key is to think of the company not just as a corporate logo, but as a set of names, faces, and people within the organization who you need to get to know and connect with in order to accomplish your task at hand.

My task was to sell our services to Kmart and ultimately form a long-term business relationship with them. Just as I needed to get to know the people at Kmart, I needed to let them get to know me so that they wouldn't think of Diversified as just another developer after their business. Over the years, I've found that succeeding in business is easier if you project a personality that makes people want to do business with you. Sometimes this personality is an unexplainable magnetism, like with Uncle Dan. But in most cases, getting people to like you is almost a scientific process. It may mean having lunch or dinner with them, taking them to a football game, or getting to know their families. The people I do business with more often than not consider me their friend because they know I talk from the heart and say what I'm thinking. People who are going to continue to give you their business have to know you and trust you, which means being straight with them. This isn't always easy, particularly during tough times when you don't necessarily have the answers they would like to hear or that you would like to give them. But you're more likely to get into trouble by trying to avoid unpleasant situations. That's why to this day I return every phone call promptly, even if I don't have the answers people want to hear. Getting people to like you is influenced by how you treat others. That means honoring everyone, from the person who cleans the rooms in a hotel you own, to the chief executive of a Fortune 500 corporation with which you want to do business.

Learning from Your Partner

Partnering with Kmart, a company that was changing the retail landscape and breaking new ground in the business world, gave me insights into strategy, marketing, and management. By observing Kmart's success, I learned a lot about how to grow strategically, but also how wrong decisions and poor implementation can affect a large organization. There's no question Harry Cunningham was a visionary, but I sometimes had to shake my head when I saw some of the policies the S.S. Kresge Company imposed on Kmart stores during their early years of rapid expansion. I can't say I was surprised that the company eventually collapsed under the weight of its management's bad judgment.

In *Kmart's Ten Deadly Sins: How Incompetence Tainted an American Icon,* author Marcia Layton Turner chronicles Kmart's steady descent into its 2002 bankruptcy. She focuses almost exclusively on recent executive misdeeds and retailing mistakes, while ignoring some of the early questionable decisions that made later failings almost inevitable.[8] In the early days, for example, management had the not-so-bright-idea of leasing 20,000 square feet within each of

---

[8]Marcia Layton Turner, *Kmart's Ten Deadly Sins: How Incompetence Tainted an American Icon,* John Wiley & Sons, 2003.

its 116,000-square-foot Kmart stores to an independent supermarket company called Allied. Just as Kmart and others were creating
giant stand-alone discount stores in the late 1960s, so too were the
major supermarket chains building large super stores. There was no
way Kmart's food store tenant could compete in only 20,000
square feet.

It took Kmart only a few years to run Allied into bankruptcy. Including a grocery section within each Kmart wasn't a bad concept; it
was the terrible implementation of the concept that irked me. The
Grand Rapids-based regional retailer, Meijer, had success selling
groceries and hard goods under the same roof. The difference was
that Meijer didn't lease out the grocery space. It actually started in
groceries, mastering this low-margin business, and gradually added
other merchandise to its mix. It had a large grocery section that could
compete with any free-standing grocery store, but was also able to
offer its customers a wide variety of products, from clothing and
sporting goods to home products and beauty items. Kmart's vision
wasn't incorrect, it just didn't execute its strategy well.

As Kmart's captive supermarket was tanking, the company gradually folded the extra space into each store or subleased it to a third
party. I tried to convince Harn and others at Kmart that building adjacent, freestanding buildings, which we would lease to a leading supermarket chain large enough to compete effectively, would give
customers a bigger complement of offerings and actually draw more
patrons to Kmart. Sure, expanding each development with more
stores would be good for Developers Diversified, but I was also certain that a first class supermarket could only increase traffic to the
Kmart. I had a hard time thinking of any downside, and an even
harder time convincing Kmart that my logic was sound.

We finally tested the waters in 1970 with two projects in Portland,
Maine, which turned out to be big successes for both the Kmarts and
the supermarkets. Even then it took me more than a year to convince
the S.S. Kresge Company to take the next step and allow us to expand our developments by building several additional attached
stores. We finally accomplished that goal in Ocala, Florida in 1971,
after which we began building shopping centers with Kmarts as the
major anchors rather than just stand-alone Kmart big box buildings.
We had moved from building a single store, to a store and a supermarket, to full-fledged shopping centers.

Losing a Friend, Parting with a Partner, Rebuilding a Team

Things were moving along nicely at this point in my life. I had taken office space in the Hannan Construction building in Beachwood, and by 1970 we had built five Kmarts and another seven had been approved. I should have known it was too good to last. In the real estate business, and in most other businesses as well, expect surprises; it'll help keep you on your toes. Sure enough, in late 1970, less than five years after Developers Diversified began operations, Howard Young died of a blood disease after a very short illness. The loss was painful both personally and professionally—I lost a partner and a friend.

Howard Young was as honest and as conscientious as anyone could ever want to have in a partner. He was also a construction genius. I never had to worry about any of his buildings being completed on time and on budget. His work ethic and standards were crucial to our early success because I had my hands full running back and forth to Detroit and all over the Northeast, Midwest, and Florida buying land, arranging zoning approvals and financing, and monitoring construction schedules at the growing number of sites under development.

Call it poor planning or that feeling of invincibility we have when we're young, but none of us had made arrangements for what would happen if one of us were to die. When Howard passed, he left a young widow and four children. Ken and I wanted to be fair, and bought out Howard's share by paying his estate one-third the value of the projected cash flow of the five Kmarts we had built, as well as one-third of the value of the cash flow that would be generated from the next seven stores we had in the planning stages. That gave Howard's widow an immediate and perpetual annual income of more than $125,000, without any debt or other responsibilities. Going forward, Ken and I now owned 50% of Developers Diversified.

Howard's death brought to light another problem, however—my relationship with Ken. It soon became apparent that without Howard, our partnership wasn't going to work. Ken's role in Developers Diversified was intended to be on the financial side, obtaining the construction loans and then converting them to mortgages once the buildings were completed. But after we built our first couple of Kmarts, the financing was easy and I was able to handle negotiations myself. During the first months of our partnership, Ken had introduced me to

Hannan Construction's bankers at the Central National Bank of Cleveland, and I had taken it from there. Kmart was flying high, and soon so were we, which made it relatively easy to get the necessary bank funds for both construction and permanent loans after completion.

Although I no longer needed any help with the financing, I did rely on Ken to complete the Kmarts on time and on budget. Ken didn't have that same experience, and without Howard it wasn't long before we started having trouble meeting our construction deadlines. Kmart was only interested in a quality site, at a fair price, and most importantly, available for occupancy on the agreed upon date. Kmart precisely scheduled the delivery of each store's merchandise and the hiring of personnel based on these projected completion dates. Even a one-day delay was extremely costly to the company and would not be tolerated.

By 1972 I was basically running Developers Diversified single-handedly, and with so many Kmarts going up simultaneously, I needed help. I brought Jim Karabec into the company to supervise construction, and instructed him to put the building of Kmarts up for competitive bid to other construction companies besides Hannan.

I had to make certain we met our timetables. I closed the Twinsburg law firm, and asked Ken Zeisler to join me as my second in command. Zeisler could see that Developers Diversified was doing well, but it was still a big step for him. He had been practicing law since graduating law school, and I essentially was asking him to make a career change. As an incentive, and because we would be closing the law firm in which he had a financial interest, he asked for a 5% ownership in Developers Diversified. I thought that was reasonable and took the proposal to Ken Young, who quickly replied that he wasn't interested in Zeisler being hired, let alone giving him 5% of the company. He said that if I wanted to grant Ken equity, it would have to come out of my share alone. I was the one running around the country buying land and negotiating leases with Kmart. I was even supervising all the construction through Jim Karabec. But if I wanted any help it would have to come out of my pocket alone. That would have left me as a minority owner, which was unacceptable to me given my growing responsibilities.

My split with Ken Young was amicable. We put all Developer's Diversified's assets on the table and divided them down the middle. Ken took sole possession of Kmarts that had a projected cash flow of approximately $400,000. I received the other half of the assets, as well as all the work in process and the liabilities.

There I was—alone again. Yet I was thrilled to be flying solo again and ready to devote 100% of my energy into Developers Diversified. Ken Zeisler began running the day-to-day operations, and as soon as we shut the doors on the law firm in Twinsburg, I hired Pat Morgan as our chief counsel. I also started hiring people to look for land, lawyers to negotiate the deals, construction supervisors, and people to lease the stores and manage the properties. Soon our staff totaled more than fifty, and we had moved into larger quarters in the Hannan Construction office building.

The next few years were among the busiest ever. With an ever-increasing staff, a booming national economy, and Kmart opening more than 200 stores each year, there was nothing we couldn't do. We had even successfully convinced Kmart to depart from its fixation with freestanding stores and allow us to make them part of shopping centers and finally shopping malls. In fact, our 1975 development in Worthington, Minnesota was the first Kmart ever to be located inside a mall. Typical of the company's shortsightedness, however, it insisted that the store not have an entrance into the mall but only onto the street. I thought this was absurd, but we developed what the customer wanted. Once we were open for a few months even Kmart could see that it inhibited store traffic. In the future they agreed to have entrances into the malls.

The Worthington project was part of Developers Diversified's strategy of moving from freestanding Kmarts to shopping centers or malls in which Kmart would be an anchor. We piggybacked on Kmart's strategy of locating stores in middle-market America by approaching the JCPenney chain, which had also expressed interest in rolling out smaller stores in midsize markets. We began building enclosed malls all over the Midwest, anchored by a Kmart and a JCPenney, and sometimes the regional store, Herbergers, along with a cadre of other national tenants like Zales Jewelers, B Daltons bookstores, and Kinney shoes.

By 1977 business was so good that I was giving thought to working another five years and perhaps retiring at the age of 55. That may sound odd coming from someone who today, at 77, gets up at 5:15 every morning to begin his daily routine so he can be in the office by 8:30 a.m. I'm as enthused about my current projects as I've ever been. But at the time, Developers Diversified, with Ken Zeisler taking on an increasing amount of responsibility, was pretty much running itself. The idea of spending more time with Iris, either traveling or working on a few big projects together, was very appealing. As usual, however, I was about to be thrown a curve.

Zeisler Departs

Perhaps I should have seen it coming, but I didn't. I was shocked when Ken Zeisler, who had become an integral part of the company after Howard's death and had become like a family member, announced he was leaving. I felt like he was turning his back on me, which stung. I had given Ken a host of opportunities over the years—first in the downtown law firm, later in Twinsburg, and then when I granted him get a 5% interest in what was now a multimillion-dollar real estate business. But it was more personal than that. During the summer of 1974, Ken and his family spent almost every weekend at my home, as the seven of us swam in the pool and barbecued together. Scott, who by this time was in law school and had worked for Ken as a summer intern, was as close to him as he was to any uncle, as was Cheryl.

In retrospect, perhaps my suspicions should have been raised in early 1975 when he came to me and virtually demanded a big raise and another five percent interest in Developers Diversified. I politely turned him down. I certainly should have smelled something fishy in May when we were all at the Shopping Center Convention in Las Vegas and he and Pat Morgan, the head of our legal department, spent most of their time without me, wining and dining Diversified's bankers and major national tenants, all on our nickel, of course. But I trusted Ken as much as I trusted anyone, and I didn't suspect a thing.

A few days after we all returned from Las Vegas Ken walked into my office and told me he was leaving, along with several key people, including Pat Morgan. It was much more of a personal blow than a business setback. I had no trouble jumping right back into the business and taking responsibility once again for the day-to-day running of the company. But I was terribly hurt personally.

When you own a business, you have to get used to the idea that some people will leave you. I have no problem when someone working for me takes another job or decides to strike out on his own. I of all people can respect that. In fact, I'm proud of all the people I've trained over the years who have gone on to become successful elsewhere. I'm flattered when they refer to their tenure working for me as getting their education at "Wolstein University." But in most of those instances people have told me up-front that they either had received a better offer or that they wanted the freedom they could only achieve on their own. I always wished them well, and we remained friends. I can think of dozens of people who fit into that category.

In Ken Zeisler's case, however, he had already leased an office when he told me he was leaving. He had also discussed possible deals with some of our business contacts. By taking Pat Morgan and several others with him, he had changed what would have simply been a split based on dissatisfaction with his current position or the desire to do something on his own into what felt like a conspiracy. It's one thing for someone to say that "I need to spread my wings;" it's another thing altogether to say "I'm taking the guy who would be my replacement and leaving you high and dry."

Although it was suggested to me, I never seriously considered suing Ken Zeisler to prevent him from setting up a competing business. I didn't want to spend the next year or more battling him in court, and I wasn't really worried about the competition. Besides, I realized that I would have been doing it out of revenge more than anything else—and that, in the end, is never good business. Yet in all honesty, what did burn me was that Zeisler expected to retain a five percent interest not only in all the projects created by Developers Diversified during the previous five years, but everything we had in the planning stages. A few days after announcing his departure, he came to my office with his lawyer and a list of every site we had ever contemplated developing. If we had so much as flown over a site, it was on his list. He expected five percent ownership in all of them, which would have meant that everything I did for the next fifteen years would have been partly for his benefit.

You can be sure there was no way I was going to allow that to happen. I knew that Zeisler was planning to fund his new company from the cash flow that his five percent of Developers Diversified. So I decided not to take any cash flow myself for the foreseeable future. If I didn't take cash flow, neither could he. Regardless of how fancy the calculator, five percent of nothing was still zero.

Once Ken realized he wasn't going to be receiving any cash flow from his old venture to fund his new one, we sat down with our lawyers and quickly hammered out an agreement. I agreed Ken could take ownership of stores that threw off $125,000 annually. As with my dissolution agreement with Ken Young just four years earlier, I retained all work in process and liabilities.

Saying Goodbye to Kmart

After the defection of Zeisler, Morgan, and the others, I had no trouble stepping right back into the nitty-gritty daily operations of Diversified, and the company didn't miss a beat. In fact, the next few years were our busiest ever, mostly because of the continued expansion of the S.S. Kresge Company, which opened 271 Kmart stores in 1976 alone. The following year, the company officially changed its name to the Kmart Corporation.

Yet despite our track record with Kmart, by the end of the decade we were beginning to have difficulty getting approval for the sites we were bringing to the table. The problem was no mystery to anyone who had been observing Kmart carefully. It had become obvious that other developers had created inappropriate personal relationships with some of the Kmart real estate executives. I've always told my people never to do anything that might result in being forced on the witness stand to either tell the truth and possibly go to jail or lie and commit perjury. There was just no way I was going to jeopardize everything I had worked so hard for, most importantly my reputation, just to add another shopping center to Developers Diversified's portfolio.

The direction Kmart was going was alarming to me. Suddenly a new group of Kmart executives was responsible for making real estate decisions, and many of our sites were being rejected in favor of inferior ones. Often I would bring them a project for review and they'd say "Oh no, we already are working on a site in that area," or "That market isn't mature enough to warrant one of our stores." I would then drop our interest in the site, only to find a few months later that they had sent one of their favored developers to gain control over that same site. They just weren't playing it straight, which was really a shame because Kmart had been an extremely well organized, disciplined, well-managed company. In the early years everyone at all levels was talented, honorable, and extremely dedicated, giving the company a solid foundation on which to build its success. The new top leadership didn't seem to have the same work ethic and discipline, and the company began to falter.

In 1980 I had fourteen full time people devoted solely to looking for new sites. I felt that people inside Kmart were tipping off other developers about the locations we were presenting them, but I never really found out for certain how other developers were finding out the specifics on the sites we identified. It got to the point where we suspected our people were being tailed as they looked for sites. I also wondered if perhaps the leaks were coming from inside my own company.

I told the top people at Kmart what was going on, but they didn't want to hear about it. The final straw came when a site we had optioned in Macedonia, Ohio at the intersection of Routes 8 and 82 (close to the old turkey farm) that served four communities was rejected in favor of a grossly inferior one in Twinsburg, which more than twenty-five years later still hasn't been developed. I knew Twinsburg real estate probably better than anyone in the world, and I knew it was a poor site that would generate little traffic.

My reputation was involved in the Macedonia site, and I at least wanted this one to be approved. This was the land that was owned by the real estate pioneer and San Francisco 49er owner Eddie DeBartolo Sr., whom I had convinced to develop the property with me. I didn't want to back out on assurances I had made him that the Macedonia Kmart would be approved.

I persuaded Walter Tenninga, vice chairman of Kmart's Board of Directors, to come to Cleveland to see both sites for himself. I had no trouble convincing him to give us the go ahead in Macedonia, but this was the last Kmart I'd ever build. I couldn't exactly expect the vice chairman of Kmart to come to Cleveland or any other city to overrule a decision every time one of our sites was rejected by his management.

I had 75 properties under option for possible Kmart stores. One day in early 1980 I came to the office, summoned everyone to a staff meeting, and announced, "We are out of the Kmart business. Terminate every one of our options." I was just not going to do business this way, and I saw the problems only getting worse.

This was a drastic step, but one which I thought necessary. After 15 years developing almost 100 Kmart stores, I was saying good-bye to the hand that had fed me well. But eventually someone working for me was going to succumb to the pressure and do something they shouldn't, and I wasn't about to wait for that to happen. It wasn't fair to put my employees in that position.

It was only fifteen years later, when Kmart started having serious financial difficulties and was on its way to bankruptcy, that some of its executives finally began being indicted on criminal charges. This came as no surprise to longtime observers of the company, who if anything felt the crackdown was long overdue. Fortunately, by the time we stopped doing business with Kmart, we had developed relationships with other retailers, including Wal-Mart which was just beginning its own growth spurt. In this instance, closing a door definitely let me focus on opening a much larger window.

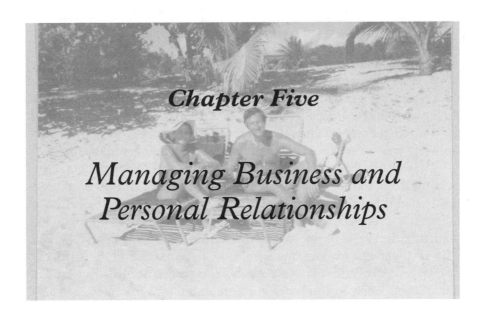

Chapter Five

Managing Business and Personal Relationships

In the wake of my break from Kmart and the unexpected, unpleasant departure of Ken Zeisler, I faced something that every entrepreneur experiences more than once—uncertainty. I wasn't exactly sure how we would replace the revenue and growth Kmart had brought to Developers Diversified, and I wasn't quite sure who would join my team to march up the hill with me. As with most serial entrepreneurs, I was never really disheartened by uncertainty. In fact, in many ways it fueled me with the energy and passion I needed to get out there and do it again. But even when I've had to face question marks, I could always count on several certainties—Iris and instinct—and now, some experience too.

Another Revolt at Developers Diversified

After Ken Zeisler left Developers Diversified in 1975, I had promoted longtime employee Jim Karabec as my second in command. In lieu of a bonus, I gave him a Kmart store we had just completed in Henderson, Nevada. A few years later he came into my office with three of my other top executives—my in-house lawyer, accountant, and the head of our leasing department. They asked me to give them the mall we were building in Hibbing, Minnesota. I depended on these four people, so I agreed. But the Minnesota mall turned out to be a difficult construction site. The original deal stipulated that the project would not need any cash equity, but because of construction difficulties and delays and new competition nearby, traffic to the center never did meet our expectations. We managed to break even for a year or two until it started operating with a negative cash flow. Since I was making up the deficit, their ownership was reduced from 100% to 50%. But I wasn't about to prop up the center indefinitely, particularly since the mortgage on the property was non-recourse, which meant I had no personal liability.

I decided to fly up to Philadelphia to make a deal with the bank that held the note. Rather than allowing the bank to take control of the center, I offered to manage it at no cost and deliver the entire cash flow to them every month. Together we would wait for business to improve. The bank, which had no desire to take ownership of a failing center, agreed. The arrangement worked fine for almost five years, until the bank had its own problems and was taken over by a larger financial institution. The new owners decided to cancel our agreement and foreclose. In vain I tried to convince them to hang in there with me until cash flow improved, but they refused. Karabec and the others asked me to put another infusion of cash into the project to save it from foreclosure, but I didn't see a turnaround in sight and I told the bank it could take ownership

Our problems weren't over yet. We had been depreciating the property and taking a tax deduction each year. Now we were faced with a tax liability because the IRS treated our debt relief the same way it would a profit. Karabec and the others wanted me to pay 100% of the taxes due, but I felt their share of ownership was their responsibility. They had asked for the asset. I had given it to them in good faith and even infused cash into it. Now they had to take the bad with the good, which in this case meant taking on some liability.

About a year later the same four employees asked for ownership of another mall. We had just entered the recession of the early 1980s and instead I told them, half-jokingly, that I was about to ask them to take a reduction in salary. Two of them resigned on the spot, while a few months later, at my suggestion, the attorney followed them. Jim Karabec stayed, with the understanding he would retire in two years. But these departures were all amicable. I felt no malice to them because their actions were bold, not mischievous. I'm still friends with every one of these men.

The nature of the commercial real estate business is such that employees see how much money they are making for the company. They sometimes begin to feel indispensable and ask for a piece of the action. If they don't get it, they often leave. I try to avoid this cycle by giving out generous bonuses to our managers once a project has been developed successfully, rather than bringing them in as equity owners.

Understanding the Human Nature of Business

When building your team, it's important to recognize that not everyone plays by the same set of rules. I can't count the number of times, particularly in the early days before I got wise to what was really happening, when people proposed a deal but in fact were meeting with us only to pump us for information. After they learned what they needed to know, they would terminate negotiations and develop the project themselves. Eventually I began keeping our expertise closer to the vest until some kind of partnership agreement had been signed, but that's a tricky line to walk. You have to gauge how much knowledge you need to display in order to win a potential client or partner's confidence, without giving away everything you can bring to the table. The temptation, especially in the early stages of building an entrepreneurial venture, is to try to build credibility by offering too much information and knowledge before an arrangement has been made. For me, the truth is I enjoy sharing my experiences with others, and I'm still not as careful as I should be about dispensing information.

I've also learned to make sure that investors are serious before getting too involved with them. Back in the 1960s I was talking to a group of young executives about a condominium project. I didn't have any money to invest, but I was offering to do all the legwork. It suddenly occurred to me that perhaps these guys were just wasting my time. I called them to a meeting and suggested that each of us ante up $200. When they all had a reason why they couldn't contribute even this small amount, I knew they weren't really serious about the venture, and I disbanded the group. That was one of the last times I tried bringing investors into one of my developments.

Though on the one hand I believe there are no buddies in business, on the other hand, almost all my buddies are *from* business. The people with whom I have lunch, play golf, or watch a Buckeyes game I've come to know through business. Today, most of them are barely half my age and have been with me virtually their entire professional lives. I don't pal around much with older guys. I know that young people like Gregg Levy, one of our key outside attorneys, and Brad Kowit, a real estate agent, spend time with me because they can learn something and perhaps even make money through me. But I don't mind. If I can help them make money, they're making money for me too.

Working with Family

Many entrepreneurs solve the problem of finding people in whom they can entrust their business by turning to family members. A son or daughter, niece or nephew, or in-law, is probably not as likely to leave you with no warning. But that doesn't mean bringing family into your business is a panacea for all your management challenges. It's true that I gained invaluable experience working for Iris's father, as well as for her Uncle. But Uncle Sol wasn't willing to give me a piece of the L & J Development Company, even though I thought I had demonstrated I could grow the business. As I explained earlier, I was disappointed, and I took his dismissal of my proposal personally. I don't know if I would have felt differently had we not been family.

I think it's almost impossible to have a normal business relationship with family. When push comes to shove, issues become personal, and that's no way to operate a business. It's difficult to treat family the same way you would another employee. That can create resentment not only from others who work for you, but also from the family members themselves, who begin to wonder why they didn't get a promotion, a raise, or more responsibility. Family dynamics in the workplace is a two-edged sword. From the boss's point of view, we're always wondering why family members aren't working as hard as other employees. If they're not, the entire staff is likely to fall to that lowest common denominator. It is difficult to run a business under these circumstances. Both Iris's brother, Lee Shur, and my son-in-law, Eugene Faigus, worked for me for almost a decade before deciding they'd each be more comfortable on their own. When this happens, the key is keeping the personal side of the relationship healthy after parting ways professionally.

Managing My Entrepreneurial Enterprise

As any successful businessperson will tell you, a company is only as good as the people who work in it. When I conduct a job interview, I barely look at the resume in front of me. I'm not looking for the person who graduated first in his class at Harvard or who has the most advanced degrees. I *am* looking for someone who really wants the job, who is hungry not only for a paycheck, but eager to learn and succeed and to rise up the ladder. I'm also looking for loyalty and honesty because I think I can teach everything else a young person needs to know.

I can even teach common sense, in part by example. I try to show people who work for me that solving problems by weighing the possible solutions and choosing the one that experience tells you is best often yields the best results. It's less about advanced calculus or deep philosophical thought, and more about common sense. To help young people develop trust in their common sense, you have to keep telling them what they're doing wrong and what they're doing right until they start to understand the process involved in making good judgment calls. Once they 'get it,' you can tell them not to ask what to do, but to figure out for themselves how to solve their problem. "Don't tell me you have a problem, tell yourself you have a problem." I suggest they attack a problem by coming up with three possible solutions, then come to me with each of them, making their case for which one is best. Usually they'll have made the right decision.

I've always tried to run Developers Diversified (and now Heritage Development) like a college. We've trained a lot of people who have become extremely successful in the business world. I try to show young people by example that there is a simple, decent way to behave in business. Probably the most important of these lessons is to respect the people you come in contact with in the course of your job. Showing my employees by example means taking them by the hand and demonstrating how I expect a job to be done. There's no job I consider beneath me. Crucial to the success of an entrepreneur is having done every task in the business yourself once so that you understand the jobs you're asking others to perform. Only then can you explain to people your expectations and determine if they are doing it correctly.

Common Sense Tips for Leading By Example

- Don't be a snob. The minute you start thinking you're better than everyone else, you're not.
- Don't judge your employees by the size of their bankbooks or their resumes, but rather by the amount of heart and pride they put into their jobs.
- Respect and reward people who perform their jobs with integrity, regardless of their title. The quality of the work performed by the person cleaning rooms at the Bertram Inn is just as important to the hotel's reputation as the quality of the manager's work with his staff and his interaction with guests.
- Don't consider yourself above any job and be prepared to show employees how to do the task you ask them to complete.
- Return every phone call, even when you dread what the other person might say. If you can't return a call promptly, have someone do it for you.
- Don't arrive late for meetings. It indicates that making a grand entrance is more important to you than other people's time. In fact, don't be on time to appointments; if possible, arrive a little early. It shows you value other peoples' time and that you are anxious to meet with them.

Last a Month; Stay a Decade   I'm probably not the easiest boss in the world to work for, in part because I expect a lot from the people who work for me. I expect them to stay focused every minute they are on the job. How do you get a job with me? By wanting it so badly that you never quit asking. That shows real hunger, which usually translates into a commitment of giving 100 percent to the company. I tell the young people who work for me that I don't expect them to give me 101 percent, only 100 percent; 99 percent will not be tolerated. But I certainly don't ask anything more of my employees than I ask of myself.

Some people can't take such scrutiny and don't last long under my employ. Many others, however, have thrived. In fact, those who last a few months with me tend to stay for many years. Jim Karabec worked for me for twenty-two years before he retired. George Kimson, who runs the Bertram Inn, has worked for me in various capacities for more than a decade. The same with Robby Benjamin, who has been with me for 18 years, almost half his life, and has become my top sales person. Myron Vernis has been in charge of Glenmoor Country Club since it opened in 1992. My company's current in-house accountant, for example, Steve Marton, has been with us for ten years, and I trust him with my personal business as well as my company's business. He has keys to our house. And John McGill has been with me for more than thirty-five years.

From hiring good people, to providing lots of hands-on experience, I've always tried to build my staff knowing that I would be spending a lot of time with them. I don't want to fight my people on every issue. We train them to have the skills needed to be successful inside the company. And we try to build a family atmosphere throughout the organization. We like to be able to have a Christmas party where people like each other, including their boss.

Motivating People   I'm not the smartest guy in the world, and I doubt I know how to do all the things people think I know how to do. But I do know how to motivate people. The more I think about my career, the more I realize that a lot of my success has been based on an ability to weed out non-performing employees and develop the loyalty of others, who I support and train to the point where they can drive the bus themselves. I don't want to do everything myself, believe me. I want to teach others how to take responsibility for themselves. Part of that involves creating an environment that fosters growth and is conducive to sharing ideas. I try to have lunch with those who work with me almost every day. That's when we tend to get our best ideas or develop a strategy for the coming weeks.

I also believe it's important to motivate employees at all levels. At the country clubs I've belonged to, the people I am most comfortable spending time with tend to be the club manager, the waiters, or the golf pro. Just by talking to them, I can learn a lot about what is going on at the club. Besides, I like the interaction. I also make it a point to be a good tipper. It works out to be a very insignificant amount of money over the course of a year, but it's the way a lot of people in the services arena make their living, so it's always appreciated. I like to park my own car, but I still make it a point to give the parking attendant a tip.[9]

Micromanaging and Delegating Contrary to popular business theory, it is actually possible to delegate and micromanage simultaneously. At one point in the 1970s and 1980s, Developers Diversified was managing more than 100 properties and 100 executives, so of course I had to delegate authority. But that never meant that I didn't follow up on the progress.

Even today it would be impossible to run a hotel, a four-star restaurant, and two of the premier country clubs in Ohio, to say nothing of the shopping center business, without giving people the freedom to make decisions and to find creative solutions themselves. But that doesn't mean I'm not constantly firing off lists of tasks for my employees to complete.

Iris and I go to the Bertram Inn, the hotel and conference center we built in Aurora in 1999, at least twice a week for dinner and discuss with the chef the menu and ways to present new dishes. We walk through the hotel, noting if the carpets need cleaning or if the furniture is located correctly. Outside, we make certain that the snow has been adequately cleared from the parking lot and, in the nicer weather, that the landscaping is manicured properly. You'd better believe that someone is following us around with a pad and pen. At the same time, by delegating responsibilities, I have plenty of time to do everything I want, including travel and focusing on our philanthropic

---

[9]I'm never really happy with strangers driving our array of classic cars that include a 1971 280 SL Mercedes, a 1989 blue Jaguar convertible, a 1997 Bentley, a 1997 BMW Z3, a 2003 Mercedes SL 500, a '93 Jaguar sports model, a Mercedes S500 4-door sedan, and a 1980 Rolls Royce.

activities. I find that a fifteen-minute meeting can go a long way toward getting others to do what I used to spend all day doing myself.

Advising College Students   In addition to doing a lot of work with the young employees at our company, I often speak to students at various universities. I tell them that I believe that if they really want to get a job with a specific company, they should be prepared to take any job at all, even if it's opening the mail or washing the boss's car. Become indispensable, work hard, and stay focused, not only at the job at hand but also at the next task and the one after that.

I also tell them to learn a business and become valuable, either to their current employer, or to someone else, or to their own business should they choose the entrepreneurial path. This is how almost all my top people came to fill their current roles. I plucked George Kimson from a small athletic facility in Akron that Scott and I owned and made him manager of our Barrington Country Club and then of the Bertram Inn. Robby Benjamin started as an intern when we owned the soccer team, and later was in charge of lot and membership sales at Barrington Country Club. He now holds dual responsibilities selling lots to builders and conducting due diligence on properties we're considering buying. His job includes handling various zoning matters and negotiating contracts with subcontractors.

Many other former employees have gone on to do great things in the real estate business. It's flattering to see these people so successful. In fact, many of them have taken to recalling their years at "Wolstein University" as their true education. When I see them at the annual International Council of Shopping Centers (ICSC) conventions in Las Vegas, it's like a college reunion as we recount each other's recent accomplishments.

John McGill: From Trainee to Partner

For me, the best example of training someone who is driven and has a lot of common sense, but who lacks the academic background many business owners look for, is my partner John McGill. John started working for me more than thirty-five years ago, and since 1999 has been my partner in the Heritage Development Company.

John says he was about five years old the first time he saw me, when I sold his parents probably the fifth or sixth house I built in Twinsburg. He remembers me showing them the lot before the house was even built. But my first memory of John was much later, in about 1967, when he was working with Scott at our various properties in Twinsburg, cutting grass, shoveling snow, and doing minor repairs. I just knew him as one of many kids doing various odd jobs for the Karabec brothers, who were in charge of home sales in Twinsburg. I learned later that John was only fourteen at the time, too young to get working papers in the state of Ohio. Jim Karabec told him to come back when he was sixteen, but John kept working anyway, and we just looked the other way.

The first time John worked directly for me was one Saturday in 1969 when I asked Jim Karabec to send someone over to the house Iris and I were building in Pepper Pike. Together John and I filled in a hole in the ground where the gas line had just been laid. After that, I always had my eye on him, as he was the hardest young worker we had. I would see him Saturday mornings as I inspected construction sites in Twinsburg. He and I were the only ones working at 7:30 a.m., so I knew we had something in common.

After John graduated high school, Iris and I offered to pay his way through college. He thanked us, but explained that with five children in the family his parents counted on his income. His father couldn't have been making more than $15,000 a year, and there were seven of them living in a 1,200-square-foot house in Twinsburg. So instead, I called John into my office at Developers Diversified and hired him at a starting annual salary of $7,500. It was the first time he had ever been in the office.

John spent his first week hauling around a lawnmower on the back of a pick-up truck to a dozen or so of our shopping centers. Soon he was in charge of a maintenance crew to make sure the grass was mowed, the parking lots swept, the walls painted, and the roofs repaired. His learning curve included getting bids from a myriad of contractors whom he would hire to take care of our maintenance needs.

Lord knows I needed people I could count on, and it wasn't long before I handed John a plane ticket and told him to fly to Bangor, Maine to inspect several shopping centers we had recently built in the state. Fresh out of high school, he had never been on a plane or signed a credit card receipt. By the following year, at the ripe old age of nineteen, he was an assistant project manager, and soon he had taken full responsibility for a few developments in Florida. By 1976, at age twenty-two, he was taking a site from conception through development, becoming one of my most trusted and important executives, along with Jim Karabec.

Doing Business During a Recession

By the time we built our last Kmart in Macedonia, the worst recession since before World War II had hit the real estate development industry hard. All through the 1970s interest rates had continued to climb, peaking in 1980 at more than 20 percent. It was a terrible time for commercial real estate. Few new projects could throw off enough cash flow to cover the cost of capital.

We were even having a difficult time finishing up the projects we had in the pipeline. In the upper peninsula of Michigan, for example, we were trying to complete an enclosed mall just as interest rates hit 21 percent. We built through the winter of 1980 in a region where the average annual snowfall was about 150 inches. We had 364 inches that winter. We were prepared to absorb the increased costs of both moving huge piles of snow and the higher interest charges, but just as the project was nearing completion, we were socked with a decision by the nearby municipalities to deny us access to the utilities we needed. Opposition to the project coalesced around their concern about the impact the new mall would have on their downtown neighborhoods. Both U.S. senators from Michigan weighed in against allowing us to open. I flew up to the peninsula and begged for a resolution. I've found that sometimes you have to hold your hat in hand and plead your case—which I did. We ultimately agreed to annex an additional piece of property into Portage Township, on which we would develop a Sheraton Hotel, which the community sorely wanted.

By the time the shopping center in Michigan opened, I had pretty much abandoned development to concentrate almost exclusively on managing our existing portfolio. I figured we'd do that for a few years while waiting out the recession. Besides, I had my hands full with a soccer team I had acquired in 1979 (see chapter seven).

I wasn't alone. The development business nationally had slowed to a crawl. I shrunk Developers Diversified from a staff of almost a hundred to a much smaller nucleus of people. Our existing shopping centers continued to generate substantial cash flow, but even the amount of cash that flowed from our 100 or so developments couldn't support our large staff. Since the environment wasn't conducive to growth, we had no choice but to lay off people and hold our breath until interest rates came down to a more manageable level.

Making the decision to let people go is a difficult one. It most often occurs when people and companies across the board are experiencing tough times. Knowing that you're adding to the stress of individuals is not an easy thing, but there are times you have to sacrifice in the short term to survive in the long run. During tough economic times, often you have to cut some jobs in order to save others. Nevertheless, the headlines always read, "XYZ Company cuts 1500 jobs," rather than "XYZ Company takes measures to save 12,000 jobs."

By this time John McGill had matured into being a very valuable employee. Even amidst these layoffs, I told him he had a job for life, or at least as long as he wanted it. I knew that meant a lot to him, but I could also see that he was becoming restless. He wasn't even thirty years old and was uncomfortable with the idea that his development days might be over.

John came into my office one morning and explained to me that while he never wanted to leave Developers Diversified, he was a developer and a creator, not a manager. He couldn't see himself spending the next few years fixing parking lots and patching roofs. He also told me he had been offered a position with CBL & Associates, a large developer based in Tennessee. He had been working with CBL, arranging to sell them properties we owned in Colorado, Kansas, and Mississippi. We had not yet begun construction at any of these sites, but Sears, JCPenney, and others had signed letters of intent, and we had completed most of the approval processes. We needed to sell them in order to reduce our debt load.

I couldn't help but be struck by the contrast between the way John was addressing his dissatisfaction versus the way Ken Zeisler had a few years earlier. While Zeisler had crept away, literally in the dead of night, John was explaining to me that he didn't want to leave unless Developers Diversified had no need for someone of his abilities and desire.

The thought of losing John prompted me to reconsider my decision to halt new development. By this time the national economy was reviving and interest rates were receding. I was also reminded by recent activity in our office that we had good relationships with more than a dozen national retailers that should not be squandered. Perhaps most important, we had begun working with Wal-Mart with the idea that they could become a replacement for Kmart as the largest anchor in most of our shopping centers.

After discussing it with Iris, a few days later I made John an offer he couldn't refuse. I knew he didn't really want to take the job with CBL. He certainly didn't look forward to moving to Tennessee. I also knew CBL was not offering him any equity. So I suggested that together we start a new company, of which John would be a 25 percent partner. His would be the sweat equity, mine would be the old-fashioned kind, and together we'd again start finding and developing properties. It was a good deal for John and for me. I now had someone to relieve me of the day-to-day grind of shopping center development, and he had the incentive he needed to thrive.

During the next ten years, John and I built more than two-dozen shopping centers under the banner of a new company called W&M Properties. Just as the rapid growth of Kmart had fueled the success of Developers Diversified in its early days, this time the ascension of Wal-Mart from small-town retailer to retail superstar helped drive W&M's success. In 1979, the year I cut my ties with Kmart, Wal-Mart had 276 stores that generated $1.2 billion in sales. By 1985 it had 882 stores with sales of $8.4 billion, and two years after that it had jumped to 1,200 stores with sales of $16 billion. Today it is the world's largest retailer, with sales of more than $250 billion annually, over 3,200 U.S. stores, about 1,100 international locations, and about 1.3 million employees. Between 1983 and 1993 John and I built twenty-seven shopping centers anchored by Wal-Marts, to go with the ninety-seven Kmarts I had built between 1969 and 1979.

Iris and Me

The one relationship that has been the bedrock of my professional and personal existence is my marriage to Iris. She has been my equal partner for more than fifty-five years, and I've been so fortunate to have her by my side during every project and through every major decision. But I'll take some credit for finding the right life partner. I may have been lucky to have that football land in front of her feet back in 1946, but marrying her was a stroke of brilliance on my part. Somehow I saw something in her right away that I liked, and I wasn't going to lose her. Never did my decisiveness, my strategy of seizing an opportunity as soon as it presents itself, pay off so handsomely.

I had reached a point in 1979, where my financial future was pretty much secure. I could have never developed another property and still lived comfortably on the cash flow from Developer Diversified's portfolio. But I also knew I wasn't through, that I still had something to prove. The difference was that now my financial independence allowed me to pick and choose projects in which Iris and I could work together. These are the projects I've enjoyed the most—the office buildings, hotels, and country clubs we've built together, and particularly the professional soccer team (which as described in chapter seven, became a true family affair).

No doubt the most satisfying project Iris and I worked on together was the building of our own home. In 1964 we had moved from South Euclid to Greenlawn Avenue in Beachwood. Iris never really liked that house, mainly because she had been looking forward to designing our second home herself. Instead, we had moved into it suddenly, after Uncle Sol offered it to us at a special price. He had built it in 1954 for his brother-in-law, who became seriously ill before ever moving in. Because it was twice as spacious as where we had been living—the same 800-square-foot bungalow we bought shortly after getting married—it felt like a mansion. The school system was excellent. It was too good of a deal to pass up. We figured that when business improved a bit we'd eventually design and build our own house nearby.

Indeed, a few years later we bought a lot in Shaker Heights—one of the nicest, most established suburbs in Cleveland. Almost immediately Iris had a case of buyer's remorse. The lot was nice, but the homes on the street sat very close together, without much privacy. She decided we should wait to find a more spacious lot that was more suitable to the kind of environment we were looking to create for ourselves. We put the lot on the market and within 30 days sold it for a $1,500 profit—a significant financial event for us at that time.

A few months later Iris found another lot in a nearby suburb called Pepper Pike. It was a beautiful piece of land, with a creek running through it, and was protected by woods in the back and a country club across the street. After some back-and-forth negotiations, the owner accepted our offer, but when I met with him for lunch a few weeks later to close the deal, he came down with a case of seller's remorse and told me he wouldn't sell it to us.

Iris and I both felt that there was only one possible reason he had reneged on the deal. Until World War II, Pepper Pike had been a restricted community where Jews, Italians, African Americans, and others were not welcome. Sometimes deed restrictions actually prohibited ethnic groups from buying certain properties in communities like Shaker Heights and Pepper Pike. By the 1960s, these attitudes had softened a bit, but obviously not completely.

Anyone coming of age during the middle of the 20th century in Cleveland, or anywhere else in the world for that matter, couldn't help but recognize the existence of anti-Semitism. I've always been aware that there are people in every community who are intolerant of ethnic groups and who believe this country is theirs and that no one else has a right to it. I witnessed discrimination in high school, and in business when some bankers and other executives were reluctant to do business with those of a certain religion, color, or ethnicity. Usually it wasn't as blatant as when we were denied the lot in Pepper Pike, but everyone knew it existed. Even today there are certain country clubs in Cleveland and around the country that do not welcome Jews, Italians, Asians, or African Americans.

But I never allowed anti-Semitism to bother me. When the property owner refused to sell us the lot in Pepper Pike, Iris and I figured the hell with him; we wouldn't want to have him as our neighbor anyway. All I could do to fight discrimination was to treat everyone equally in my own business and personal life and judge them by their competence and integrity rather than their religion or the color of their skin.

Iris was heartbroken when we lost the lot, but it only made her more determined to find a piece of land on which to build our dream house. She soon found what we were looking for on Fairmont Boulevard in Pepper Pike. The site was owned by, who else, Forest City. I negotiated to buy three adjacent one-acre lots for a total of $45,000. The deal was a good one for Forest City because that's what it needed to extend the water and sewage lines to the area.

We hired the architect, Richard L. Bowen, who would later design a number of our more prominent commercial buildings. Iris and I built the house ourselves, acting as our own general contractor. Howard Young was nice enough to show an interest and made a number of helpful suggestions, including widening the living and dining rooms slightly. Iris stayed on top of every detail, and the house was completed in ten months. The day we moved in, just before Thanksgiving 1969, Iris and I worked hard to put everything in its right place by nightfall. By the time the movers left, Iris had dinner on the table as if we had been living there for years.

We hadn't quite created our Eden, however. One day, about three years after we moved in, Iris called to tell me there were bulldozers in our backyard. Apparently, I didn't own as much land as I had thought. In fact, the small storage shed I had built in the back yard turned out to be located on property owned by Forest City, and just beyond that they intended to put in a street.

Iris and I were horrified, as our privacy and idyllic setting were about to be shattered. Fortunately, by this time my company had built a number of Kmarts and was in the process of building more. Iris and I had even paid off the original $75,000 home mortgage. I negotiated with Forest City to buy eight lots for an average price of about $20,000.

A few years later we had to buy another dozen lots to prevent Forest City from putting in a street to the east of our property. Now we owned a rectangular 30 acres. In 1985 I gave two acres to our son Scott, on which he built a house that Iris helped him design. He still lives there today with his wife and four children. The street Forest City started to pave actually became his driveway.

Recently we've gone the other way. In 2002 Iris and I began developing nine lots into a cul-de-sac on the far eastern edge of the property in such a way that we'll never notice any of the houses.

It turned out that Iris is a real estate entrepreneur in her own right. In the 1970s we had paid about $650,000 for the 30 acres , and later we spent another $350,000 to develop the street, including getting the necessary permits and clearances. All told, we invested about $1 million in the land, and today we're about to sell a small piece of it for $4.4 million.

Having Fun with Iris

Now it was time to start having fun with Iris. Our first vacation as a family was when we drove to Atlantic City in a our tiny Plymouth. The kids were very small, but a few years later we drove with them to Florida and had a wonderful time on the beaches of Sarasota. I had $500 in my pocket and we made it last. We splurged on a separate motel room for the kids at $11 per night. In those days I was always worried about spending money on vacations because we had so little in the bank. There was no one but me to support our family of four and that worried me. I had no backup. But you never seem to miss the money spent on vacations; you always cherish the memories.

Probably the best trip we took with the kids was a cruise on the USS United States in 1966. We drove to New York, having booked the two smallest state rooms on the lowest deck. As we boarded, we noticed that people were dressed as if they were going to the opera, many of them standing next to huge trunks of clothing. Some of them seemed to have man-servants standing silently nearby. The four of us were in sneakers and shorts, lugging our suitcases. Suddenly we heard our names being paged over the loudspeaker. Iris and I were sure we were going to be bumped from the cruise and would have to sheepishly turn around and drive back home. It turned out they had overbooked the ship and were offering us a free upgrade to a huge room in the upper deck. The four of us had a blast.

The first time Iris and I left the country was in 1974. Developers Diversified was doing a lot of business with Palevsky Building Hardware, and they invited the Young brothers and me and our wives on a charter trip to Italy. The six of us flew to Rome and a few days later traveled by bus to Florence. We then had a few days by ourselves, so Iris and I left the group and took a train to Naples, then a boat to the island of Capri. Being alone with Iris was the best part of the trip.

A few years later we started making regular visits to Europe. We fell in love with Lake Como, and have returned many times to Villa d'Este, a 16th century villa turned into one of the most celebrated hotels in Europe.

In the mid seventies we also started exploring the Caribbean. Al Rosen, a former all-star third basemen for the Cleveland Indians, turned us on to St. Maarten, where he had a condominium in a wonderful resort called La Samana. In 1980 we bought a place ourselves. We sold it once we built our boat, but we've probably been to St. Maarten fifty or sixty times in the past twenty-five years. I like places that feel like home, where I know the restaurant owners and shopkeepers and feel comfortable walking on the streets. Since building our boat, we've toured every island in the Caribbean.

I don't pretend to be the most sophisticated traveler in the world; in fact, in some ways Iris and I remain extremely naïve. I was skiing with Scott in California, and we ran into a severe snowstorm. We drove over the mountains to Reno to catch a plane to Salt Lake City. In the cupboard at the condo where we were staying we found a mirror covered with white powder. I was terrified, and we flushed the powder down the toilet.

But I do think Iris and I have formulated some helpful travel tips over the years.

Getting The Most Out of Traveling

- Treat travel like a business, with the same devotion to preparation and focus.
- Learn the rules of the land and use them to your advantage.
- Familiarize yourself with the tipping practices in each country you visit.
- In many countries, you are expected to negotiate when buying a piece of jewelry or any other item. Just like in any negotiations, be prepared to walk away if you don't like the deal.
- Check every item on your restaurant and hotel bills.
- Don't allow yourself to be taken advantage of just because you don't speak the language. It's not that difficult to make yourself understood.

Owning a Plane

Another enjoyable part of travel over the years was owning our own planes. The first airplane I owned was a Citation One, a five-passenger jet I bought in the early 1980s. A few years later I traded it in for a nine-seater Falcon 20. I sold it a few years later at a considerable profit, but it wasn't one of my smartest moves. The fuselage on the Falcon is built to last 100 years, and I could still be flying in it if I had kept it. It had a top speed of only 350 miles per hour, but it was a beautiful plane, particularly after Iris got through remodeling the interior and repainting the exterior. But I let my ego get in the way of good judgment. I convinced myself that bigger is always better and traded it in for a 15-passenger Gulfstream II, a wonderful plane formerly owned by McDonalds founder, Ray Kroc. Iris completely gutted it and redecorated it beautifully. We took it to Europe twice, to Portugal, Spain, and Italy with our children.

I eventually turned the Gulfstream over to a management company because I wasn't using it anything close to the 400 or so hours per year that makes owning a plane cost effective. A number of Hollywood personalities and sports figures chartered the plane, and at one point Van Cliburn put a piano in it and took it to Russia. Unfortunately, when the banks were breathing down my neck in 1992 (see chapter nine), I sold the Gulfstream at a big loss. Another reason I sold it was that we had no accurate way to determine if we were getting our fair share of the charter income. Recently I bought a one-eighth share in a Citation 7, a two-engine seven-seater jet with a cruising speed of 500 miles per hour. I've contracted for 100 hours a year in the air at a fixed price.

The Deil Gustafson Story

One of the wackiest trips Iris and I ever took was to Acapulco as the guest of Deil Gustafson. I met Gustafson in 1971 when I was trying to find locations in Minneapolis for Kmart. We negotiated back and forth by phone concerning a piece of property he owned, and I made a date to meet with him in Minneapolis to finalize the deal. I arrived at his office in Minneapolis only to be told he had left that morning for Las Vegas, where he was negotiating to buy the Tropicana Hotel. I decided to chase him to Vegas, where I literally cornered him at the Tropicana. We made the deal and became good friends. I think he was impressed that I had chased him down and didn't let him off the hook. I wrote him a check for a half million dollars and liked to kid him that it was because of me that he was able to buy the Tropicana. Gustafson was always urging Iris and me to visit him in Las Vegas and stay at the Tropicana, as his guest. We took him up on his offer a couple of times and were treated like royalty. Our room and meals were always comped, and during one trip he gave us the use of a boat on Lake Mead packed with food and drink.

Deil also invited Iris and me to Acapulco, where he was throwing a big party at a villa he had rented. All his Hollywood friends were there, including Merle Oberon, Irving Wallace, Mario Puzzo, and others. We were immediately uncomfortable. I think we were the only married couple there. Our discomfort increased when we got to our room and there were no blinds or shades on the window. We were on the ground floor and there was no privacy. It must have been a kinky Hollywood thing. We moved to a hotel the next day.

Gustafson was a character. When he bought the Tropicana it was so run-down that he described it in the *Wall Street Journal* as "an old elephant that needed a stab in the rear." But he renovated it, building a beautiful new theatre to stage the Folies Bergere. Deil was forced to sell the hotel in 1979 because of his ties to the Kansas City mob. Then in the mid 1980s he served more than three years in prison for skimming from the casino. His misfortunes continued when he lost an arm in a boating accident. He passed away in 1999.

Planning for Our Personal Future

With the ability to provide for my family the way I had always hoped, I began to get serious about deciding how and where to invest our disposable income. I've never been one to speculate in the stock market. The real estate business is risky enough that I don't need to gamble with my money a second time. I also didn't want to have all my cash tied up in my company. You never know what's going to happen to commercial real estate or how your banks will behave. I had worked too hard to end up with nothing.

In the 1980s I began to invest in museum-quality art. It seemed to me this was something that could only go up in value. The artists were dead, so they certainly weren't making any more of it, and museums and collectors would always create a demand. I developed a relationship with a local art dealer, who helped Iris and me buy some wonderful pieces by masters like Picasso, Avery, Dubuffet, Max Ernst, and Jackson Pollack. We created a personal, financial safety net by putting all of our art in Iris's name, as well as the boat, office building, and house. Should anything ever have happened to Developers Diversified, we had assets that were safe.

We bought almost all the paintings through a local dealer, who turned us on to some wonderful pieces. Almost all of them have increased in value and have given Iris and me a great deal of pleasure. But remember when I wrote that you should be knowledgeable about every aspect of your business? I should have studied a bit more on my own rather than blindly trust a stranger. At some point he must have decided that lining his pocket with my naiveté was too tempting to pass up. In the mid 1980s he showed me a painting by the French impressionist, Eugene Boudin, that he said was a real steal. It was a steal alright. According to our dealer friend, it was worth $850,000, but he assured me he could get it for $505,000. He told me it was such a bargain that he would buy it back from me at the purchase price at any time. It wasn't even the kind of art I like, but relying on his expertise, which hadn't steered me wrong yet, I lowered my guard and made the purchase.

Yet something didn't feel right. He was too eager. My suspicions were confirmed when after I bought it I had it independently appraised for $200,000.

The dealer, of course, denied he ever said I could return the painting to him. After some investigation, I discovered I had also overpaid for the previous painting he had sold me, a Milton Avery. I sued him in civil court but lost. He brought all his cronies to testify, and his lawyer did a good job of making the case about a rich guy suing a poor guy rather than a professional taking advantage of a neophyte. You can't win them all. By the way, I still own the Boudin. The highest appraisal I've been able to receive is $250,000. And he lives across the street from us.

Wine and Birthdays: Enjoying the Finer Things in Life

In a smaller way, Iris and I also began collecting wine. I first got interested when we visited the French Caribbean island of Guadalupe. I felt I had to educate myself so I could intelligently order wine at meals. Back in Cleveland we started visiting wine stores, and one of the owners suggested we buy wine futures. I had never heard of wine futures, but you're actually buying the wine before it's processed, betting it will be a good year and it will go up in value. I figured I could always drink it, so I took a flier on two cases of 1970 Lafite Rothschild and Chateau Mouton-Rothschild for $15 per bottle. Thirty-seven years later we have all but five bottles left, and they're worth between $500 and $1,000 each, perhaps more. We really should drink them.

Iris and I started going to wine tastings. Our experience came in handy once we opened the country clubs and the Bertram Inn and began being wined, if not dined, by numerous vineyards. Over the years we've become more knowledgeable, and have accumulated about 2,500 bottles of mostly French and Italian reds and whites. To accommodate them all, we've gradually expanded our wine cellar at our house. During the last renovation we dug down and created a walk-down, naturally cooled, underground room to store them all.

Iris and I were having fun during these years. Rather than give each other gifts on special occasions, we prefer to give each other memories. For my 40th birthday she surprised me with a party at a local restaurant, inviting all my high school friends. I reciprocated on her 50th by renting a prop plane and flying about thirty-five of us to Detroit. Iris had no idea where we were going, and I wouldn't tell her, as I mixed bloody marys and passed out boxed breakfasts. From the downtown Detroit airport we took a bus to a 65-foot cabin cruiser on the Detroit River, and we cruised up into Lake St. Clair. On the way back we changed clothes and stopped at the Detroit Yacht Club for dinner. When we returned to Cleveland, another fifty people or so were waiting to surprise Iris at our house.

For my 60th birthday Iris invited eighty people to Sammy's restaurant, overlooking the Cuyahoga River. She completely redecorated the restaurant, brought in live music, and served a tremendous array of food. She even arranged with the fire department for a permit so she could have "Happy Birthday Bart" spelled out in fireworks on the shore of the Cuyahoga River.

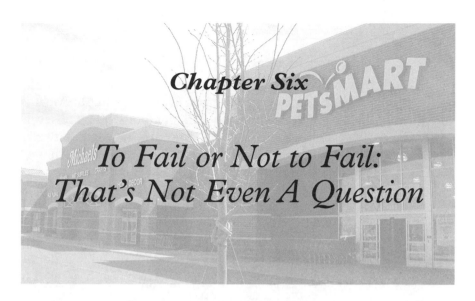

Chapter Six

To Fail or Not to Fail: That's Not Even A Question

The topic of failure in business has been debated passionately for decades in business books and universities. Most experts seem to believe that failure is OK, citing that it makes individuals stronger and gives them insights and lessons from which to learn the next time around. I'm sure that for some that is true. I've always subscribed to the opposite philosophy—avoid failure at all costs. To me, there's nothing remotely alluring about failure. Frankly, I don't like it. I don't want to be around it. I'm afraid of it. I don't think it's necessary.

I've been able to avoid failure by relentlessly focusing on problems as they arise and doing whatever it takes to solve them (while staying true to my own legal and moral compass). I'm not saying that if you experience a setback or a full blown failure that you shouldn't get up, dust yourself off, reexamine the terrain, and try again. But if I can avoid it altogether, all the better.

The real estate business provides the perfect case study for exploring the highs and lows of entrepreneurship. With both figurative and literal potholes at every corner, it has on many occasions sorely tested my "it's not OK to fail" philosophy. This was demonstrated during my first experiences in Twinsburg, and at most of the 200 or so commercial properties I've developed since. Recently John McGill and I were involved with two particularly challenging projects that illustrate the kinds of roadblocks often placed in a real estate developer's path to success. They are by no means the largest or most important projects we've ever developed, but I think they demonstrate the combination of flexibility and persistence necessary to overcome problems as they arise.

The Breed Called Entrepreneurs

- Entrepreneurship is not for the faint of heart. You can't back away from a fight at the first sign of conflict. You can't worry about being loved by everyone. Entrepreneurs are in business to make money, not to win popularity contests.
- Entrepreneurs go through almost daily struggles, but that doesn't mean they are not succeeding or that they can't win the fight in the end.
- Entrepreneurs who expect to make it in the long run have to be willing to roll up their sleeves and do whatever is needed to keep their company and employees focused in the right direction.
- Entrepreneurs have to wear many hats. Sometimes that means going on sales calls or cleaning the restrooms. Sometimes it means pounding nails or digging foundations.
- Entrepreneurs need to stick to their personal ethical convictions about doing what they think is right and saying what they believe to be true, regardless of the consequences.

Testing Our Patience in Parma

In early 1999 two tenants with whom we had often worked, Home Depot and the Giant Eagle supermarket chain, independently expressed interest in expanding into Parma, Ohio, a middle class suburb about 15 miles south of Cleveland, adjacent to the towns of Broadview Heights and Seven Hills. In March, John McGill brought to my attention the perfect location, a 33-acre site on Broadview Road, which consisted of seven separate parcels with six different owners. We spent the next few months drawing up a site plan[10] and negotiating 3 to 6 month options to purchase each of them. Little did we know how many times during the next 30 months we would have to negotiate renewals to extend these options.

In May 1999 we had a preliminary, informal meeting with Parma's Mayor, Gerald Boldt, and a few of his key staff. They were

---

[10]Today, these plans can be created in-house using off-the-shelf computer drafting software. When I first started out in Twinsburg they had to be drawn by hand on large sheets of paper, photocopied, and painstakingly changed with whiteout or started from scratch each time a change was made.

particularly impressed that we expected our development to generate 400 jobs and almost $1 million in annual tax revenue. They expressed enthusiasm, with one important caveat. Because the parcel of land had very little frontage on Broadview Road, we were proposing that the stores face south, just behind Gettysburg Estates, a 41-home subdivision. The Mayor suggested the City would be more likely to support the project if we flipped our design so that the parking lot, rather than the two big box buildings, backed up to the subdivision. The Mayor also wanted to increase the buffer between the parking lot and the nearest home with a landscaped mound.

We understood their concerns and wanted to address them, but we also made it clear that we'd need a number of zoning variances in order to make it work. In the first place, the size of the parking lot would have to be reduced from the seven parking spaces per thousand square feet as required by Parma's zoning code, to the industry standard of five spaces. We would also need a setback variance so that the lot could sit just five feet from the southern property line, rather than the prescribed 20 feet. And finally, we would have to move the overhead power lines, which involved the added complication of needing the cooperation of the City of Seven Hills, which owned the property across the street over which the power lines would be strung.

At this early stage both sides seemed amenable to the compromises that would have to be made, and John and I felt we were walking away from this initial meeting with an agreement on what needed to be done. Since it was already mid-September, however, the Mayor asked us to wait until after the November elections before formally submitting our proposal. We weren't delighted with the three-month delay, but we agreed to cooperate.

We were confident enough about the development that we used those three months to solve the power line problem. Initially, we approached Seven Hills seeking an easement, but when that town's City Council asked us to purchase the land, we eventually agreed on a $266,000 price. We felt that the property had some value over and above our need to redirect the power lines, and we liked the idea of controlling our own destiny in this regard and not having to rely on yet another governmental body for permits and approvals. I also liked the idea that the City of Seven Hills was planning to use the funds to build a community center.

Immediately after the first of the year, Parma's Planning Commission recommended approval of the development. A few weeks later it was formally passed by the City Council in a 5-4 vote, which came down to the last city councilman breaking a 4-4 tie. Finally, after a few compromises and some patience, we had the green light.

NIMBY Syndrome

Not so fast. This green light quickly turned to yellow, and we had to figure out how to prevent it from turning red when confronted with every real estate developer's chief bugaboo–the NIMBY (not in my back yard) syndrome.

Of course, local communities across the country have the right to create their own zoning regulations, and ultimately to accept or reject any proposed development. People living closest to a site are, for obvious reasons, the most likely to attend zoning or planning board meetings to have their voices heard. This is democracy at work, and often at its purest since individual citizens have an opportunity to stand up in a public forum and make their views known to their elected officials. They can readily affect change based on the rationale behind their concerns. There are some people in every community, who will oppose every development on the principal that any growth is bad. Sometimes it seems as if it is their full time job. Much more irritating is when the opposition is comprised of anti-growth forces from outside the community.

At least in the case of our Parma development, the most vociferous opposition seemed to be coming from residents of Gettysburg Estates and other nearby homes. After the 5-4 vote, they circulated a petition and collected the necessary number of signatures to put the rezoning variances we needed to a town-wide vote. By law, they had 30 days to submit the petition to the board of elections.

Our lawyer, State Representative Tim Grendell, found a technical flaw in the petition, and the board of elections subsequently rejected it. This was a mistake on our part. In retrospect, we probably would have been better off allowing the rezoning to be placed on the ballot. Our successful effort to block a public referendum only angered the leaders of the petition drive and made them much more militant in their opposition to our project. Our proposed development would have benefited Parma in a number of important ways, and I'm confident we cold have successfully made our case in a city-wide referendum. But at the time, we were reluctant to accept the delay a vote would have caused (please see Figure 6.1).

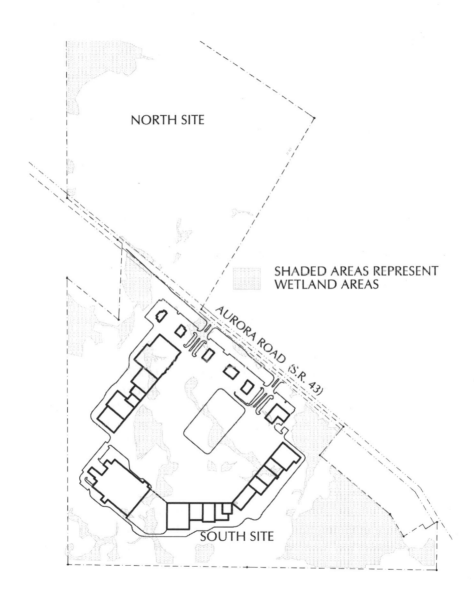

NORTH SITE

SHADED AREAS REPRESENT
WETLAND AREAS

AURORA ROAD (S.R. 43)

SOUTH SITE

How I Became an Expert on Wet Lands

Our real problems didn't begin until we started the process of obtaining wetland approval from both the state and federal environmental protection agencies, which the development's opponents quickly latched on to as their best chance to defeat the entire project.

In any industry, it is crucial to do your homework before making any kind of substantial investment. In any real estate development, for example, you don't want to pay for an option on a piece of land before being certain that the soil will support the type of development you have in mind. You also want to be sure there is no existing easement, legal restriction, or right of way that might doom the project before it begins. In Parma, we had already hired independent consultants to investigate such factors as soil, road access, and the availability of utilities. We also had determined that there weren't any kind of title problems such as oil or gas leases that might preclude us from moving forward. And perhaps most important, we had conducted a thorough study of the impact the development would have on the site's 3.8 acres of wetlands.

Wetlands are precisely what the name implies–wet land. Generally, they refer to an area where saturation with water is the dominant factor of the soil and is crucial to the types of plants and insects that live in that soil.[11] In order to develop wetlands, one must fulfill a rather lengthy approval process with the United States Corps of Engineers, the investigative arm of the U.S. Environmental Protection Agency, and in Ohio, also the State Environmental Protection Agency (OEPA). As a first step, we organized a walk through of the Parma site with both relevant agencies, and all parties agreed that there were 3.8 acres of wetlands that would be affected, including two streams. The law requires developers to either mitigate the environmental impact on the wetlands on site, which typically means recreating them elsewhere on site, or if that is impossible, to protect wetlands elsewhere in the state, preferably in the same watershed.

In this case, we couldn't entirely mitigate on site the impact the development would have on the wetlands, so we proposed to comply

---

[11]For regulatory purposes under the federal Clean Water Act, wetlands is more specifically defined as "those areas that are inundated or saturated by surface or ground water at a frequency and duration sufficient to support, and that under normal circumstances do support, a prevalence of vegetation typically adapted for life in saturated soil conditions."

with the law by preserving 11 acres of wetlands in Twinsburg and 3 acres in Mantua, Ohio. This was a typical solution under the Clean Water Act. We were also prepared to leave the Parma site in a better condition, environmentally speaking, than when we had found it. We proposed improving the remaining wetlands, as well as donating a nine-acre strip of land to Parma for a hiking trail leading to the 180-acre West Creek Park. We also offered to monitor the creek, its two tributaries, and the site's wetlands for five years in order to measure the project's impact on water quality. This would include testing both the habitat and the water to make certain that storm runoff from the development did not damage West Creek or its streams. We agreed to file regular reports with the OEPA, which would give the State much greater control of the site's water quality than if the seven separate parcels were developed piecemeal. The U.S. Corps of Engineers told us that this kind of long-term compliance was unprecedented in a state wetlands permit.

The U.S. Corps of Engineers issued us a provisional permit, but that was little more than a comfort blanket since the OEPA also needed to issue a permit for it to have any real value. That was easier said than done.

In March 2001 the OEPA administrator assigned to our case, who by state law has a tremendous amount of discretion because the wetland guidelines are so ambiguous, advised us that our project in Parma did not justify the potential harm to the wetlands. When we asked what criteria he was using, he told us that the project did not meet "public need." But he never could articulate exactly what that meant.

In May, the OEPA held a public hearing in Parma. Although Mayor Boldt had on numerous occasions expressed privately his support for the project, he was always conveniently out of town any time it actually came up for a vote. Nevertheless, we were surprised when he announced he would not support the development because of the impact it would have on the wetlands.

We were dumfounded, both by Boldt's turnaround and the fact that the mounting opposition seemed to equate these wetlands with some sort of Holy Grail. Anyone truly familiar with the site knew full well that this was in no way a vibrant, vital, or extraordinary oasis, but rather a muddy conclave filled with garbage and old shopping carts. In fact, the OEPA's own research showed that the stream running through the property had more than 300 times the acceptable level of E. coli, and equally high counts of fecal coliform bacteria. What's more, the problem was most severe closest to Gettysburg Estates, whose faulty septic systems were causing the problem in the first place. The situation was so dangerous that the environmental biologist we hired told us she had never seen a stream with so much sewage contamination. She was so concerned that she and her staff inoculated themselves for hepatitis before returning to the site a second time.

As a result of all these tests, we modified our proposal to include not only the relocation and cleanup of the stream, but also the construction of a pipe to the subdivision so that the city could extend its sanitary sewer system and eliminate the septic systems altogether. We offered to design the system and proposed that the extension of the municipal utility be paid for with tax increment financing (TIF). The City would pay for the improvements through a bond issue to be retired by the development's property taxes. This is precisely what the City eventually did, but not before many more months of denials and delays. At the time our proposal was barely heard over the growing "save the wetlands" roar.

John and I had meetings in Columbus with every OEPA official involved, up to and including Chris Jones, the director who would make the final determination. During the next few months we agreed to most of the technical changes they requested, but there continued to be an undercurrent in our negotiations that the permit would in the end be denied. Sure enough, Commissioner Jones issued a proposed denial on November 1, 2000. He argued that the wetlands and the two streams on the property were acting as a filtering agent for the sewage from the Gettysburg Estate's forty-one homes.

The ruling made absolutely no sense, because we had proposed to clean up the streams that the subdivision was currently using as little more than a sewage treatment plant. Our only recourse now was to file an administrative appeal, which meant a full-blown trial. Our attorney began a formal discovery process, deposing witnesses and preparing our arguments, while the State Attorney General did likewise. None of this was making us particularly optimistic, since according to Ohio law the administrative appeal would be heard by an OEPA official who reported directly to Commissioner Jones.

By this time, the issue had become totally politicized, as it became increasingly clear that the opposition to the development was based on something other than concern for the wetlands. On that issue we had the facts on our side. We would we be cleaning up a filthy, swamp-like cesspool generously called a wetlands, and would be mitigating the elimination of the site's true wetlands by protecting wetlands three times the size elsewhere in the state, as prescribed by law.

It didn't help our cause when U.S. Congressman Dennis Kucinich joined Mayor Boldt in voicing his opposition to the project, which raised the issue's profile, caught the media's attention, and undoubtedly increased turnout at the various public meetings held on the issue. Everywhere I turned, it was wetlands, wetlands, wetlands. The opposition had latched onto that topic because it was much easier to rally the public troops behind a back-yard environmental issue than their real objections. The additional traffic the two large stores would generate and whether in the minds of Parma residents (particularly adjacent property owners) a new grocery store or home improvement center was necessary may have been legitimate concerns, but they were not the arguments being used to criticize our plan.

Fight or Flight

Toward the end of 2001 Parma's City Council seemed prepared to kill the deal completely. At this point we knew we could either do nothing, and likely forfeit two years and almost $2 million, or continue to spend money and fight. The media portrayed it as a battle between environmentalists and anti-environmentalists, which was nonsense. In our minds, it was a fight between those who were playing by the rules and those who weren't. We weren't ready to walk away.

In November and December we filed lawsuits against the U.S. EPA and the OEPA, as well as the homeowners adjacent to the site, for allowing hazardous sewage to flow through property on which we now had legal control. We also sued the OEPA for denying our permit. Our suits highlighted how ironic it was that the project's opposition was in effect arguing that we shouldn't be allowed to clean up the wetlands because we would be ruining the wetlands.

It was clear we weren't going anywhere, and with the facts on our side, in May the OEPA began talking to us about a settlement. The following month we entered into an accord that required us to go through yet another 45-day public comment period, followed by another public hearing in August, after which the director assured us he would finally sign the necessary permits. In other words, the fix was in. The OEPA just wanted Parma's residents to have one last chance to voice their concerns.

Unfortunately, no one told the residents of Parma that the fix was in, which essentially made the public hearing a farce. It was local

American democracy at its worst. John and a few others from our office sat in the back row, listening to speaker after speaker, including a very passionate Congressman Kucinich, oppose the project, usually trumpeting the wetlands canard. All the while we knew full well that no matter what was said at the public hearing, the OEPA had already assured us that our signed permit was sitting in a drawer in Columbus, ready to be mailed to us as soon as the 45-day waiting period had expired. I felt badly that sincerely concerned citizens thought the public hearing was their last bona fide opportunity to defeat the development. The fact that they were, knowingly or not, pursuing their own ruse about imminent damage to the wetlands made the situation a little easier to swallow.

Crafting Win-Win Options

At 10:00 a.m. on September 13, 2001, ten days after the public hearing, the OEPA permit was faxed to our offices. Two years of hard work had paid off. Our celebration, however, was short lived. Coincidentally, a few hours later we received another fax, this one from Home Depot informing us of its decision to terminate its commitment to locate in the Parma shopping center. The two-year delay had forced us to extend our agreement with the company fourteen times, which in turn had forced Home Depot to pursue another location, two miles to the south. It hadn't helped that media reports about the wetlands controversy sometimes referred to the development as the "Home Depot Project," or worse, nicknamed the retail chain "Home Despot."

Now we really had a problem. At this point, we had spent twenty-six months, countless man-hours, and millions of dollars obtaining permits from state and federal environmental agencies and the variances and rezoning permits we needed from local authorities. Now we were about to receive final site approval from Parma's City Council. All for a project in which they had scared away our major tenant and jeopardized the success of the venture.

But the City of Parma didn't know that. The poker game had now officially begun. We knew full well that if we announced Home Depot's departure from the project, the opposition would do cartwheels and we'd have to start all over again with another, smaller site plan. That was not an option for us; we were not about to repeat voluntarily the process of the past two years. And with $2 million invested, we would not be forced to abandon the project altogether.

We still had a few cards to play. First, while there were rumors that Home Depot was having cold feet, it had agreed not to make a formal announcement. Second, it was possible that we would find a substitute anchor store–Wal-Mart, for example. We decided that our best strategy was just to continue the process for getting final approval for the plans and see where it would lead. After all, the Parma City Council had granted preliminary approval based on receiving four items—a rezoning certificate for the buildings, a setback variance for the buffer between the homes on both the north and south sides of the site, a special use variance for our parking lot, and wetlands permits from both the state and federal environmental agencies. We had met all these requirements and were entitled to receive a final site plan.

Ignoring the Home Depot situation in early 2002 we appealed to the Cuyahoga County Common Pleas Court for relief. Our position was that we were entitled to final site plan approval because we had fulfilled all the conditions laid out for us two years and $2 million ago. The judge looked at the evidence and ordered the City to reach an agreement with us or risk having one imposed on them.

Once the Judge suggested that it would be in Parma's best interests to reach a settlement, we gave the City three options, any one of which we were willing to accept:

- *Develop the property as originally planned.*
- *Walk away.* John and I would agree to walk if Parma acquired the 33 acres from us at a purchase price of $4 million, giving us a modest profit and satisfying those worried about the wetlands. If the City chose this option, it would have to come up with the cash and would forego almost $1 million in annual tax revenue.
- *Compromise.* We would downsize the project, leaving only a supermarket and other parcels that we would lease to smaller stores or restaurants. The City would buy 23 acres from us for $1.8 million (compared with 9 acres the City would have received for park land at no cost under the original proposal). Home Depot was no longer in the picture, and we hadn't been able to find an alternative anchor. But we figured that after all the controversy, this alternative wouldn't be palatable to Parma's elected officials.

We doubted Parma would agree to Option #2 either, but there was precedent for putting it on the table. In the fall of 2001 a new effort to defeat the project had started to take shape when Mayor Boldt and others began talking about acquiring the 33-acre site under the right of eminent domain. Congressman Kucinich encouraged the idea with a vague promise of federal money. At one point he even introduced a bill in Congress to declare the site a national park. But that was just grandstanding on the part of Kucinich and Boldt. Parma was at the time struggling to cope with a serious budget deficit, and was in no position to come up with the necessary funds. Once we had called their bluff by offering to sell the entire property to them for $4 million, talk of purchasing the land quickly subsided, only to be revived again as one of the options we now put on the table. While we would have jumped at the chance to get our money out of the project, we knew the City was unlikely to come up with $4 million for an undeveloped piece of property that wasn't going to generate tax revenue.

We were counting on the City choosing our third option. We had already approached Giant Eagle to make certain they were willing to move into the development without Home Depot. They had told us they were, although with a 67,000-square-foot store rather than the 80,000 square feet originally planned.

This option put the parking lot 348 feet from the nearest home, compared to less than 100 feet in the original plan. Even at its reduced size, the revamped shopping center still would provide almost $250,000 to Parma in annual property and other taxes.

We had to think long and hard before offering Option # 3 because we knew it would put us in negative cash flow territory. Between the options on the land and consulting fees, to say nothing of our own overhead and $750,000 in legal fees, our total investment had ballooned to $2.7 million. What's more, our rate of return calculations had been based on a 300,000-square-foot development. But at least proceeding with the downsized project would give us a chance to recoup most, and eventually we hoped all, of our investment. We made it clear, however, that this option would have to be imposed by the court so that we would not have to return to the planning board or city council for approval of another site plan.

To no one's surprise, Parma chose alternative three. We fully leased the center and recently made a deal to sell the building that houses the Giant Eagle supermarket. Once that closes, we will have turned a seven-figure loss into a seven-figure profit. Patience does indeed sometimes pay off in the long-run.

A Changing Real Estate Industry

Our experiences in Parma, though at times absurd, are not unusual in an increasingly regulated real estate industry. Over the years, the nature of business has changed. Understanding these changes and being able to adapt is key to long-term survival.

A friend of mine recently attended his first shopping center convention. He was impressed as 40,000 people descended on the convention floor—a far cry from the hundreds of people who attended in 1968 when it was held around the pool at the Fontainebleau Hotel in Miami Beach. In those days I would meet with potential tenants, in a tiny cabana. It was just Iris and me, with Iris keeping my schedule, greeting visitors as they arrived, and serving hors d'oeuvres and coffee.

After spending a day walking through almost two million square feet of exhibition space, my friend characterized the nature of the business as "40,000 people trying to convince Wal-Mart to build on their site." Of course this is an exaggeration, but accurate in concept nonetheless. The real estate development business can basically be boiled down to buying a piece of property and convincing serious tenants to lease space in the buildings we construct.

Ah, if it were only that easy. Failure is around every corner, behind every zoning battle, every soil sample, every retail bankruptcy. It is the extremely rare development that proceeds without a single misstep.

The Media is the Message

Sometimes the media can serve to exacerbate those missteps. Most business leaders know all too well the give and take nature of media coverage. On one hand, advertising and public relations specialists help court the media to highlight the accomplishments and offerings of a company. On the other hand, companies' problems are often caused or exacerbated by misleading or downright incorrect media reports. Managing the two sides of media coverage is tricky at best.

Take this simple test. Think about any newspaper article you've read on a subject with which you happen to be intimately involved. Perhaps it was about the company where you work, the town where you live, or a topic on which you are an expert. Read the article carefully and see how many factual errors you can find, and any important errors of omission. I'll wager you can find more than one. It should make you wonder about the rest of the articles you read every day on subjects you know nothing about. Not all reporters want to get both sides of a story. Once they get the negative side, they've got a juicy story and have little reason to cover the opposing view.

So how do you handle the backlash of negative publicity? What do you do when the media makes false statements about you, your company, or a proposed project? I've learned over the years that it is important to focus on the things you can do something about. Once a story casts you in an unfavorable light, you just have to hold your head high and don't let it bother you. That can be easier said than done, but I've found that getting on with my business and focusing on achieving the next task at hand is the best way to confront a media attack and put it behind you.

Although I had some experience in dealing with negative media coverage in Parma, it certainly wasn't enough to prepare me fully for what happened with our proposed shopping center in Bainbridge Township, a suburb 25 miles southeast of Cleveland. No project I've worked on during the past fifty years was covered in the media more inaccurately and with more misinformation.

The Bainbridge development began just as Parma had, with a major tenant expressing interest in a particular area. In this case, both Wal-Mart and Kohl's were looking for a site that could serve four communities—Solon, Twinsburg, Aurora, and Bainbridge Township. John and I knew of one property that met that requirement; it was an 85-acre parcel adjacent to the Six Flags amusement park set against the Solon town line. The land had been on the market for years, ever since the Grandview trotter racetrack had burned to the ground about thirty-five years earlier.

John and I lost no time signing up Kohl's and Wal-Mart and optioning the property for $50,000 against a sale price of $17 million. That same month, August 1999, at an informal meeting of the Bainbridge Township trustees, we presented a site plan for 450,000-square-feet of retail space. We were just entering the early stages of the Parma project at the time. Little did we know how much time, money, effort, and emotion these two projects would demand.

Immediately it became apparent that our biggest obstacle was going to be the town's zoning requirement of 40 percent lot coverage, meaning that the buildings and parking lot and retention areas could occupy no more than 40 percent of the entire property. This was an unusually strict requirement that predated the municipal water and sewer infrastructure to a time when it had made sense to preserve a substantial portion of a development's acreage for septic runoff and clean water wells.

We asked for a zoning change that would allow us to develop 70 percent of the 85 acres, a much more typical ratio. For several months we went back and forth with the town's trustees, eventually telling us that they might consider a 50 percent lot coverage, but never the 70 percent we needed.

We began to seek alternatives. On the south side of the street sat a 130-acre undeveloped site on which we took an option. The two properties were physically divided by Route 43, but the state road was dedicated by an easement, so we believed the two lots were actually contiguous. In real estate parlance, an easement simply means an interest in a piece of property that allows for a specific, limited use. If we could have the two parcels declared one contiguous site, we would be able to meet the town's lot coverage requirement without a problem.

While these negotiations continued, there were several other issues to be resolved. One was that regardless on which side of the street we built, we'd have to work with either the municipality of Aurora or Solon to bring in municipal water and sewer lines. Solon was notoriously anti big box, so we focused on Aurora, with which we had a longstanding relationship due to the successful Barrington Country Club we opened in 1994 (see chapter eight). Indeed, the Mayor of Aurora immediately gave us positive feedback when we approached her about paying a $500,000 fee to allow us to tie into the City's water and sewer infrastructure. The City Council even suggested we try to annex the land to Aurora. We knew that was a long shot, particularly since Aurora and Bainbridge Township were in different counties. We filed a petition to annex anyway, thinking it might give us some leverage in our continuing negotiations with Bainbridge to build what we now were calling the Marketplace at Four Corners.

Bainbridge promptly agreed to support us in building the center on the 130-acre property, mainly because it would move the project away from the residents of Bainbridge Township and closer to residential communities in the adjacent towns of Solon and Aurora. This was a win-win for Bainbridge Township, since it would receive the economic benefits of the development with little of the geographic impact (please see Figure 6.2).

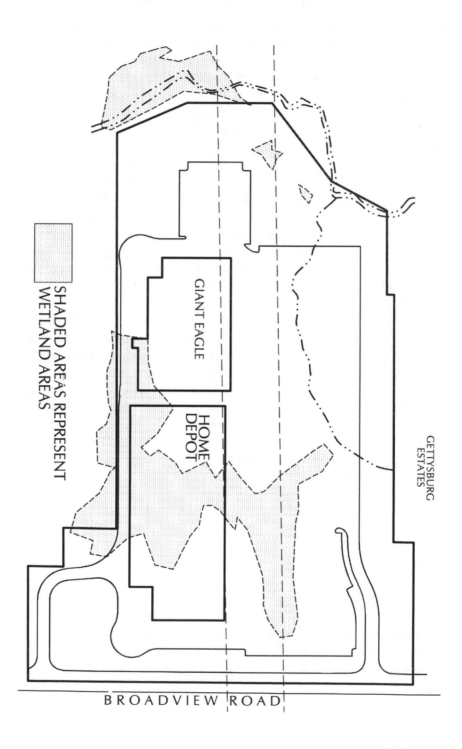

Addressing Environmental Concerns

Our biggest concern, however, was an issue that now seemed to follow us wherever we went—wetlands. We had already successfully received approval from both the federal and state EPA authorities concerning 11 acres of wetlands, 2.9 acres of which we would be impacting, on the north side of the street. But if we built on the other side of the street, we would have to begin the approval process all over again.

Our only non-negotiable position was that if we agreed to move the development to this new site, Bainbridge Township would support our request for the new wetlands permits. We weren't about to repeat our experience in Parma, where local opposition was a major factor in the difficulties we were having there. In this case, we entered into a memorandum of understanding with the township that they would strongly support our wetlands permit.

In June 2000 the U.S. Army Corps of Engineers visited the 130-acre site, walking through it with our consultants to review our delineation of each wetland. The first step was to decide what was and was not a wetland and set their boundaries. Initially it appeared we would be impacting 13 of the 35 acres of wetlands, but by redesigning the construction plan slightly we were able to reduce that to just under 10 acres.

Once the U.S. Corps verified our site plan, we forwarded it to the OEPA. Despite our problems in Parma, we didn't expect a similar battle in Bainbridge Township. In more than 100 tries before, we had never been denied a wetlands permit. Parma was a fluke, we thought confidently, and this time we had the full support of the local government.

The first inkling of just how wrong we were occurred when the OEPA project administrator appeared for his first walk through—repeating the walk through already conducted by the US Army Corps of Engineers. On the job for just 30 days, this was the first time he had ever delineated, classified, or even walked through a wetlands in an official capacity. We sensed we were in trouble when he couldn't stop 'ooing' and 'aahing,' and saying, "Wow, look at all these beautiful trees." We wanted to tell him that "beautiful trees" were not an endangered species, and that even if they were, they had no relevance to the wetlands permits we were seeking.

Throughout the summer we lobbied the OEPA to rule on our permit request, but the agency kept dragging its feet. The issue was their classification of each wetland. The OEPA uses a three-category system, with number one being the least vital to the environment and number three being the most. Under Ohio law, a category 3 wetlands can only be disturbed if the development can demonstrate a strong public need, benefiting the entire state. We didn't anticipate a problem, however, because we were avoiding the site's sole category 3 wetlands altogether. Our consultants assured us that under state regulation each of the wetlands we were impacting would be classified as a category 1 or, at worst, a 2.

In September the OEPA finally made a ruling. We were informed that we had been using the wrong version of the Ohio Rapid Assessment Method (ORAM) used by the state to categorize wetlands. Our consultants had been using the current 4.1 version, which didn't take trees into account. Silly us. Instead, the project administrator had decided to use version 5.0, which did incorporate trees, even though it was still under review by the OEPA. Was it just dumb luck or something more orchestrated? Who knows. What I do know is that under the new scoring method, the only wetland site that we couldn't avoid destroying because it was located right smack in the middle of the property had been reclassified from a category 2 to a category 3.

We appealed the decision, but after another two months of foot-dragging, the OEPA told us they could take no action until after a public hearing, which they scheduled for December 2000. We were further frustrated when a snowstorm cancelled that meeting, and we couldn't persuade them to reschedule it until February 2001.

After the public hearing, we immediately submitted our written comments and hoped for a speedy decision. Just like with the Parma development, John and I went to Columbus to present to the project administrator and OEPA Director Chris Jones, someone not unfamiliar to us, a mitigation package that we hoped would 'wow' them. In words, tone, and attitude, we made it clear to Jones and his staff that we didn't want an adversarial relationship; we were ready to compromise in additional ways to make this work.

We agreed to pay for widening State Route 43, which ran along both our property and the Six Flags Amusement Park, and to make substantial improvements in the region's water, sewer, and flood prevention infrastructures. We also approached the wetlands issue head on. In a typical mitigation, a developer is asked to replace one and a half acres for every acre disturbed by a project; sometimes the ratio is two to one. We proposed to protect 4.2 acres for every acre we disturbed. This was unprecedented, and at between $18,000 and $22,000 an acre, an extra 14 acres would cost us an additional quarter of a million dollars, not an insignificant sum. But we felt it was a small price to pay in order to speed up the process. We were much more concerned about the carrying charges on land valued at $14 million than we were spending $250,000 to strike a deal that would move the project forward. We were particularly eager for a decision to be made one way or the other. Though we were confident that, in the end, our arguments and common sense would prevail, even a denial would allow us to begin the appeal process and keep the process moving.

The Paul Bunyan of Bainbridge

In June 2001, John and our environmental consultant met in Buffalo with the U.S. Army Corps of Engineers to work out the details of our federal permit so at least that would be finalized. At the end of the meeting John asked whether there was anything to prevent us from cutting the trees in and around the wetlands. We had already cleared the rest of the site. We were still confident we would prevail in court if it came to that, and we didn't want to waste any more time before starting construction once we finally did receive all our approvals. The U.S. Corps of Engineers confirmed that we could cut the rest of the trees by hand, without using heavy machinery in the wetlands themselves. We could even reach into the wetlands and remove trees, as long as we didn't actually enter the wetlands or remove the stumps.

We knew we also needed permission from the Geauga County Soil and Water Conservation District, which confirmed its approval in a June 13, 2001 letter which read in part, "After discussions with Mark Scalabrino of the U.S. Army Corps of Engineers, cutting of trees may be done in the wetland areas but earth disturbance of any kind may not occur in these areas." That was fine with us. We made certain that the OEPA was copied on the approval letter, and we proceeded to carefully cut and remove the trees.

Still, the OEPA spent the entire Spring moving at snails' pace, all but ignoring our direct appeals to both the agency and the Governor. In July, after we had finished removing the trees and were ready to begin construction save for this last permit, I called Chris Jones. He told me he had good news and bad news to tell me. The good news was that he had our Parma permit sitting in a drawer waiting to be mailed immediately following the public hearing I mentioned earlier in this chapter. The bad news was he was going to deny the wetlands permit for Bainbridge Township. We were stunned, but not nearly so flabbergasted as we were over what happened next. Almost immediately the OEPA issued a press release headlined, "Developer Cuts Trees After Denial."

What denial? We wanted to know, but before we could get answers, the story had taken on a life of its own. Soon the media was branding Heritage Development, and John McGill in particular, as outlaws. Spurred by the statement from the OEPA, the media spun the story so that it reported we were ravaging wetlands by illegally destroying every tree in sight.

"But what about the law–L-A-W?" asked an editorial in the *Cleveland Plain Dealer* on August 9, 2001. "That's what McGill has trampled. The EPA and the Ohio attorney general's office, which are investigating McGill's' actions, are right to say that they won't let him get away with this brazen challenge to their authority."

We tried circulating the letter from Geauga County that had given us permission to cut the trees; we also urged the media to call the U.S. Army Corps of Engineers to get its side of the story. But no one seemed very interested in the facts. The media lived up to their reputation of never allowing the truth to get in the way of a good story.

Now the gloves were off. We decided the courts were our only recourse. Immediately we filed a defamation suit against the OEPA, naming both Chris Jones and the project administrator as defendants. More importantly, in August, as soon as we were officially denied our wetlands permit, we appealed to the Geauga County Common Pleas Court. This meant an expensive, full blown trial, but we felt we had little choice.

Then a funny thing happened as each side began taking depositions. After the judge reviewed the case and discovered that we had had the legal right to cut the trees within the wetlands, he told both sides that he was prepared to force a settlement if we couldn't reach an agreement. That understandably made the OEPA extremely nervous. The large, healthy trees in this one wetlands were the primary reason it had been categorized as a number 3. But since we had legally cut the trees, the one justification for the category 3 no longer existed. If the courts ruled in our favor, which seemed increasingly likely, a precedent would be set enabling developers to create category 1 wetlands out of almost any site by simply cutting the trees. In fact, the Parma City Council saw what was going on in Bainbridge Township and passed a law requiring permits for the clearing of trees, with a $150 fine per tree for each violation.

$1 Million "Fine" for Something We Never Did

Perhaps then it should have come as no surprise that just after the first of the year, the OEPA finally seemed willing to talk with us about a settlement. The agency waited, however, until the 41st day of hearings before getting serious, which, intentionally or not, made the process as expensive as possible for us, as well as taxpayers. At any rate, it was clear that whatever compromise the OEPA was willing to make, it needed the media spin to be in its favor because our effort to obtain a wetlands permit had become a prominent issue throughout the community. The OEPA certainly couldn't be seen as caving to the wishes of a developer.

The details of the settlement were relatively easy to conclude, particularly considering the amount of time it had taken to get to this point. We agreed to contribute $1 million for a variety of environmental causes. Half would be deposited in an escrow account for the Geauga Park District, $250,000 would go to the Environmental Education Fund and to a wetlands regulation program, and the rest would be used to pay the OEPA's legal and staff fees. We also agreed to purchase 30 acres of wetlands in the Twinsburg Bog and donate it to a land conservancy, and to build five acres of quality wetlands from scratch to replace the wetlands we were disturbing.

The primary dispute now was that the OEPA insisted that the $1 million be labeled as a "fine." They needed to save face, and a "fine" that included us reimbursing the OEPA for the taxpayer funds it had spent fighting in court with us over their permit denial would send the message that they had won and we had lost. This was absurd, of course, but at this point our first priority was to stop the delays and get the project moving. We were ready to begin construction immediately, and feared that any further postponement would cause a repeat of Parma, with some of our major tenants bailing on us. We had already spent more than $2 million on the project, and another year or two delay, even if we prevailed in the end, would be disastrous. If the OEPA wanted to categorize the settlement as a "fine" in order to protect their political butts, that was OK with us. We knew in our hearts we had done nothing to warrant a fine.

Entrepreneurs who might find themselves facing a similar situation need to remember the goal toward which they are working. For us, paying a "fine" even without having done anything wrong was the right business decision. The fine let the other party save face, allowed us to get on with developing the land, and put an end to legal expenses. Today the Marketplace at Four Corners is a popular, successful

700,000-square-foot center with major tenants that include Wal-Mart, Kohl's and Marshall's.

Never Walk Away from a Fight

I've developed a reputation over the years of never avoiding a fight, particularly when I think I'm right. More specifically, people know I don't walk away from a development once it's begun. Entrepreneurs take note. Building a reputation for never giving up has often helped us successfully negotiate a compromise that has allowed us to move forward with a difficult project. If the other side knows you're not about to go away and has reason to believe that you may ultimately prevail, their own best choice is to negotiate the best settlement possible.

I use the same philosophy when faced with nuisance lawsuits. Once you develop a reputation of being quick to settle any lawsuit even if you believe you are in the right, you only invite further lawsuits. If I get sued for the sole reason that the other side thinks I have deep pockets, I immediately counter sue. I'd rather spend more money on legal fees than a quick settlement would cost than be an easy patsy, which will prove more costly in the long run anyway as you get a reputation as an easy mark.

Sometimes Just Walk Away

None of this, however, means I won't settle a lawsuit if I think I'm in the wrong, or walk away from a project if its potential success proves less sure than we initially believed. In that case, the trick is to walk away with as much initial investment back in your pocket as possible.

A few years ago, for example, Home Depot expressed interest in locating a store in Chardon, Ohio, about 35 miles from our office. We optioned a site and proceeded to tackle a complicated rezoning process, which included a referendum on the November ballot. We developed a master plan—including a connector road requested by the City Council and our donation of a small parcel where a community recreation center would be built through tax increment financing. The public referendum ultimately passed in our favor by a small margin.

We then ran into a problem because our option on the land was expiring and we did not have renewal rights. We weren't prepared to exercise the $8 million option because we hadn't yet received final site plan or wetlands approval. Nor had we negotiated lease agreements with our proposed tenants. We were in the middle of our battles in Parma and Bainbridge Township, and we weren't about to take a chance in Chardon.

We fell victim to our own success. Now that the public referendum had passed, the value of the land had increased to such an extent that the owner thought he could get a better price from another developer. Suddenly he wasn't willing to renew our option.

The seller had pulled the rug out from under us, but we retained an important wild card. We had kept an option from another owner on a five acre parcel with road access to the larger site, without which no development could proceed. We ultimately agreed to assign this option for a payment of $350,000, which represented our total investment in the project plus a fee of $50,000. When you walk away, it's better to walk away with something than with nothing.

Other times a project that appears desirable at first blush sours upon further review. A few years ago we entered into a preliminary purchase agreement to buy a mall in North Randall, Ohio. It was in a transitional neighborhood, but we saw it as a potential redevelopment. We thought we could operate it for a short time at a small profit until we could develop plans and obtain the necessary approvals to tear it down and begin again. Our due diligence, however, revealed that the seller had seriously misrepresented the mall's income stream. The movie theater, for example, instead of having 13 years left on the lease as represented and $900,000 in annual revenue, actually had six years remaining and slightly more than $600,000 in revenue. Likewise, we had been told that the Dillard's department store had six years left on its lease and generated $500,000 in annual revenue, when in fact it had just given its default notice and hadn't been paying rent for several months. We had negotiated a price based on an erroneous income stream, and decided to walk away from the deal after an investment of only about $25,000.

Building a Boat and a Boat Company

If there's one thing I learned from my dealings with projects such as Parma and Bainbridge, it's that creative solutions can almost always be found in order to make the best of a bad situation. Rarely do you have to abandon a project altogether. This is true with real estate projects and also with personal decisions, large and small.

In 1989, after briefly considering the purchase of a second home in Florida, Iris and I started thinking instead about owning a yacht. We like to travel, and a yacht would serve both purposes–a second home while we were in Florida and a way to travel in ultimate comfort. We visited a number of friends on their yachts, as well as several boatyards and boat shows both in Florida and in Europe. We identified Burger Boat in Manitowoc, Wisconsin as the Rolls Royce of U.S. boat manufacturers.

Harry B. Burger had founded Burger Boat in 1863, building sailing craft for commercial fishermen. In 1901 he entered the pleasure boat industry, and by the 1960s the company had become the premier American manufacturer of aluminum motor yachts.

Burger wasn't the least expensive yacht builder by any means, but it was the best. Aluminum was considerably more expensive both to build and maintain, but the company had long resisted the move to fiberglass. The fiberglass process uses reusable molds and is therefore unsuitable for customized designs. Our boat, which I naturally named "Lady Iris" before we had even signed a contract, was going to be one of a kind—like the woman for which it was named.

Little did I know, however, that just as we began work on Lady Iris, Burger Boat was beginning to slide into serious financial difficulties. In 1986 the last family owner, Henry E. Burger, with no heirs interested, had sold the company to oil and gas millionaire John McMillan, who wanted to move it to Florida. This was a poor business decision since the craftsmen, many second, third, and fourth generation workers, were not about to pick up and move to Florida from their homes in Wisconsin. Without its employees, there was no Burger Boat Company. These were true craftsmen, experts in everything from woodworking, to upholstery, to welding, to naval engineering.

McMillan ended up running the company from his Coral Gables home, which was almost equally foolhardy. Even with hands-on management, shipbuilding is a tough business. As the saying goes, the quickest way to make a million bucks in the boat business is to start with two million and get out fast. Apparently McMillan experienced this first hand and sold the company to the Tacoma Boat Building company, which only made matters worse. A public company, Tacoma was just emerging from bankruptcy as the 1980s recession was in full swing. It bought Burger for the cash flow, eventually sucking as much cash out of it as possible, to the tune of $13 million. With just twenty minutes notice to its employees just days before Thanksgiving, Tacoma closed the shipyard, laying off 140 workers.

We now had a real emergency on our hands. In January 1991 Iris and I, along with our lawyer Al Adams, flew up to Manitowoc, Wisconsin to see for ourselves what exactly was happening. The answer was nothing—no activity, no workers, nothing. On previous trips we had been invigorated by the activity and the enthusiasm that filled the air. This time the shipyard was virtually empty. It was heartbreaking to see Lady Iris, heretofore subject to the tender care of dozens of busy craftsman doing what they loved, now sitting alone in the middle of winter in a giant unheated shed, a forlorn shell of what we still envisioned she would one day become.

The most obvious solution was to find another company that could finish the job, using the same specifications Iris and I had so meticulously approved. I explored various ways to transport our half-finished boat to another shipyard either by truck or barge. This was no doubt the most economical way of getting our yacht finished, but it didn't sit very well with either Iris or me. Lady Iris was going to be a unique, special yacht, in no small part due to the talented craftsmen of Manitowoc. I respected these people; they were hard workers who had been poorly treated by Burger Boat's last owner. The closing had devastated the entire community, and I could sense that both the workers and the local government would jump at a chance to help create an environment in which to finish Lady Iris.

I grilled Al Adams about what it would mean for me to in effect take over the company until Lady Iris was completed. I didn't want to assume any of the company's obligations, particularly its pension plan or union bargaining rules; I just wanted to get my boat built. There certainly were plenty of unemployed workers who were more than willing to help me.

I sat down with a leadership group and explained that I had a way of continuing their employment and healthcare benefits. I had incorporated the Manitowoc Boat Company, with the intent of handing it over to the workers as their own operating company. I then negotiated with them an hourly rate and put in place a purchasing process so that they would have a system for submitting invoices, which I would pay weekly, along with their hourly wages. The workers' biggest concern was their health insurance and vacation pay, both of which they had lost when the company closed its doors. I guaranteed them both benefits as part of our deal.

The process of building the boat of our dreams was frustrating at times, but Iris and I had fun, and in the end it was extremely rewarding. As usual, Iris completely furnished the vessel herself and was intimately involved in the design, which gave us a spectacularly beautiful, unique boat. She inspired several structural innovations, including designing three stairways that separated our quarters from the guest rooms and from the crew's quarters, which gave us privacy unique even on a luxury yacht. She also designed a high-tech office for me upstairs, as well as a complete walk around on deck so we don't have to travel through the cabin to go from one side of the deck to the other or from the rear deck to the galley or crew's quarters.

Motivating the Workforce

When we had signed the original contract, Burger management told us that they hoped we'd visit during construction, noting that the next time they saw most customers was when they arrived to take possession. We assured them our modus operandi was much more hands-on.

Once we had organized the workers for the sole purpose of finishing Lady Iris, we felt it was important to do everything we could to inspire them. It was Iris's idea to have a series of parties to allow them to get to know us better, and insisted we fly to Wisconsin twice a month to check their progress. The day I ceremoniously welded the first piece of the keel we flew up a number of friends and family and had a huge party in the shipyard with the workers. Another time we entertained the work crew after hours at a local restaurant. As our timetable began to slip, Iris had sweatshirts made for every worker with a picture of Lady Iris and the projected completion date. We missed the date by a long shot, but we got it finished in a first class manner, and amidst all the frustrations, we derived a great sense of accomplishment.

Ultimately, the cooperation between us and the workers established a bond that inspired them to stick together and try to revive the company. Shortly after Lady Iris was launched, they tried organizing a new company themselves and finding a new owner. Finally David Ross, a boat enthusiast who had sold his technology company a few years earlier and agreed to acquire Burger Boat with a promise to invest $750,000 to upgrade the shipyard. Since its rebirth, Burger has built more than thirty luxury yachts. Many of the craftsmen who worked on Lady Iris are now back working at the company, and probably some of their children as well.

Recouping My Losses Legally

I pursued the two former owners of Burger Boat in court to force them to make restitution for the year's delay and cost overruns that had been caused by their negligence. They hadn't even had the decency to alert me to the company's problems, but instead had just left our boat unattended without so much as a phone call. They had also completely taken advantage of Burger Boat's workforce.

Nasty people hire nasty lawyers, and the two former owners were totally unresponsive during depositions. The judge didn't take too kindly to that, and after several reprimands from the bench he issued a default judgment. One defendant admitted wrongdoing and wrote me a check for $950,000. The other one offered me $200,000, which I rejected. As he had threatened, he promptly filed for bankruptcy. We chased him to his home state of New Jersey, where we won a judgment in bankruptcy court that his bankruptcy had not absolved him of liability. In a subsequent trial we had to prove I had suffered damages.

After a three-day trial, the court ruled against us, despite the fact that the boat was delivered almost a year behind schedule, I was forced to take control of its construction myself, and I had no warranty. Trying to win a case as an out-of-towner against a Garden State native with a New Jersey judge presiding was tougher than organizing and running a boat business. I filed an appeal with the Federal Court of Appeals, but it too ruled unanimously that I had not been financially damaged.

An Entrepreneurial Approach to My Health

A person's most important decisions usually concern his or her own health. They too should be treated like any business decision. Do a lot of research, rely on expert advice, include and listen to your top management team, look for creative solutions, and resolve not to fail.

I had my first bout with cancer when I was in my early thirties— right about the time I left Sol and started developing houses in Twinsburg. Iris noticed a cyst on my back, and I immediately had it removed. It tested positive, but we had caught it early and it never reoccurred.

My problems in early 2000 were much more serious. This time I had symptoms. I couldn't go five minutes without having to urinate, and when I did, the burning sensation was terrible. At one point I could barely drive the two miles from home to office without wanting to pull off to the side of the road.

I had a very unsatisfactory experience with the first doctor I saw. First off, he gave me a very cursory examination. Secondly, he very matter-of-factly told me my prostate was enlarged and was forcing itself on my bladder, causing the pain. It wasn't anything to worry about, he said, and he sent me home with some medication, dismissing the need for further tests.

I wasn't about to leave it at that; it was obvious to me that something was wrong. I called my personal physician, Dr. Michael Nochomovitz, and told him how dissatisfied I was. He referred me to Dr. Michael Oefelein, a young doctor in the urology department at University Hospitals, a nationally known hospital affiliated with Case Western Reserve.

In the interim I already had a routine physical scheduled with my internist, Dr. Bruce Cameron. He suggested that when I saw Dr. Oefelein I should have him perform three different tests: a biopsy, an ultra sound, and a PSA blood test. A few days later, without me saying anything, Oefelein did all three tests, giving me confidence that he was focused on giving me the best care possible and that he actually knew what he was doing.

The biopsy tested positive, and I was now given three options on how to proceed. I could have the prostrate radiated, I could have it removed, or I could do nothing in the hopes I would outlive the cancer. They always say you'll die from something else before you die of prostate cancer, except that it kills 40,000 American men every year.

Doing nothing wasn't my style. I wanted it out right away. I received the bad news on a Wednesday, and on Friday I sat in the car in the University Hospitals parking lot waiting for the phone to ring to tell me that the results of the tests I had taken the previous day were back and that I could immediately go in for a pre-surgery appointment. I had the surgery the following Monday.

My health problems weren't quite over, however. I had always had a large Adam's Apple, but rarely thought much about it. A few years ago my grandson, Harrison, said something about it, and it bothered me. Leave it to a 10-year old to blurt out what everyone else is too polite to say.

Three months after my prostate surgery, Iris suggested I see a throat specialist, who told me it wasn't an enlarged Adam's apple but a thyroglossal cyst that I probably had had most of my life. He removed it and said it showed an "insignificant" amount of cancer. He assured me that it was nothing to worry about and that I didn't need to take any action. But after my prostate experience, I didn't think "cancer" and "nothing to worry about" belonged in the same sentence. By this time I was using Dr. Nochomovitz as a sort of medical traffic cop, and he recommended I see Dr. Baja Arafah, a thyroid specialist. After seeing the results of the biopsy, Arafah told me I should have my thyroid removed.

Now I was really confused. I called for a meeting with everyone to join me at the table–Iris, Nochomovitz, Oefelein, Arafah, and Dr. Pierre Lavertu, the surgeon who would actually perform the operation. Collectively they recommended that the thyroid be removed, and in September 2000 I had the operation.

That was quite a year. My prostate was removed in June, the thyroglossal cyst in August, and my thyroid at the end of September. But since then, I've thankfully been cancer free. I continue to be extremely vigilant about getting specific, aggressively-scheduled checkups that include a PSA test every three months and a visit to Dr. Arafah every six months. In addition to an internal examination twice a year, I also have my bone density checked to make certain that the medication, called synthroid, that I take to replace the thyroid function is in balance with the combination of medication, calcium, and a rather rigorous exercise regime that I follow to improve my bone density.

Iris too has had her own health problems. In recent years she's had a serious back operation, another operation on her hip, and knee replacement surgery. None of that has slowed her down. She still does all our laundry herself, weeds the garden, and cleans our 10,000-square-foot house without help.

Taking Control of Our Future

Iris and I recently called together all of the specialists that have taken care of our various health care issues over the years. Rather than try to communicate with each doctor individually, we wanted all of them to communicate with us simultaneously, to give us a complete picture of our health and for them also to hear each others' opinions. We discussed our medical histories, current medications, and current issues and ailments, and we asked a lot of questions. We came up with a plan for both Iris and me, including which tests each of us would have to undergo to move on to the next stage of devising our health care plans. Asking tough questions and being proactive had helped me in business in the past, and has recently helped me in managing my own health.

This "don't take no for an answer" attitude also came in handy when Iris and I recently decided to find a cemetery where we could build a mausoleum for ourselves. We had a terrible time finding a suitable site. The Conservative Jewish cemeteries around town had a rule against being buried above ground. I asked my own Rabbi about it, and he said that since in ancient times Jews were buried in caves, he didn't have a problem with a mausoleum. Still, it wasn't easy. I tried everything, including investigating the possibility of buying property adjacent to an already existing cemetery. Finally a friend of mine suggested we join the reform synagogue, Tifereth Israel Temple, which would give us the right to purchase a plot in the Mayfield cemetery and build whatever we wanted because they had no rule prohibiting being buried above ground. Iris and I were thus able to create our final resting place where we wanted it, how we wanted it.

Bottom line—you need to take control of your situation, whether we're talking about personal, business, or health issues. You have to be your own advocate in the boardroom, doctor's office, or courtroom. No one else is going to look after you; no one is going to have your best interest upper most in their mind, except possibly your spouse or children. Don't give up, don't delay, and don't quit until you're satisfied with the information and the answers to your questions.

Revisiting Pohnpei

In the Navy, 1944 — Dating Iris, 1946

Relaxing at the beach with Iris, 1947

Wedding day, September 11, 1948

Expecting our first child, 1950

Cheryl's Bat Mitzvah, 1963

Twinsburg Called Great Growth Area

By BILL SCHWARTZ

REAL ESTATE
NEWS and VIEWS
BOB BRENNAN, Real Estate Editor

Lady Iris

Cheryl and Eugene Faigus wedding day, 1969

The Israel Bond's Israeli Development Award

Running my first marathon, 1979

At the ISCS convention with Iris

Getting involved in politics

Father and son

Cleveland FORCE 1987-88

To Iris and Bart Wolstein
With best wishes, *George Bush*

My friend, Bob Dole

Glenmoor Country and Resort, Canton, Ohio

My buddy, Jack Nicklaus

The Chapel at Glenmoor C.C.

The Heritage headquarters,
Moreland Hills, Ohio

Toledo Hilton Hotel

Iris S. and Bert L. Wolstein Building, United Cerebral Palsy

Iris S. and Bert L. Wolstein Hall, Weatherhead School of Management

Iris S. and Bert L. Wolstein Research Building,
Case Western Reserve, Cleveland, Ohio

Prize-winning cover of University
Hospitals of Cleveland magazine

Hebrew University in Jerusalem, Israel

The Ohio State University, Big Ten
Football Champions, 2002

Watching the Buckeyes from our loge

Archie Griffin, two-time Heisman trophy winner

My childhood home, 1776 S. Taylor Road, Cleveland Heights, Ohio

Our backyard, Pepper Pike, Ohio

Strolling in Capri, Italy

Mother's Day with our grandchildren

Granddaughter, Kimberly Faigus, Wedding Day, December 2002

Chapter Seven

May the Force Be With You

In the early 1970s, had someone asked me how I would define myself, many things would've come to mind—everything from real estate developer and entrepreneur to husband and father. But major league sports owner? Sure, most men probably fantasize about owning a sports team at one time or another, but actually doing it is a whole other story. For me, the fantasy became reality in the autumn of 1979 when Iris and I were vacationing in Italy, staying at the Villa d'Este on Lake Como. We received a call from Scott saying, "For $25,000 we can buy the Force."

"The Force?" I asked. I had no idea what he was talking about. Sure, the first "Star Wars" movie had just premiered, but I was pretty sure that the force wasn't something I could buy for $25,000. The Force, it turned out, was the Cleveland franchise in the Major Indoor Soccer League (MISL) that had just completed its first season. Though I didn't know much about soccer (I wasn't even aware they played indoors), I was interested.

I had always been an avid sports fan, and for several years Scott and I had been talking about acquiring a major league sports franchise. I thought owning a professional team would be a fun thing for Iris, Scott, and me to do together. Developers Diversified had by this time built about a hundred shopping centers and the business was almost running itself, with Jim Karabec and John McGill taking care of the company's day to day operations. For me it was beginning to become more and more difficult to get excited about building a 99th, 100th, or 101st shopping center, so I was on the lookout for new challenges.

Contemplating the Cavaliers

Two years earlier I had come close to buying Cleveland's professional basketball team, the Cavaliers. Scott had interned for the team one summer after graduating high school, so he had some knowledge of the franchise, and later got wind it was being put up for sale.

The team was actually a public company, but Nick Mileti owned the largest block of stock. Anyone who bought his shares would control the franchise. Mileti was a sports promoter, who at one time, using other people's money, had owned the Cavaliers, the Barons and Crusaders hockey teams, the Coliseum where all these teams played, and the 50,000-watt radio station, WWWE. He even briefly owned the Indians baseball team. Mileti didn't have any serious money himself; he did all this with smoke and mirrors, as far as we could tell.

At any rate, once we learned the Cavaliers might be for sale, we met with Mileti to talk about price. By this time the newspapers were reporting that there were a variety of groups interested in taking control of the team, so we quickly made an offer—$10 for each of Mileti's 300,000 shares. The next thing we knew, Mileti had sold his shares to someone we had never heard of—Lou Mitchell from Columbus, Ohio—who had paid about thirty percent more than we had offered.

Mitchell hadn't owned the team a week before he showed up at my house one evening, begging me to take it off his hands. He told Scott and me that he had made a big mistake and was in way over his head. We started negotiating with Mitchell, but we told him we needed a little time to do our due diligence. Before we knew it, a cousin of Mileti's, Joe Zingale, had jumped into the fray. He took Mitchell off the hook, although we knew from our negotiations with him that Mitchell must have suffered a significant loss for owning the team for about a week.

Zingale, however, had his own problems. Before he had even paid for the shares, he showed up at our office, acting like he had done us a big favor. "I now have control of the team," he blurted out, "and I'm ready to negotiate with you." He wanted us to pay less than we had offered Mileti, but more than Mitchell was asking. I suggested we form a partnership to own both the Cleveland Cavaliers and to build a new arena, but Zingale had no interest in that. He just wanted to flip the team and make a profit.

We had no intention of paying Zingale for stepping in and buying the team, and we told him so. We thought it was obvious that he was in way over his head, just as Mitchell had been. He may have been more financially capable of making the deal than Mitchell, but we felt he was just looking to make a quick profit and never had any intention of putting up any cash. We told him we'd match what he had paid for the team, but not a nickel more.

That same night Scott and I happened to have tickets to the Cavaliers game at the Coliseum. Zingale was introduced with grand fanfare as the new owner. It was comical because we were certain he would never take ownership.

Sure enough, within a few weeks Zingale had sold out to Ted Stepien, who was part of the consortium we had put together to make our offer to Mileti. But he had insisted on running the franchise, and the other members of our group had balked at that, citing his lack of experience. Stepien, the owner of a very successful classified advertising company, instead decided to buy the team by himself. I had no intention of getting into a bidding war with him.

All in all, it was like a Chinese fire drill. First Mileti, then Mitchell, then Zingale, all in the space of a few weeks. Stepien ended up losing a fortune with the Cavaliers. In the mid 1980s he sold his advertising company to the Gund family for less than it was worth in order to include the Cavaliers in the sale.

The Force: Finding a New Passion

When Iris and I returned home from Italy, a videotape was waiting for us, showing highlights of the previous MISL season. As soon as I saw a bicycle kick, I was hooked. In a bicycle kick, the player, with his back to the goal, jumps up and in a somersaulting action kicks the ball toward the goal as he is in the air upside down. What a cool sport, I thought.

Like most sports fans, I had never even heard of indoor soccer much less seen it played. But I thought that with some hard work I could make a go of it. The price was certainly right, particularly since Scott negotiated a deal whereby if after a year we were disenchanted with the team, the MISL would buy it back from us for $500,000. I figured we couldn't lose.

I didn't count on two factors. In the first place, within the first year we invested a lot more than $500,000 in trying to turn the franchise around. Selling it even for a half million dollars wasn't as financially appealing as we once thought it would be. And in the second place, I didn't anticipate that Iris, Scott and I would all fall in love with the sport, the team, and the thrill of owning a professional sports franchise.

Before agreeing to buy the Force, I made it clear to Scott that I was only interested in taking on this new challenge if he and I were in it together. I wasn't looking for a full time job, and had no interest in embarking on this adventure, which I knew would take a lot of hard work, by myself. Scott agreed, and suddenly I was the owner of the Cleveland Force soccer team.

I joined the MISL with my eyes open. I knew indoor soccer was an obscure sport and at the time the Force was probably its weakest franchise. The original owners, Eric Henderson and Frank Celeste (the Ohio Governor's brother), had paid $25,000 for the franchise but didn't want to battle the flow of red ink. I inherited a team which in its inaugural 1978-79 season boasted a record of five wins and nineteen losses. With an average of barely 3,000 fans a game, the Force had the lowest season ticket sales of any team in the league.

I didn't know the first thing about selling tickets or running a team or even the rules of indoor soccer. I didn't even know how to watch the team play. For the first few games I took a seat right behind the bench, until I realized I couldn't see anything from that vantage point. I then moved our seats to near the top of the lower deck at mid-field, near all my friends. For our first home game, we mailed out 5,000 free tickets, only to play during a furious snowstorm. To get to the Richfield Coliseum, about 30 minutes from downtown Cleveland, you had to navigate some considerable hills. There were three automobile accidents from our office alone, including Scott who skidded onto the emergency lane and seriously damaged his car. Fortunately no one was hurt. We played the game, but not many of our free tickets were used.

At our second home game I sat next to the league's commissioner, Earl Foreman, who turned to me and said, "You know you have less than a thousand people here? You've got real problems."

No kidding. He didn't have to tell me we had problems. We had inherited a coach, Eddie McCreadie, who was a nice guy and very bright, but not exactly the most reliable fellow on the planet. He had been a hall of fame player in England, and brought along a number of English soccer players who seemed like they were his drinking buddies more than world-class athletes. More than once during our first season he disappeared, and we had to call around to the local hotels to find him. Other times his girlfriend would plead with us to help her locate him. My first official act once I bought the team was to invite all the players and coaches to my home for a barbecue. That must have had the neighborhood buzzing. Let's just say these guys had some rough edges.

What made me think that with no experience in the sports arena that I could turn this disaster of a franchise around? Why would a 52-year-old who could finally relax and enjoy life take on a struggling professional team in an unknown sport and try to make a go of it? Why invite the headaches? Why gamble the money?

When you come right down to it, owning any sports team is an ego trip, plain and simple, and that was part of it, to be sure. I thought that if I made the Force a success, I'd get some respect and doors would open for me within the Cleveland community. But mostly I wanted to see if I could be successful in a business I knew nothing about. After our first year, people told me the Force was one of the worst franchises in America, not just in soccer, but in any sport. I had to laugh at that. I didn't care. I thought I could make it work if I put my mind to it. After all, that strategy had always paid off in the past. Besides, isn't it an entrepreneurial trait to look for new challenges that will show the world we can succeed where others have failed?

I knew a turnaround wouldn't be cheap, although I didn't anticipate that during the first year we would lose a whopping $900,000. But that just made me more determined. I was certain we could do better the second year, and we did, sort of. The good news was that we doubled our attendance; the bad news was that we increased our losses from $900,000 to $1.2 million. Now I knew we were in for a struggle. It also showed me that increasing attendance wasn't going to be enough. We were also going to have to generate significant revenue from sponsorships and other advertising.

I didn't buy the Force to make money. The question was whether our initial losses were money down the drain, or an investment in startup costs. Only time would tell, but I was intent on making it the latter. All eyes were on me, and I was afraid to fail.

Do-It-Yourself Marketing and Sales

I spent the 1979-80 season learning what I could about the 'business.' In fact, just calling it a business, and subsequently turning it into one, were our most important initial tasks. The previous owners had been passionate about the game of soccer, but they had run the team as a hobby. I had to clean house completely and put together a management team that understood the difference and had the dedication to turn this sports team into a profitable business venture. We hired Paul Garofolo, who had experience in both the league office and with the Pittsburgh franchise, as a salesman. He proved himself and soon climbed the ranks from head of public relations, to assistant general manager, and finally to vice president and general manager. Rob Benjamin started out as an intern and became director of marketing. Bob Shemory joined us in 1981 as director of community relations, which became an increasingly important position as we aggressively tried to reach out to the community.

I quickly realized we couldn't just open the doors of the Coliseum and expect the people of Cleveland to wake up in the morning and say, "Gee, I think I'll go buy a couple of tickets to see the Force play today." It was going to take a lot more than that. We were going to have to get out there and *sell* tickets. The time had come for me to sell the Force, not to investors, but to the public. We would have to make an emotional connection with the community and go one step further than creating customers—we would have to create fans, Force fans.

Our first step was to beef up our sales force. I gave them instructions to make a list of the largest Cleveland-area businesses and to call each company once a month to try to sell them season tickets and advertising on the radio or TV, in our printed program, or on signage at the Coliseum. I drilled into them that just because someone says no to you today, doesn't mean he or she will say no to you next month or next year. It was no different than struggling to build a shopping center and fill it with tenants. Remember, persistence pays off; continually going back to the same company until you get a yes really works.

I felt that I had to set the tone for the sales force and took it upon myself to take the lead in selling tickets and sponsorships. There was no sale too small for my personal attention. I called the top people at Coca Cola, Anheuser Busch, McDonalds, and the largest local banks. We would meet with Pepsi at lunch and Coca Cola at dinner and each time have to remember which product to order. We threw everything we could think of into the marketing packages we were selling, including season tickets, signage on the playing field and in our practice facilities, and advertising in our own newspaper, the game program, and on television and radio.

I wasn't above using a little leverage when necessary. The first to buy season tickets and sponsorships were people who did business with Developers Diversified—our lawyers, bankers, insurance agents, accountants, and contractors—which made these early games like homecomings because most of the people in attendance were our friends. Most people came right from work and wore suits and ties, making the games quite upscale, especially for a sports event. We even sold roses for the dating crowd.

One time Paul Garofolo had been trying to sign one of the large local banks to a $50,000 sponsorship, but had been repeatedly stonewalled. Paul had taken my advice and returned again and again, but the bank's marketing director just wouldn't give him a straight answer. I called Paul into my office and told Developers Diversified's chief financial officer to pull our money from the bank. Fifteen minutes later the bank president called to ask what was wrong. I had always gotten along well with this banker, and I told him point blank that we weren't selling poison. I explained to him that we had a great product for a very reasonable price that an organization like his could use to its advantage. He understood the promotional benefits the Force could provide the bank, and later that afternoon Paul took him a sponsorship agreement, which he signed almost without reading.

Another case in point was Steve Qua, owner of Rolls Royce and Buick dealerships in the Cleveland area. Steve, a big fan of the Force, was trying to persuade me to buy a Rolls Royce. When I was younger I said I'd never own a Cadillac, much less a Rolls; I never thought I was the type to drive such an expensive car. One day he called to ask if he could drop off at my house a beautiful 1980 Silver Shadow with 2,000 miles so I could try it out for the weekend. Iris and I figured what the heck, and just as Steve suspected, we were wowed by the car's performance. It was like nothing I had ever driven.

I agreed to buy the car on the condition that when we made our pitch about the Force to the Buick Dealer's Association, Steve would stand up and say to the others that he'd been to a Force game and that the team's enthusiastic family audience was a perfect match for Buick. I knew Steve enjoyed himself every time he attended a game, so I wasn't asking him to do or say anything he didn't believe. We ended up selling the Buick dealers a five-year, $125,000 sponsorship package, which helped justify in my mind the expense of the Rolls.

I was totally committed to filling the arena—I would go anywhere, anytime to sell two season tickets. Sometimes I felt like I had to get on the table and dance to sell tickets, but I guess everyone has a line that they're not quite willing to cross. Yet we were relentless. Companies that started with four season tickets often ended up with twenty-four because of the demand from their employees and clients. We insisted people at least try our product because we knew that once our performance on the field improved, people would enjoy themselves.

We tried everything to sell tickets, very much like our early experiences selling houses in Twinsburg in 1959. At the 1980 home opener every adult received a free glass of champagne and the kids a Coca-Cola. We also initiated all sorts of discounts to drum up demand, even though prices were a bargain—in 1980 they ranged from $4.50 to $7.50. At one game kids under 15 who showed up in soccer uniforms were admitted for half price. Companies could get steep volume discounts, which they could use to reward employees, entertain clients, or build morale with inexpensive company outings. We also had two for one specials, free giveaways, and radio contests. We put coupons on milk cartons and in the *Cleveland Plain Dealer* that entitled people to four tickets, four hot dogs, four Cokes, a pennant, and a parking pass for $29.95.

Particularly during the early years when it was difficult to sell advertising and season tickets, we used barter arrangements to get companies involved. In return for advertising, we were given everything from free meals and airline tickets, to hotel rooms and rental cars. If we needed a new television, we'd go to an appliance store and trade them for an advertising spot. During the 1986-87 season we had a $20,000 credit at the Tavern of Richfield inside the Coliseum. That's a lot of hamburgers and fries.

One of our more ingenious ticket promotions occurred after we partnered with the University of Akron's marketing department. Together we designed a questionnaire to help us learn more about our customers, specifically what prompted them to buy tickets, what they liked about the experience, and what factors were most important in their decision-making process. The survey listed all sorts of reasons why someone might have chosen to attend that game, such as the Force's current win-loss record, the quality of the opposition, whether or not there was a free giveaway, or the importance of the game in the standings. The students talked to fans and recorded their answers.

By far the most critical reason people named for attending a Force game was ticket discounts. People wanted to feel like they were getting a deal, which I think was probably more important in the early years because the Force was new and people hadn't had a chance to become die-hard fans as they had with the Cleveland Indians, Cavaliers, or Browns. As a result of our survey, we came up with a plan whereby we doubled the price of the seats behind the two goals, then offered them as a two-for-one special if purchased in advance. We flooded the community with two-for-one coupons, making them available at fast food restaurants and drug stores all over town. From then on, these seats were consistently sold out. The promotion had the added benefit of showing a packed stadium on every local television sportscast that featured goals in their highlight reels.

Since we had doubled the cost of these tickets before embarking on the two-for-one program, people were in essence paying the same price as they would have prior to the offer. But we were now appealing to something that was apparently even more important to them than actual price—the *feeling* that they were getting a deal and the *perception* that they were saving money. Once we got people to a game, it was up to us and the team to make them feel that they'd gotten their money's worth in terms of entertainment and fun.

After a while it became much more important to me to win a game than it was to build another shopping center, and I was spending almost all my time trying to make the Force a success. While still keeping constant tabs on the details of the various projects being pursued by Developers Diversified, I met every day with the Force staff, located in the basement of the Heritage, on everything from ticket and merchandise sales, to game day operations, to player personnel. Mostly, I enjoyed looking at the big picture, coming up with new ways every day to make the Force a success.

Fortunately, I was not alone. No doubt the best part of owning the Force was the joy of accomplishing great things together with Iris and Scott. Scott's strengths complemented my shortcomings brilliantly. I was comfortable as a salesman, trying to use personality to sell a product, in this case a professional soccer team. I had done it with homeowners in Twinsburg, bankers, and with retailers, and now I was certain I could do it selling tickets and sponsorships for a soccer team.

As much as I was Mr. Outside, Scott was Mr. Inside, taking care of all our player contracts and sponsorship agreements. While I concentrated on ticket sales and other revenue generating activities, he negotiated all the player contracts, the arena lease, and our radio and television deals. We both had our hands full trying to recruit better players.

As usual, I also had Iris by my side every step of the way. It wasn't long before she and I were spending almost every waking hour thinking about ways to improve the Force, both on and off the field. We arrived at every home game hours before it started, greeting fans and employees and making certain everything was in order. I never failed to shake every hand in the handicap section and to circulate in the stands, thanking people for coming. We began to develop relationships with our customers, making them feel welcome and valued. It was a great, inexpensive way to make them feel special and create a connection between them and the team. We were increasing the Force's fan base one fan at a time.

Iris Brands the Force

Iris stepped in and created marketing magic by quickly expanding the Force product line. She designed an entire line of children's clothing, which we sold at department and sporting goods stores, at the Coliseum, and in the soccer shops within our own practice facilities. Soon she added soccer equipment, pennants, pens, and other promotional items, all emblazoned with the Force logo, which she had also designed. During the games, Iris would personally check every concession booth to make sure her growing array of Force merchandise was properly displayed.

During the 1982-83 season, after Iris became involved on a full time basis and began running B&W Products, the merchandising arm of the Force, it had total sales of more than $66,000, about ten times what it had generated the year before. Iris transformed herself into a true businesswoman, importing dozens of items from Asia and growing her merchandise line to eventually include almost 100 different items. By the 1986-1987 season, her sales topped $200,000.

Iris had her hand in everything seen by the public, including all of our advertising, uniforms, and players' warm-up outfits. She was also responsible for the complimentary food we served the press corps before and after each home game. For the uniforms, she designed a wide stripe that circled the shirt. Inside the stripe on the back was the player's name, and on the front was the Force logo. We were also the only team to have travel uniforms—navy blue blazers, striped ties, yellow shirts, and beige slacks.

Improving Our Product on the Field

Regardless of how great the marketing was or how much logo merchandise we were selling, we knew that unless we improved the product on the field, meeting our business goals would be impossible. Again, common sense prevailed and told us that we had to create a winning team if we wanted to create die-hard fans. During the first few player drafts, Scott and I sat at the table as if we knew what we were doing. But we learned to take other people's advice on evaluating talent, a strategy that worked *some* of the time. For example, we paid a lot of money to buy Luis Alberto from the New York franchise. He was a star player for the New York team, but was a bust for us.

Scott and I traveled the world looking for the best players. We recruited two players from Israel. Iris and I went to Yugoslavia with a Yugoslavian friend who volunteered to help us evaluate the talent playing at the professional outdoor league there. In Brazil, Scott and I were certain we were looking at the best players in the world, who would surely lead us to a championship. But most of the players we recruited from South America weren't nearly as talented as we were led to believe and were mostly just interested in coming to the United States. We were still in the learning stages, and none of these were issues we could solve overnight.

After the Force compiled a 48-68 record during our first three seasons, we finally promoted Eddie McCreadie to general manager, and hired Timo Liekoski as coach. I never agreed with Timo's strategy of playing not to lose rather than playing to win, but I couldn't argue with his results. His first season we were 29-19, and we never again had a losing record.

Timo was an excellent judge of talent. By 1983 the outdoor North American Soccer League had gone out of business and many of the best professional soccer players in the world became available. We signed superstars Kai Haaskivi from Finland and Craig Allen from the Island of Guernsey, which really helped our performance on the field. We also signed Antonio Carlos Pecorari, also known as Tatu. He was a truly phenomenal player from Brazil, but he never actually played for us because the Dallas franchise stole him out from under us by circumventing the very specific MISL rules concerning signing new players. Unfortunately, the commissioner was unwilling to step in and enforce the rules, I think because he was concerned that the Dallas franchise might fold. He knew I wasn't going anywhere.

We sued in Federal court, arguing that we were entitled to compensation commensurate with Tatu's superstar status. I met with the judge to explain the MISL's contractual rules to him, but he awarded us only $40,000. When I bumped into him about a year later he told me he had become an indoor soccer fan and had been following Tatu's career. He admitted I had been right about Tatu being a franchise player.

Timo did a good job of sprinkling European talent into our American lineup, which gave us a nice mix of players to promote. Still, we had a terrible time getting local sports reporters to pay attention to us, despite constant pestering by Paul Garofolo and me. In these early years it was nearly impossible to convince them that our improved performance on the field, particularly compared to the dismal showing of the other Cleveland professional sports teams, warranted increased coverage. I know the sports reporters at the *Cleveland Plain Dealer* were sick of my constant haranguing and of Paul's constant calls and visits to the newsroom. But we kept at it.

After awhile, we decided to attack our publicity problem from another angle. Rather than try to compete for coverage in the sports section, where competition from other teams was intense, we thought that we might have more success getting coverage in other sections of the news. So, we broke down every section of the newspaper and identified angles to our story that would fit areas on which they focused. We approached the *Plain Dealer*'s food editor, for example, who assigned a story about the ethnic recipes the players' wives were preparing during the Holiday season. Then the fashion editor agreed to highlight our players in photo spreads, and we partnered with local department and clothing stores for our players to wear their clothing. Another time we had a front page picture at Sea World of one of our players sitting on Shamu, the whale.

Butting My Head Against the Wall

Yet it was still tough going. I made phone calls and knocked on the doors of Cleveland's power brokers, pleading with them to purchase season tickets. I'm sure that some people in the community thought I was too aggressive in expecting local companies to support the team, but I was frankly startled when they showed little interest. I felt we had a community asset that would be in everyone's interest to support. But we had a difficult time persuading the same companies that would think nothing of spending $100,000 for a season box to watch the Browns or Indians to spend $2,000 on season tickets to the Force. Support was so weak that in 1982 we explored the possibility of playing half our home games in Cincinnati or Columbus. It was even a struggle to get on radio or television. We had to buy the airtime and sell our own advertising.

We worked hard for every ticket sold. In the basement of the Heritage we had a computer hookup to Ticketron so we could not only print out tickets as we sold them, but also provide ourselves with an up-to-the-minute assessment of the number of tickets that had been sold. On game day, I would go to that computer every hour and press the button to get the current count. Then at the Coliseum, standing in the concourse, I'd stare out the window, counting the cars coming into the parking lot. When I saw a long line, I'd go crazy making sure we had enough ticket sellers to handle the walkup crowd. The customer, whether it was a business client or a dinner patron or a homeowner or a man buying a hot dog for his son at a Force game, was paramount. I wanted them to feel comfortable, and to come back for more.

As usual, there were all sorts of crises to attend to. One Sunday we were scheduled to play the St. Louis Steamers, but the team called that morning to cancel, saying that a snowstorm had stranded them in Baltimore. But the weather was fine in Cleveland, and we had sold 8,000 tickets. I'd be damned if I'd forfeit all that revenue or disappoint more than 8,000 fans, particularly after I learned the weather had cleared in Baltimore and the forecast for Cleveland was sunny. Scott and I spent the entire day at home on the telephone with the Commissioner and the owner of the Steamers, scrambling to find a charter company that would fly the St. Louis team from Baltimore to Cleveland. I was talking to the charter company on one line, and Scott was on the other yelling at the Steamers' general manager, telling him that they had an obligation to play the game.

We finally convinced the commissioner to order the Steamers to play. I paid for the charter flight myself. We had to delay the game more than an hour, but we managed to keep our fans happy. We entertained them with our popular mascot and kept making regular announcements as to the Steamers' whereabouts.

"They're in the air."

"They've boarded the bus."

"They're in the parking lot."

The icing on the cake was that we went out and walloped the Steamers on the field. One of our Israeli players, Simon Look, scored five goals playing the best game of his life.

Darth Vader: Giving Fans What They Want

By far our most successful marketing ploy was our mascot, a Darth Vader look alike, who before each game would run from the tunnel onto the field. The lights would dim, Star Wars music would blare, and smoke would billow as he led the players onto the field with great fanfare. I got chills, along with everyone else in the stadium, as Darth Vader appeared. No one will ever convince us that we weren't the first to create this kind of pre-game extravaganza with lights and music and smoke. Now it's de rigueur at virtually every National Basketball Association and National Hockey League game.

It got to the point where people would come out to see Darth Vader as much as the Force. He was just a big teenager in a costume, but he signed as many autographs as some of the players. I realized we were onto something when before one game a little old lady yelled at me to sit down because I was blocking her view of Darth Vader.

After *Sports Illustrated* ran a picture of our mascot in 1984, we received a cease and desist letter from George Lucas' Lucasfilm organization, the owner of the Star Wars franchise. They wanted us to pay $8,000 a game for the right to use Darth Vader's likeness. That was as much as we were paying to lease the Coliseum on game day, and there was no way we could afford it. Our solution was to create a new mascot, and we planned all sorts of hoopla to introduce him. At the next pre-game, a James Earl Jones sound alike playing the part of Darth Vader bade farewell, saying "My work is done here; the force is established." We had spent $5,000 creating a new blue and gold costume, with a cape, full facemask, and points coming out of his head. I felt like Coca-Cola must have felt after they introduced New Coke. People booed when this Star Wars-like character appeared instead of Darth Vader. Fans wanted their old mascot back.

Scott contacted Lucas' attorney, only to learn that they had been classmates at the University of Michigan Law School. They negotiated a one-time fee for the use of the Darth Vader image, and we strategized how to resurrect our fallen mascot after his short absence. One night in 1987 before a semi-final game against the Minnesota

Strikers, Star Wars-like music began to fill the packed stadium. Fans started hanging over the railings to find out what was happening. Suddenly Darth Vader appeared and everyone started screaming. The noise was really deafening. It was like Elvis was in the building.

Developing Demand by Bringing Soccer to the Community

While the Cleveland business establishment never did embrace the Force, we had much better success once we targeted our core audience–suburban families with children who play soccer. We focused on public relations, sponsorships, promotions, ticket sales, but most importantly on building awareness and excitement around the game of soccer within individual communities. Indoor soccer was not even a professional sport until 1978, and we realized we needed to promote the sport, as well as the team and its individual players.

We purchased the Four Seasons Racquet Club in Warrensville Heights to be used as the Force's practice site, but we also used it as the launching pad for an indoor amateur soccer league. By 1983 we had bought four more facilities, all former tennis clubs. The tennis boom of the 1970s was over, and we were able to buy them at a good price. In fact, Scott structured a transaction whereby our investment firm, Diversified Equities, syndicated the five facilities to other investors so we were able to control them without putting up any cash.

These former tennis facilities were perfect for indoor soccer because they were large structures without any poles or beams in the center. We renamed the facilities the Force Fitness Institutes, and between league play, instructional programs, and other events, we eventually had 38,000 people a week going through them.

We started week-long summer camps which were extremely popular. During the summer of 1982, more than 3,000 kids attended one of 56 camps spread throughout the Cleveland metropolitan area. Bob Shemory played a significant role in developing our camps, clinics, and facility business, which grew into the largest program of its kind owned and operated by a professional sports team. The first year, each camper paid $110 per week.

In addition to becoming an important profit center, the camps also generated other revenue streams. Sponsors like Burger King, Pepsi, and Nestle took advantage of grassroots sampling opportunities by distributing either food or goody-bags with samples to the camp kids and their parents. The giveaways became walking billboards.

The Force players worked with the kids on various skills in their role as camp instructors. By the end of each weekly session many of the kids had developed a case of "hero worship," begging their parents to take them to see "their friend" play in a game at the Coliseum. We made it easy for parents picking up their kids at camp to buy tickets to individual games and to our Camper Reunion Nights.

In 1980, we began the Force Indoor Soccer Leagues with 38 teams. By 1987 we had more than a thousand teams and more than 15,000 amateur players. Indoor soccer really began to take off as a participatory sport during the cold Cleveland winters. The facilities were packed every day after school and on weekends. Even adults began playing, and soon more than half the players were over 21. Twenty percent were women. We parlayed that popularity into interest in the Force by sometimes allowing amateur teams to play in the Richfield Coliseum before our games. We also offered discount tickets to the Force at each of our five facilities.

One of the most important marketing strategies we undertook was building a bond between the players and the public. Our goal was to create and foster an emotional connection between the Force and its fans, especially young ones, so that they would constantly think about going to a Force game. We hoped that they would, in fact, bug their parents to take them to upcoming games. To ensure that fans developed an emotional attachment to the team, we signed our players to 12-month contracts and obligated them to make personal appearances at the camps, clinics, and schools.

Another successful marketing strategy was the creation of our own newspaper. In its early days it was difficult to create circulation, but as the success of our camps and clinics grew, we began to create lists of everyone who visited the Force Fitness Institutes, our season ticket holders, advertisers, and anyone who had ever filled out a two-for-one coupon. What started out as a four-page newsletter mushroomed into a 44-page tabloid size newspaper, and by 1984 we were sending it to a mailing list of 50,000 people. Since we sold ads on almost every page, it became an important profit center for us.

Turning Point

As owner of the Force and a tenant in the Coliseum, I had access to premium seats to any event held there. Iris and I frequently went to concerts and saw the likes of Michael Jackson, Phil Collins, and Neil

Diamond. In early 1982 we went to hear the Rolling Stones. The place was packed, just bulging at the seams, with an energy that I envied. I remember turning to Paul Garofolo and telling him wistfully, "Just once I'd like to see this at a Force game."

By the 1982-83 season, our new coaching staff, headed by Timo Liekoski, had orchestrated a major overhaul of the team. In December we enjoyed the best winning streak of our tenure, and people finally seemed to be paying attention. On the Saturday after Christmas we had a crowd of more than 12,000 fans to a game against the Chicago Sting. We were so excited to see the size of the crowd, but equally disappointed by the magnitude of the loss: Force 3, Sting 10. Liekoski was quoted in the paper the next day saying that the loss was a fluke and that we were much better than what we had showed on the field. Then the next week we played the Sting again in Chicago and lost 11-2. Iris and I attended the game with our daughter Cheryl, her husband Eugene, and their two daughters Kimberly and Tiffany. We were embarrassed at the team's performance.

Our overall record that year, however, was 29-19, and we made the playoffs, only to face our nemesis, the Sting, in the first round, for a best of three series. Tuesday's game was at the Coliseum, Thursday's in Chicago, and then if necessary Saturday's game would be played back in Cleveland.

On Tuesday night we drew only 7,000 fans, and I was feeling more disheartened than at any other time since buying the Force four years earlier. I had tried. We had done our best for four years, spending an extraordinary amount of time and absorbing substantial financial losses. I had invested $5 million in the effort, and what did I have to show for it? We had had some success, to be sure, particularly in introducing a new sport into northeastern Ohio. But it just didn't seem like the Force was catching on. It wasn't like we had much competition. This was a time in Cleveland when every other professional sports franchise—the Browns, the Indians, and the Cavaliers—had poor records almost every year. We had given Cleveland a playoff contender, and done everything we could think of to boost attendance. Yet still people weren't showing up. Making matters worse, we lost the first game to the Sting 9 to 5.

It was very frustrating. We had an advance sale of only 800 tickets to the Saturday game, which we assumed wouldn't be played anyway. I thought we'd lose in Chicago Thursday night, after which I was seriously considering calling a press conference and packing it in.

Iris, Scott, and I watched the Chicago game at home on television, thinking it might just be our swan song. Two minutes before the half we were losing 4-2, when we scored two quick goals to tie the score. But our second string goalie hurt his leg and couldn't return. Our first string goalie was already out with an injury, so we knew we'd have to play the second half with our third string, Lou Cioffi, who for the year had an average of more than ten goals scored against him per game. It looked hopeless.

In the second half Cioffi played like no one had ever played the game before. Every shot on goal hit something–the post, Cioffi's head, the cross bar, Cioffi's hip, something. Cioffi and the other Force defenders shut out the Sting in the second half, and we won the game 5-4.

The game got prominent play in the *Cleveland Plain Dealer* and on all the local television stations. It had been televised live in Cleveland and broadcast on a 50,000-watt clear channel station that reaches probably 38 states and half of Canada. The radio station even replayed the game in its entirety that evening. It was now less than 48 hours before the rubber game to decide which team moved on to the next round.

For the first time it seemed like there was a buzz about the Force, that people were talking about us at the water cooler. Iris, Scott, and I and the entire staff were excited, in anticipation of a good walkup crowd for Saturday evening's deciding game.

Paul was the first to arrive at the office on Friday morning. At the time we had an elderly couple named Julius and Virginia clean the Heritage for us. They were the sweetest people. They called Iris and me Mr. and Mrs. W., and Paul was Mr. Paul. "Mr. Paul, you have big problems," they said to him. "Your phone system is broken. All your lines are blinking."

Paul could see they were right. All twenty lines were indeed blinking. Paul pressed line one. "Good morning, Cleveland Force," he said instinctively.

The person on the other end of the line told him he was looking for tickets to tomorrow's game. Paul then pressed the second line. "Is this where I can buy tickets?" the voice asked. Paul went up and down the rows of buttons, and on each line someone was asking about tickets to the third and deciding game against the Chicago Sting.

By then we were at about thirty-six hours to game time and counting. All day and into the night, and all morning Saturday, our entire staff answered the phones, taking ticket orders. The volume was too much for us—we had to recruit people from Developers Diversified to help out. Iris and I pitched in as well.

As game time approached, the Coliseum was a madhouse. At one point the television news reported a major accident on I-271 and announced that they had sent their chopper to investigate. A few minutes later they told their viewers that it wasn't an accident at all, but cars backed up for miles on the interstate on their way to the Richfield Coliseum to watch the Force play.

From an advance sale of 800 tickets, we had a paid crowd of 19,106. It felt like the rock concert crowd I had envied just a few months before, but now they were cheering for the Force. We sold more than 18,000 tickets in less than 48 hours, with the largest walkup crowd in the history of the Coliseum. The building wasn't equipped to handle such a large last-minute crowd, and many people didn't get to their seats until just before half time. It was a cold winter day too, but we piped the radio broadcast outside and into the corridors and even those standing in the long lines remained enthusiastic. We also sold a lot of hot chocolate.

We won the game 7-5, and we were the talk of the town. We lost in the next round of the playoffs to Baltimore, but it didn't matter. That magical evening marked a turning point for the Force.

Talk of the Town

Finally we had a product people wanted, which made the sales process so much easier. We spent the summer making a concerted effort to boost season tickets. Suddenly doors that had heretofore been slammed in our faces were now open to us. During the summer of 1983 we sold more than 2,000 season tickets, and the next season our average per game attendance more than doubled, from 6,609 to 13,675. No longer could fans expect to just arrive at the game and get a good seat. No longer could companies afford not to advertise with us if they wanted to reach our growing fan base.

The first year we owned the franchise, the Force game program contained only two ads, but by 1981 it had fourteen ads, and all games were on radio, and many on television. By 1986 the game program was filled with more than 90 pages of advertisers. Instead of having to sell our own television advertising, we made a $250,000 deal with Gaylord Broadcasting to televise every game the following season on WUAB Channel 43, the primary free sports channel in Cleveland.

We had great success selling signage on the dasher boards around the playing field for $5,000 per season. We started getting $7,500 for signage on the boards near the goal, and $10,000 from Anheuser Busch for a sign integrated into the goals. The company got its money's worth. Each time a scoring shot was shown on television or in the newspaper, there was Budweiser's logo, as clear as could be.

Total team revenue went from $1.7 million during the 1982-83 season to $4.4 million in 1986-87, when we turned a profit of close to $600,000. (See the charts on the following pages for income and attendance breakdowns.) We continued to keep careful tabs on our expenses and revenue. Either Scott or I signed every check in order to be on top of each penny that went out the door.

We even came up with a scheme to fill the Coliseum for exhibition games, never an easy task. We sold the Revco drugstore chain on the idea of buying the entire house for $50,000. We advertised only in our own newspaper, telling people to pick up their free tickets at their local Revco stores, which were flooded with customers looking for the coupons. We learned that "free" is the most powerful word in the English language. We had never drawn more than a few thousand for an exhibition game, but for this one we had more than 18,000 fans, making it the first time an indoor exhibition soccer game had ever been sold out.

In 1985 when we hosted the MISL All Star Game, we convinced the Cleveland City Council to approve the installation of brackets on the light poles downtown so we could string banners to promote the event. The brackets are still there, and banners announcing various events are now a regular occurrence downtown. Beginning in 1986 we also sponsored the Budweiser Soccer Classic that showcased the

The Force
1978-88

Year	Total Attendance	# of Games	Average Attendance	Won/Loss	Revenue
1978-1979	37,393	12	3,116	5-19	$ 55,000
1979-1980	49,280	16	3,080	12-20	$ 100,000
1980-1981	97,680	20	4,884	21-19	$ 350,000
1981-1982	110,030	22	5,002	15-29	$ 760,000
1982-1983	158,619	24	6,609	29-19	$1,700,000
1983-1984	328,201	24	13,675	31-17	$3,000,000
1984-1985	310,284	24	12,929	27-21	$3,600,000
1985-1986	307,040	24	12,793	27-21	$4,000,000
1986-1987	366,887	26	14,111	33-18	$4,675,000
1987-1988	315,807	28	11,279	30-26	$3,800,000

1986–87 Estimated Revenue Breakdown	
Season tickets	$884,640
Other gate	$315,360
Radio	$225,000
Television	($41,000)
Exhibition season	$6,100
Expansion fees	$15,000
Loge boxes	$34,200
Summer camps	$183,000
Merchandising	$363,000
Dasher boards	$217,000
Game programs	$185,000
Sponsorships	$1,400,000
Miscellaneous	$102,400
Budweiser Classic	$200,000
Playoffs	$586,000
TOTAL	$4,675,700

top college players from around the country. Both the all-star game, which was nationally televised, and the Budweiser Classic, drew sell out crowds.

On April 5, 1986, in a game against the Minnesota Strikers, we had the largest crowd for a sporting event in the history of the Coliseum. Paul Garofolo and Bob Shemory gave me a jug mounted on a wooden plate full of 20,174 pennies to represent the record crowd. Later that year Iris celebrated my 60th birthday by serving birthday cake on the floor of the Coliseum to fifteen thousand people. I got a standing ovation, everyone sang happy birthday, and I couldn't keep the tears inside. Then we served about 10,000 pieces of birthday cake to the fans.

During the next few years we regularly outdrew the Cleveland Cavaliers and the Cleveland Indians. We were highlighted in *USA Today* and other national publications as the model franchise in any sport, not just soccer. In a 1984 *Sports Illustrated*[12] article, David Stern, the Commissioner of the National Basketball Association, was asked how concerned he was about the growing popularity of the National Hockey League. His response was that he was much more worried about indoor soccer. *Sports Illustrated*, the *Wall Street*

---

[12]Jaime Dian, "This is No Mistake By the Lake," Sports Illustrated, January 30, 1984.

Journal, Inside Sports, and *USA Today* routinely referred to the Force as the MISL's "showcase" or "Cadillac" franchise. *Cleveland Magazine,* comparing us to the City's other professional sports teams, called us "an island of professionalism in a seemingly unending sea of swill."

We also continued to do well on the field, posting winning records during each of the next five seasons. We never won a championship, but we were the only team to be in the semifinals four years in a row. On a personal level, never winning the title was disappointing, but from a business standpoint I always thought coming in second or third wasn't the worst thing that could happen. Whether you're a sports team, a radio station, a retailer, or any other kind of business, if you're number one everyone wants to knock you off your pedestal, and where do you go from there except down? I think you could make the argument that a business is actually better off financially if it comes in second in the marketplace. It keeps the team hungry and keeps the ultimate goal in sight.

Negotiating a New Lease on Life

One continual frustration was our lease arrangement at the Richfield Coliseum, which was owned by the Gund family who by this time also owned the Cavaliers. Ironically, a few years earlier I had offered the two banks holding the $37 million mortgage $1,000 to take over the mortgage, which would have put me in control of the building. They were operating at a huge loss, and I thought they might be eager to unload the property at any price. The Gunds ended up buying it for under $500,000, or so I heard.

By 1981, we were the building's major tenant, and when we had a decent crowd at least, we were the ones driving the concessions and filling up the suites. We estimated we were responsible for more than $2 million in yearly revenue to the Coliseum, none of which we shared.

In the early 1980s, with the Force still very much in the red, Scott and I approached the manager of the Coliseum and told him we needed some sort of relief if we were going to continue to operate the team and the use the facility. We proposed two possible solutions. Either the Gunds would become a partner in the Force, or we would become a partner in the Coliseum. Although the Coliseum building was unprofitable, by taking partial ownership we would receive a substantial tax benefit to help offset some of our losses.

The Gunds had no interest in becoming a partner in the Force, but they agreed to give us half ownership in the Coliseum. The Coliseum was losing money anyway, so the Gunds weren't really giving up anything. But the tax advantages were important to us. In return, we agreed to a long term lease, as well as an increase in our per-game rent, although we ultimately would be paying half that rent to ourselves because we would own half the building.

Gordon Gund and his attorney told us they couldn't execute the agreement until the first of the year, 1983, when Nick Mileti and his group would no longer have partial ownership of the building. To show their good faith, they agreed that our rent for the upcoming season would be deferred until the deal was finalized.

In early 1982, Scott and I traveled to the Gund offices in Princeton, New Jersey to finalize both our fifty percent ownership of the Coliseum and the new lease. Both Gunds were at the meeting, as well as a number of their top people. We were handed the new lease, and Scott asked, "Where's the contract?"

"What contract?" Gordon asked us.

"The contract you agreed to whereby we become partners in the company that owns the Coliseum," replied Scott.

Gund claimed he had only meant that we could become a part owner in the land surrounding the building, but not the building itself. Well, that was just absurd. Scott would have never agreed to that because the land was worthless to us. We were looking for depreciation for tax purposes, but there were no tax benefits to owning the land because land can't be depreciated.

It was clear to Scott and me what had happened. Scott had first started talking to the Gunds amidst rumors that we might fold the team if its financial performance didn't improve. Gordon Gund certainly didn't want that to happen, and it was in his best interests to help us out. But by the time we got around to signing our new agreement, we had beaten the Sting in the playoffs and a ticket to a Force game was suddenly a hot commodity. With our success, we had ironically lost our leverage. The Gunds knew we had nowhere else to play, and I think that's why they were no longer inclined to sell us half the building.

Whatever their reasoning, Scott and I were stunned at the about-face, and after going back and forth on the issue and getting nowhere, we left the meeting without signing anything. A few weeks later we had another meeting, this one with Gordon Gund in the Gunds' suite at the top of the Coliseum. Scott and I had already decided that if they were not going to honor our agreement for partial ownership of the Coliseum, we would fold the team before signing the new lease, which we had only agreed to in the first place because we would own half the Coliseum.

Scott and I were met at the door by a butler in a tuxedo and ushered into the suite. The table was laid out formally, with the red wine already poured. We had started to eat when Scott reiterated that all bets were off if they refused to honor our signed agreement to become a partner in the Coliseum. We tried to make Gordon understand that we would never have agreed to own only half the land and not the building because the entire reason for the deal was for us to gain the depreciation deductions. Besides, our letter of agreement, which they had already signed, clearly stated that we would become "partners in the Richfield Coliseum."

Gordon Gund asked Scott if that meant he was reneging on the new lease to which we had agreed. I thought Scott was going to lose it; he was really angry. Scott told Gordon he hadn't even known what the word "reneging" meant until he met him.

We left the meeting not certain if we were going to have a place to play the following season. There was no way we could accept the increase in rent without the quid pro quo of being given half ownership in the Coliseum.

But it all worked out in the end. Either because of Scott's outburst, or perhaps because Gordon knew he was in the wrong and felt a little guilty, a few days later we received word that the Gunds would agree to a new lease that was much more favorable to the Force, including a sharp decrease in rent.

League Can't Keep Up

The Force was only the second U.S. professional soccer team ever to show a profit, and the only one to do it two years in a row. This is what ultimately led to our downfall, as the other teams within the MISL failed to keep up with us.

The biggest problem was that the makeup of the league had changed drastically since we had joined. During the early years of the MISL, I belonged to a club with some of the biggest names in sports—Eddie DeBartolo Sr., owner of the San Francisco 49ers and Pittsburgh Penguins, owned the Pittsburgh Spirit; Jerry Buss, owner of the Los Angeles Lakers, owned the Los Angeles Lazers; Joe Robbie, owner of the Miami Dolphins, owned the Minnesota Strikers;

Donald Carter, owner of the Dallas Mavericks, owned the Dallas Sidekicks. Stan Musial and Joe Garagiola were original partners in the St. Louis Steamers.

By 1986, however, none of these other owners remained involved in the MISL, except for Jerry Buss and me. The Kansas City franchise now had thirty owners, while Wichita had 40 and Tacoma had 20. There were no longer any "check writers" among the other owners, no one who had the stature to make things happen.

Even worse, the votes at the ownership meetings began regularly to go against us. One early rebuff was when we were searching for a new commissioner. As chairman of the search committee, I suggested two candidates, but the other owners rejected them both. Instead, they hired someone with a terrific resume, but with no sports experience. He was a former undersecretary of state and newspaper publisher, but he lacked the drive necessary for the difficult task of putting our fledgling sport on par with the other professional leagues. We needed a promoter, a dealmaker, someone who would make it his life's work to see the MISL succeed. Instead we got someone who when I tried to speak with him during the height of the season, I finally located him on vacation in Hawaii. The last thing we needed was a commissioner who vacationed in Hawaii just as the playoffs were about to start. We terminated his contract, but the next commissioner we hired was no better.

Another constant dispute was over the number of games we should be playing. Most of the other owners were always trying to shorten our season, reasoning that since they were losing money, they'd lose less money if they played fewer games. But their reasoning made no sense. The only added expenses of playing an additional game were travel, which was about $4,000 per game, and rent for the home games, which in our case was $8,000. If their average ticket price was $6, they only had to sell 2,000 tickets to break even. But I couldn't make them understand that the more games we played, the more revenue they'd produce and the less money they'd lose.

I tried to prevent these issues from becoming adversarial, but it was difficult. There was a lot of resentment over the Force's profitability. But it certainly wasn't our fault that we were profitable. We wanted them to succeed. We constantly told the other owners, "Guys, we can't play by ourselves. We need you to be successful too."

The beginning of the end occurred over our effort to obtain a New York City franchise in Madison Square Garden. To have a team in Manhattan playing at the most famous arena in the world would have been a tremendous coup for the league. The media exposure, as well as the access to the owners of every professional basketball and hockey team, would have been invaluable to us.

Earl Foreman, Scott, Paul, and I flew to New York to meet with Jack Krumpe, who ran the Garden. We pitched Krumpe hard, and much to our delight, he told us he was interested in an expansion franchise, but with three conditions. First, Krumpe wanted all television rights for the New York area so he could put the games on the Madison Square Garden cable network. Second, he didn't want to enter the league for two years because he had another twenty months left on his commitment to the Ringling Brothers circus. And third, we had to agree not to put another franchise in the New York area for those two years. The MISL had already experienced two aborted attempts in the New York area, one at the Meadowlands in New Jersey, just across the river from Manhattan, and another in the Nassau Coliseum on Long Island.

We were all extremely excited. Krumpe's conditions were totally reasonable, and we could immediately use his commitment to trumpet the league among other potential owners, advertisers, and the television networks.

As the chairman of the expansion committee, I presented the good news to the other owners. At the same meeting, however, there was a proposal made to put new ownership into the Nassau Coliseum in Long Island for the upcoming 1986-87 season. That would violate one of Krumpe's conditions, I told them, and I argued strenuously that we should not turn our backs on Madison Square Garden.

To make matters worse, the proposed ownership structure of the Nassau franchise was a strange one, to say the least. Stan Henry, the owner of the Pennysaver, along with a former player, Shep Messing, wanted to sell season tickets that would include stock in the new team. Someone could buy, for example, a season ticket that cost $400, but they would pay $1,000 and receive season tickets for two years while becoming a shareholder. I didn't see any possible way such a scheme could work, but the other owners disagreed. I felt no satisfaction when the Nassau team didn't make it through its first season, folding at the all-star break.

The final straw occurred after Scott was asked by the other owners to negotiate with the MISL Players Association a reduction in the league's $1.275 million salary cap. After some intensive negotiations, Scott shook hands with the head of the union on a per team salary cap based on revenues that for the upcoming season would give each team savings of more than $250,000. At the time, no professional sports league had a salary cap based on gross revenues, but we thought this was an innovative way for struggling teams to save money and, at the same time, protect players should the league's fortunes improve. The other owners, however, rejected the deal out of hand.

The Fat Lady Sings

On July 22, 1988 I announced that the Force was ceasing operations. It was a difficult decision, but in the end I felt I had little choice. On one hand, Scott, Iris, and I had had some wonderful times over those nine years, watching the Force at the Coliseum, traveling with the team, and experiencing the thrill of victory. There's really nothing in business to compare with the high of victory in professional sports, which in our case was victory on the field and as a business. On the other hand, I didn't want to spend another year in a league that was crumbling around me.

We were certainly proud of our accomplishment in turning one of the worst professional sports franchises into one of the best, but we had taken it as far as it could go. There was actually a sense of relief after we folded the team. I know Iris was certainly relieved. We had wonderful fun, but it took an extraordinary amount of time and focus to make it work. And losing was always hard on us. Iris and I couldn't even talk to each other after a loss. Sometimes the players would be laughing or just taking it easy, but Iris and I would be devastated.

My only regret is that If the league had retained its original owners and taken some of our marketing and business suggestions, I think that today indoor soccer would be a major professional sport on equal footing with the National Hockey League. Instead, the 1989-90 season was the league's last.

For me, however, there were some lasting benefits. Owning a sports team puts you in a very elite group of visible individuals. It gave me recognition in the community, which in a subtle but powerful way seemed to make it easier to borrow money, make a deal, and get people to listen to my proposals. Suddenly I was seen as a player, and most everyone would take my call.

A Proposal for a New Arena

That doesn't mean I had clear sailing, particularly in Cleveland. In 1986 Developers Diversified proposed building a $90 million,

20,000-seat arena on the old Central Market site downtown. Owning the Force had taught me that the only way for a franchise to be truly profitable was to own the arena or stadium where my team played. I tried to get the City of Cleveland behind the proposal. The Richfield Coliseum was a perfectly adequate site for the Force and the Cavaliers, but it didn't benefit Cleveland in any way because it was located in the suburbs, twenty miles from downtown. Scott, John, and I spent months and more than $150,000 putting our proposal together, tying up the land, and reviewing more than a dozen arenas around the country. We hired Gino Rossetti, the Detroit architect who had built the Palace in Auburn, Michigan where the Detroit Pistons basketball team plays. He later designed the new soccer stadium in Los Angeles. We even created an architectural model to show how the arena and a baseball stadium could fit on the site, and made a detailed presentation to Cleveland Tomorrow, the leadership group made up of fifty of the area's top CEOs.

I could never get the City or any of the movers and shakers downtown to focus on the plan seriously. The next thing I knew the City had created the Gateway Corporation to build a project similar to what I had been proposing, on the identical parcel of land. We didn't fight them because we were still hoping to be involved in developing the 20,000-seat arena Rossetti had already designed to be built next to the baseball stadium. I told the Gateway people that I could build the arena without any public funds, but they weren't interested in that either. The City ended up giving the Gunds a sweetheart of a deal, which was so unnecessary. At the time, the Force was outdrawing the Cavaliers, and I was prepared to move the Force and a minor league hockey franchise into the new arena. But they wouldn't listen to me on that score either.

Losing on the Convocation Center

I wasn't any more successful in my efforts to persuade Cuyahoga County to build a 20,000-seat arena. At the time, I was on the board of Cuyahoga Community College. Governor Rhodes had come up with a strategy for funding worthwhile cultural facilities, but the funds had to be allocated through an educational institution. Cuyahoga Community College, for example, gave $4.5 million that had been allocated to us by the state to the downtown Playhouse Square Theatre. In return, the college had the use of the theatre for $1 per year. The arrangement worked very well for both the college and Playhouse Square.

I suggested that Cleveland State University (CSU) use the same strategy with its $40 million state grant, but CSU insisted it wanted to use the money to build a convocation center for its exclusive use. This made no sense to me, and I lobbied hard against the proposal, meeting with the president of CSU and its board of directors, as well as Mayor Voinovich. I argued that CSU should instead make a deal with the Cuyahoga County Commissioners that would allow the County to use the money to build a much more substantial 20,000-seat arena. In exchange for the $40 million, for a dollar a year CSU could lease the facility for all the dates it needed for its sporting and graduation events, leaving plenty of open dates to attract professional sports team.

The president of the university told me my plan wasn't feasible because the school needed the building for intramurals. But that was ridiculous, and I told him so. CSU could have built a building for $3-4 million to use for intramurals and graduation ceremonies. To spend all that money on a center that would be used for events that drew no more than 2,500 people just didn't make sense. Our plan would have given CSU the building it needed and also created an arena that would have brought business and jobs downtown.

I tried to get the Mayor, the Governor, Cleveland Tomorrow—anyone I could—to see the logic of what I was proposing. I had no axe to grind. I was just trying to get the powers-to-be to act in the public's best interests. But no one would listen. It didn't help matters that the Gunds used all their political influence to get the legislature to put a caveat on the money so that the CSU arena couldn't have more than 13,000 seats. They didn't want any competition for the Richfield Coliseum or for the new downtown arena Gateway was preparing that the Gunds ended up controlling. Cleveland ended up with two buildings within walking distance of one another, a convocation center that is a real white elephant, and a downtown arena that benefits the Gunds more than the City. Oh well, I tried.

Pursuing the Cleveland Browns Franchise

My next stab at owning a professional sports team was in early 1998, after bumping into John Hicks at a golf outing in North Carolina. Hicks had been a consensus All American at The Ohio State University in 1973, when he won the Lombardi Trophy as college football's out-standing lineman of the year. He had gone on to have a career in the National Football League that included being named the offensive rookie of the year in 1974, before retiring and getting involved in the real estate business in Ohio.

Through several rounds of golf, Hicks suggested to me that I should be the new Browns owner. He arranged for me to meet with former offensive tackle turned Ohio State Senator Dick Schafrath about the possibility of making a bid for the new Cleveland Browns franchise. The NFL had already announced that it would be granting an expansion team to Cleveland. The city had been promised it ever since Art Modell moved the Browns to Baltimore two years earlier.

Schafrath and I met for breakfast. He told me he could put together a group that included hall of fame running back Jim Brown and ex-Browns offensive tackle, Mike McCormack, who had been the Carolina Panthers' first president when it had entered the league two years earlier. McCormack agreed to become our first general manager.

We were among the first both to make an announcement that we had pulled together a group interested in the new franchise and to make an official bid to the NFL. Subsequent bidders included former Browns quarterback, Bernie Kosar, Indians owner Richard Jacobs, Cablevision chairman Charles Dolan, and New York real estate developer Howard Milstein.

The new owners of the most recent NFL franchises, the Carolina Panthers and the Jacksonville Jaguars, had paid $204 million to enter the league in 1996. Factoring in the new television contract, as well as the historic tendency for the value of NFL franchises to increase at a significantly higher rate than inflation, all the bidders assumed that the cost of the Cleveland franchise would fall somewhere between $320 and $360 million.

Soon, however, the purchase price seemed to enter the stratosphere. Jerry Jones, the owner of the Dallas Cowboys, called and asked me to meet him in New York so he could persuade me to bid $800 million for the Cleveland franchise. Tampa Bay owner Malcolm Glazer also called and suggested that I come to Florida to discuss with him the idea that I should bid $1 billion if I wanted to be sure to get the team. These numbers were just crazy and a bit insulting. I thought to myself, if that's how little they think of me, why would they want me as a partner?

At these prices, I was no longer really interested. Besides, once Shaker Heights billionaire Al Lerner expressed interest, it was obvious that he would end up with the franchise. For months Lerner had been denying he was interested, something the number two person at the NFL had confirmed to Paul Garofolo and me when we met with him in New York. I had always made it very clear that if Lerner threw his hat in the ring, I was no longer interested. I certainly had no intention of getting into a bidding war with him. Besides, he was clearly the best candidate. He was local, like I was, and had more money than the rest of us combined. He had had a small interest in the Browns when the team was owned by Art Modell and was tight with both NFL Commissioner Paul Tagliabue and Cleveland Mayor Michael White.

Now everyone realized that the fix was probably in all along. The fact that neither Tagliabue nor White had ever even spoken with me about my interest in the Browns should have made me suspicious.

At this point I was just looking for an exit strategy. The bid had already been expensive, when you consider the lawyers and accountants we had to hire to put our financial package together and all the travel costs for me and my team, which included Jim Brown, Dick Schafrath, and Mick McCormack. They were all with me in Atlanta in August 1998 when I presented our proposal to the owners. I introduced them and spoke of my experience with the Force and the kind of similar dedication we would devote to an NFL franchise. The other owners seemed to love our presentation. After I was finished, New England Patriot owner Bob Kraft came over and gave me a hearty congratulations. The photograph of Jerry Jones with his arm around me with large smiles all around made the sports pages all over the country.

The owners also liked our financial bid, or at least they liked the total number we came up with. Goldman Sachs asked us to make an official bid, and we ended up setting the price others would follow. I offered a whopping $500 million. I knew full well it wouldn't be accepted because it included very little cash and proposed that the NFL become a partner. But it set the price. It's funny; if Al Lerner had just called me and offered me a small ownership stake in the team, I would have been happy to pull out of the bidding. Instead, our proposal prompted Lerner to increase his bid from $450 million to $530 million, which was ultimately accepted. So the NFL ended up with a good price and the best owner.

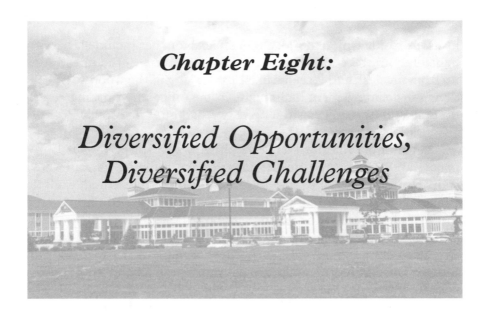

Chapter Eight:

Diversified Opportunities, Diversified Challenges

Almost as soon as I split from Ken Young in 1971, Iris suggested that I move into my own office building. The irony that I was putting up building after building for others, yet still renting space from Hannan Construction, bothered her. By the mid 70s I guess it bothered me too, enough to be on the lookout for a suitable site. Since my days with Sol, I had had my eyes on the corner of Chagrin Boulevard and S.O.M Center Road in Moreland Hills. It was just 3.1 miles from our house at a terrific intersection, where an office building could be constructed without other buildings bearing down on top of it. I spent the better part of two years cultivating a friendship with the lawyer representing the owner, who was reluctant to sell. I made up my mind I was going to get this site and wanted to be certain that when the owner finally did decide to sell it, I'd be the first guy he'd call. That's exactly what happened, and in 1978 I bought it.

I turned the design responsibilities over to Iris, knowing she wouldn't let it become just another boring commercial edifice. Rather, she would fill it with the type of pizzazz unique to Iris. She had some very specific ideas how the building, which she named The Heritage, should look, starting with a two-story contemporary design of hard-fired iron-spot brick that would blend into the primarily residential neighborhood. She instructed our architect, William Dorsky, to make an immediate statement with a winding stairway just off the entrance. No detail escaped her, including working with Dorsky to put in reverse reflective glass, highlighted by a modernistic look that hints of an old fashioned silo. Other special touches include large sky-lights in both the conference room and my office. Sometimes I look up from my desk and it seems like I'm working in the woods. Iris kept saying that since I spent half my life in the office, my working condi-tions should be as nice as the home we had built in Pepper Pike ten years earlier.

Much of the interior of The Heritage was inspired by our Euro-pean travel. Iris picked up the idea for the building's cantilevered stairway in Switzerland and the sprayed-plaster textured walls in France. She imported all the carpeting from England. She covered the walls in woven, suede and herringbone fabric, which nicely com-plimented the natural white oak woodwork. The artwork is mostly American contemporary, but Iris chose a massive, 15-foot tall mu-seum quality freeform sculpture called "The Clench," by the Aus-tralian, Clement Meadmore to dominate the entrance. In the two-story lobby she placed two 24-feet trees–a Netida Ficus and an Areca Palm, both imported from Florida.

Iris had always hoped Scott would one day work with me, so she insisted we build and furnish an office for him. While it remained empty for quite a few years, I think it was a silent reminder to the three of us that there would always be room for him at Developers Diversified.

Beginning when he was 12, Scott worked for me during the sum-mer, first at manual jobs at construction sites, then as he got older running back and forth from the law firm in Twinsburg to the County Clerk's office to file documents. By the time he was enrolled at the Wharton Business School at the University of Pennsylvania, he had made it very clear that he had no interest in coming to work for me. "I'd like to work *with* you Dad, but not *for* you," he'd tell me.

Although I shared Iris's thought that it would be great to have Scott by my side and perhaps even take over the business one day, I admit I had mixed feelings about the idea. I love Scott like only a fa-ther can love a son, and he's a brilliant businessman in his own right. But at the time I think I wondered whether he had the hunger nec-essary to be an entrepreneur. In my case, that hunger had always been driven by a strong desire to cross Taylor Road and prove I was as good as any of my schoolmates. But I learned that there are many types of fuel that drive people to succeed. Scott's didn't have to be the same as mine; it just needed to be inside him.

Like many children of entrepreneurs, Scott wanted to make it on his own. He felt strongly that before we worked together he should ob-tain the kind of education and experience that would bring something new to the table and complement my strengths. He did that, first by graduating cum laude from the University of Pennsylvania and then cum laude from the University of Michigan law school. Since 1977 he had been working as an attorney at one of Cleveland's top law firms, Thompson, Hine & Flory. In fact, Scott worked under Jim Schoff, who coincidentally had six years earlier helped me draft the dissolution agreement with Ken Zeisler. As a result, Scott became much better versed in the legal and technical nuances of securities, partnerships, and syndications than I ever was or ever wanted to be for that matter.

Diversified Equities is Born

Together Scott and Jim built up a practice at the law firm that focused on venture capital investments and other kinds of partnership agreements. They specialized in syndicating businesses, which meant selling them to groups of investors and taking over their management. The businesses were organized in such a way that they generated passive losses and large tax deductions for their investors. They syndicated businesses like real estate, equipment leasing, cable television, and oil and gas ventures that Congress had determined should receive special tax benefits, either in accelerated depreciation write-offs or tax credits.

After several years together, Scott and Schoff thought they could be more successful on their own. I think they also felt that being at a large firm restricted them from pursuing more entrepreneurial opportunities. In 1981 we figured out a way for them to have the best of both worlds—the support of a larger company and the freedom of doing their own thing.

I agreed to join them in a new company we'd call Diversified Equities, and the three of us became equal partners. The deal was that they would provide the sweat, and I would provide the equity, including guaranteeing them each an annual draw of $70,000. The tax law made the kinds of tax shelters they were creating very popular, and it seemed like we couldn't really fail as long as they just continued what they had been doing at Thompson, Hine & Flory.

The new arrangement was a good one for all of us. Jim Schoff liked to call me Diversified Equities' social and financial chairman because not only did I co-sign the bank loans for each new investment, Scott and Jim also used my contacts in the real estate business in their pursuit of various projects. I left them pretty much to themselves, but whenever they needed the extra credibility of some grayer hair, I'd go along for a meeting with a banker or potential investor to offer my two cents on a possible deal they wanted to pursue.

Getting Diversified

Their first order of business was to syndicate 25 of my freestanding Kmarts by placing wraparound mortgages on them. Though it's called creative financing, it's really quite simple. Each Kmart was given a high value, after which a new mortgage, called a wraparound, was placed on the property. The first mortgage stayed in place, which I continued to pay using the fixed monthly amount I received from the tenants. The difference between the payment on the first mortgage and the payment on the new wraparound mortgage was mine to keep. The syndication was set up in such a way, with such a large mortgage, that it produced heavy paper losses, which allowed huge tax deductions for the investors that far exceeded the value of their initial investment.

Scott and Jim also began to be more creative about the kinds of businesses they syndicated. While still concentrating on ventures that lent themselves to large depreciations and tax losses, they ended up managing everything from a cable company, to a fleet of river barges, to our five Force Fitness Institutes. Most of these deals were successful and we generated millions of dollars in profits, certainly enough to justify my ongoing investment. Perhaps most important, the office we had built for Scott in the Heritage building was finally occupied!

All this abruptly changed, however, in 1986 when Congress passed the most significant overhaul of the Internal Revenue Service code since World War II. Among its many reforms, it eliminated precisely the kind of tax shelters in which Diversified Equities had been specializing. Suddenly Scott and Jim started to stress the first word of the company's name, Diversified, more than the second, as they made all sorts of different investments, everything from buying a steel pipe mill packed in crates, to a radio station, to representing athletes, to a computer company. They even organized a National Bowling Challenge event.

The Renaissance on Playhouse Square

While this kind of helter-skelter diversification would sometimes produce less than stellar financial results, some of our more straightforward real estate investments were among the most meaningful of my career. In 1988, Scott and I were approached by an office building developer, Ross Farro, who was having trouble getting financing for a deal he had put together to build a 15-story office building on Playhouse Square. The Playhouse Square Center, on the eastern edge of downtown Cleveland, is the country's largest performing arts complex outside of New York City. It includes five historic theaters that date back to 1922, which draw more than a million people a year. Farro had already designed the office tower and had received most of the permits and tax incentives from the City that the project needed. But the banks were balking at the financing, and suggested he find another partner. They recommended us.

Once a deal was struck, it was our job to take over the completion of the architectural drawings, negotiate a construction contract, finalize the financing, and construct the building. We ultimately named it "The Renaissance," and Iris became involved. This was our only building in downtown Cleveland, and we wanted to make a statement about the kind of developers we were. Rather than just design another cookie-cutter stone building that would disappear among equally non descript downtown buildings, we worked with architect Richard L. Bowen to change the design to include an impressive lobby and an elegant auditorium. Most importantly, we wanted the building's façade to strike an imposing contrast to the other newer buildings in downtown Cleveland. Iris always had to inspect personally the material she was purchasing, so we ventured out to a quarry in Quebec City to select every piece of granite ourselves. It must have been 30 degrees below zero that day, but it was worth it.

We had no problems honoring the financial package Farro had put together with the City of Cleveland, but not everything went so smoothly. When Scott initially introduced me to the project it was with the understanding that Farro had an insurance company committed to providing $6 million of the financing. That meant I would only have to sign a mortgage commitment and not come up with any cash. But after intensive negotiations, we decided to reject the insurance company's onerous terms, which meant an equity investment of $6 million was required, and that became my responsibility.

We also had some early trouble keeping the building occupied. When it opened in 1988, Laventhol & Horwath, one of the larger accounting firms in Cleveland, had rented three floors. The company had signed a ten-year lease and had just completed some extensive construction work, including an elaborate spiral staircase that connected each of their floors, all at our cost. A few days after the building opened, Iris and I happened to be attending a play at one the theatres on the square across the street, and we noticed moving vans parked outside. We assumed it was people moving into the Renaissance, but it seemed the furniture was going *into* the vans, not *out*. The next day we learned the truth. Laventhol & Horwath had vacated the Renaissance in the dead of night. Soon thereafter it became public knowledge that it had paid out $57 million to settle various lawsuits accusing it of shoddy auditing, and a few months after that, it filed for bankruptcy.

In the long term, however, the experience of building and owning the Renaissance proved to be very positive. A few years later I was repaid my $6 million investment after we refinanced the mortgage. The building has always maintained a high occupancy rate and thrown off enough cash flow to cover maintenance and debt service costs. Much of its success can be attributed to Ross Farro, who retained a 20 percent interest in the building and has been an excellent partner. He works hard to find tenants and to keep maintenance up to a high standard.

But most importantly, the Renaissance has given us a higher profile than most of our other projects. Particularly when we travel outside of Cleveland, it is our signature developments like the Renaissance and the Glenmoor Country Club that are most impressive on our resume.

The Hotel on Playhouse Square That Never Was

The Renaissance was an important addition to its immediate neighborhood, and I felt good about the contribution we had made to downtown Cleveland. Soon after it opened, the Playhouse Square Association approached us about getting involved in building a hotel on land it owned on the square, next to the Renaissance. As with the Renaissance, we were brought in after another investor had financial difficulties. In this case, it was Columbus developer Richard Bernstein. He had crafted a proposal to build a 192-room hotel on the site but had forfeited his option on the property for non-performance.

Downtown Cleveland has for decades presented an extremely difficult business environment. We knew we'd need plenty of help from the City in order to make this project financially viable. I was willing to take a risk, but not a guaranteed loss. We estimated that under stable business conditions, a luxury hotel would average a 62% occupancy rate. (Even the outside consultant hired by the City estimated only a 66% occupancy rate.) The City agreed that we needed a creative financing package to make the numbers work, including a real estate tax increment financing (TIF). The City ultimately endorsed a financial package that made sense for both sides. It included a real estate tax abatement, a $5.5 million low interest loan, and a $4 million short term loan. A $5.5 million federal grant had also been awarded before we got involved. Only final approval of the TIF stood in our way of immediately beginning construction.

We were confident enough that the entire financial package had the support of the relevant government agencies to proceed with a redesign of the original architectural plans. After the success of the Renaissance, we were only interested in building a truly first class hotel. Iris worked with Richard Bowen again to design top floor suites aimed at the stars who came to perform in Cleveland in connection with the Rock and Roll Hall of Fame and the theatres across the street. She spent many hours approving the building's interior detail, everything from the quality of the mattresses and the bed sheets to the design of the drapes and the color and quality of the towels.

We were days away from beginning construction when the Cleveland City Council met to approve the $4.5 million in tax increment financing bonds. We had everything in place, and we were prepared to break ground immediately after final approval of the TIF.

The TIF represented the last hurdle in a complicated public and private financing arrangement. We were all confident we had the necessary votes, and it was one of the rare occasions that I attended a Cleveland City Council meeting myself. In fact, the TIF should have been the easiest package to get approved, since the bond would be paid out of future real estate taxes from the hotel.

At this eleventh hour, however, at the advice of the bond counsel, the City Council added an unusual condition for granting the TIF. They insisted that I personally guarantee the bonds. They had pulled a fast one me. My personal guarantee would turn the $4.5 million grant into a loan, and that option had never been on the table.

To me, it was typical politics. Michael White was the Mayor at the time, but in my experience, no matter who the mayor is at the moment, it's difficult to get things accomplished in the City of Cleveland unless you are a member of a very small group of insiders. In all of my work with politicians, I never get the feeling that they have the public interest foremost in mind. It's all about politics—getting reelected and consolidating their power. The best interests of the public always seem to be their third or fourth priority, rather than their first.

At any rate, the failure on the part of the City to approve the financial incentives we needed to build the hotel was so unnecessary, especially given the fact that they had supported the tough proposals and ultimately botched the easy one. The next day, Mayor White blasted me in the *Cleveland Plain Dealer* for walking away from the project, even though he had, in essence, been the one handing me the proverbial walking stick. The project had been risky even with the TIF, and I saw no reason to change a deal to which everyone had agreed. We had already invested about $200,000 in legal and architectural fees, to say nothing of our own time and effort. But your first loss is sometimes your best loss. Better to get out now than be on the hook for a multimillion-dollar hotel that would be financially insolvent from its inception and that didn't have the support of the city government. A half dozen years later a hotel did go up on the site, a more pedestrian building that became part of the Wyndham chain.

For years I think the Playhouse Square Foundation blamed me for the impasse, and at one point even vetoed my nomination to join the board of the Playhouse Square Association. But eventually they saw I wasn't such a bad guy after all. The Renaissance proved to be an important financial contribution to the square, and I supported the association's efforts to make it a Community Improvement District, which meant the tenants in the area could be taxed to pay for maintenance, landscaping, advertising, and security costs. We didn't need the security so much ourselves, since our office building was closed at night, but I think they saw that I wanted to be a good corporate citizen. In fact, they made me president of the Improvement District. In 2002 the Playhouse Square Association presented me and Ross Farro with its annual Distinguished Service Award in recognition of the contribution made by the Renaissance, which had been the first new construction in the theater district in more than 60 years.

The Rise and Fall of the Flats

Another major investment orchestrated by Scott and Jim was in an area of downtown Cleveland called the Flats—so named because it was the "flat" land located on either side of the Cuyahoga River, near where it flows into Lake Erie. Diversified Equities started to acquire one property after another along the waterfront. We renovated an old warehouse, subdividing it into Headliners nightclub and Max and Erma's restaurant. Joe's Crab Shack and an Irish pub called Fado's leased land from us and built their own buildings. We tore down a large building at the corner of River Road and Main Street to create a parking lot for more than 500 cars. A couple of years later we bought the old Custom House and occupied that too with restaurants and shops. We also built a boardwalk along the river at the back of restaurant row. All in all, by the late 1980s the east side of the Flats boasted more than a dozen flourishing restaurants and bars and several shops for household goods.

For years the area was packed almost every night. In fact, the parking lot we developed became a cash machine, as there was hardly anywhere else to park. With some relatively upscale tenants, we attracted working professionals, young families, college students, and empty-nesters. The Flats became the place to be.

As with most projects, we did hit some snags. There was a run-down bar called Kindler's on one side of the parking lot that had been there for years. I bought it for $400,000 and made major renovations, including building a new deck for outdoor dining, turning the upstairs into a party room, and putting in new tables, chairs, and fixtures downstairs. But I never found the right person to run it. I tried everything, including hiring prominent chefs, but nothing seemed to work. I always had the feeling the people working there were making more money than I was, thanks in part to an old bartender trick. When the owner's away, bartenders sometimes get friendly with the clientele and end up only charging patrons for the first drink. The second one is 'on the house.' More times than not, however, people leave some money for the drink, which the bartender then pockets. There is no easy way to stop this without spending more money on prevention than you're losing in revenue. I eventually closed the restaurant, but not until several other tenants leased the space and tried unsuccessfully to operate it. It now sits there unoccupied.

Unfortunately, our strategy of attracting families and business people flew in the face of what others were doing in the Flats. The area eventually began filling up with a different demographic group looking for loud music, cheap beer, and ways to cause trouble. They hung out at places like "The Basement," which really should have been called The Unfinished Basement. It was a dump, but they loved it. The place was a zoo, even on weekdays.

While the growing popularity of these dives kept our parking lot filled, it didn't do much for our tenants, who were growing increasingly disillusioned with the neighborhood. In addition to a changing customer base, some of our tenants were experiencing cash flow problems during the winter months. The Cleveland waterfront is a nice place to be from April to October, but November to March can be less than ideal. Some tenants were willing to try to stick it out as long as they could, but as traffic decreased during prime weather months, they weren't able to make enough to see them through the off-season. It also didn't help when an inebriated Clevelander fell over a side railing and drowned. Even though it occurred on the west side of the Flats, across the river from our properties, it stigmatized the entire area.

I've learned that restaurants need a 'hook' to attract customers. Whether its special events or special menu items, restaurants need to create a reason for customers to seek them out. At the Leopard, for example, our restaurant at The Bertram Inn and Conference Center, we focus on gourmet food and tableside presentation that is hard to find any place else. That's our hook, and it keeps our customers coming back.

By the mid '90s, the kind of patrons we were looking for had defected to the trendy restaurants being opened in the nearby Warehouse District. Gradually, most of our tenants closed their doors, and today we are stuck with property that cost us about $10 million but which today is generating almost no income. At its heyday, our parking lot had an annual cash flow of about $600,000. Today it has a negative cash flow.

This is just another example of the dangers of getting into a business where the overriding factors of success are beyond your control. I like projects that will be successful if I work harder than anyone else because I know that no one will outwork me. I can control how hard my staff and I work, but not what happens on land I don't own. The situation is analogous to the indoor soccer experience, where we were as successful as any franchise in any sport. Yet no matter what we did, we couldn't control the performance of the rest of the league, which ultimately dragged us down with it.

Barrington Country Club

Another successful Diversified Equities project was the Barrington Country Club. In 1988 Scott, Jim, and I took an option on 200 acres fronting Route 82 in Aurora, Ohio, about 25 miles Southeast of downtown Cleveland. I had had my eyes on the property for years, passing it on the way to visit friends, but every time I inquired about it, I was told that it was owned by farmers who had no interest in selling. Something had obviously changed, and I gave Scott and Jim my full support to option it when it became available. Almost immediately I started to discuss acquiring an adjacent 400 acres owned by the Warner & Swasey Corporation. We must have had a dozen meetings with company management before finally agreeing on a very reasonable per acre price.

By merging the two parcels in Aurora, which totaled more than 600 acres, visions of golf balls began dancing in my head. A first-class golf course would be a great way to generate sales of the luxury homes we wanted to build. I was already thinking about building a country club just outside of Canton, so I guess I had golf courses on my brain at that point.

Barrington was originally a joint venture between Diversified Equities and me. Scott and Jim did a good job of building a first class gatehouse and model home, from which we began selling lots for luxury homes. Our next step was to build the clubhouse, which we kept to a reasonable size in order to operate it economically. We did include a 40-seat restaurant that could accommodate up to 200 people for weddings or other events. Although we wanted the clubhouse to be economical, Iris made it elegant with her special design touches.

Once the club was open, Scott and Jim needed capital for a number of other activities they were pursuing. I was happy to buy out their interests in Barrington because I've always been most comfortable running a business enterprise by myself, without any committees or other investors to answer to.

As happens to so many entrepreneurs who dive into a project or take over a business, Barrington became almost a full time job. I'm not complaining; I enjoyed managing it and helping to turn it into one of the premiere golf courses in Cleveland. I loved the camaraderie I felt when I entered the clubhouse, talking to both employees and members, and when I played golf on a course I had so intimately been involved in designing.

During the nine years I owned Barrington I visited it at least three or four times a week, and Iris and I had dinner there at least twice a week. Together we'd review the service and quality of the food. I'd also meet with the general manager, the accountant, the food and beverage manager, the chef, and the golf pro at least once a week. When I played golf there, I'd constantly make notes about the condition of the course and any maintenance that was needed.

Selling Barrington

Unfortunately, my experience in recent years has not been nearly as pleasant as the first nine years I owned Barrington. As anyone who has ever operated a country club knows, they are notoriously difficult to run at a profit, or even at breakeven. More typically they are operated for the benefit of their members and as a loss leader in order to generate sales of homes surrounding the golf course. When I owned Barrington, we spent almost $1 million a year taking care of the golf course, which was probably the largest budget of any course in the greater Cleveland area. But my goal was to make it the premier golf course in northeast Ohio, and to achieve that we had to be willing to pay for the privilege.

Certain members of Barrington, however, were never satisfied. In order to survive we had to do what every club does—schedule corporate golf functions on Mondays and intersperse weddings and other non-member activities during the rest of the week. We closed the club most Mondays to make room for these kinds of events, as did most other clubs in the area. But the membership board resented this and our other attempts to generate revenue. It was only after I sold the club to them that they began to understand how difficult it is to keep a first-class club operating in the black.

The fact that Barrington was an equity club put me in an odd position. In an equity club, members buy equity in the form of a membership fee, in our case $50,000. The membership is a commodity and can be given back to the club at any time for resale at the going price, which is defined as the greater of either the price you paid for it or 80 percent of the sale price. So if, for example, you paid $50,000 for your membership and the club sells it for $50,000, you get your $50,000 back. If it's sold for $80,000, you get $64,000, with the remaining $16,000 going to the club. The only kicker is that once you decide to sell, you are put on a resigned list, and you have to wait until the club sells your membership before getting your money. If the club has sold all its memberships, yours can be sold to the first buyer that comes along. But if it still has memberships in its inventory, as Barrington still does, only every fifth membership sold comes from the resigned list. That's still better than if you belonged to a typical country club in which you have no equity. In that case, if you stop paying dues for any reason you simply lose your membership.

The legal structure of our equity club also stipulated that the membership fee be treated as an option payment. At the end of ten years, members had to exercise that option or lose their memberships. In the case of Barrington, the option agreement required the members to purchase the club from me during 2003, ten years after its completion, at eight times the cash flow earned during the preceding 12 months.

As my ownership tenure was drawing to a close, the members and I found ourselves in a strange position. Superficially at least, it would seem to be to the advantage of the members if the club was unprofitable and had very little cash flow in 2002. This would, in turn, reduce the price they would have to pay for the club the following year. On the other hand, it was to my advantage to operate the club profitably, both on an ongoing basis and in order to get a fair purchase price. But what the membership board never seemed to understand was that both sides had a strong interest in having Barrington operate as profitably as possible. It would certainly not be in their best interest to inherit a club that was bleeding money. In fact, if this were the case, they would need to generate even more cash flow once they obtained ownership because they would have to mortgage the property in order to purchase it.

At any rate, I was willing to sell the club a year early, but I balked when the membership board asked me simply to *give* it to them. I didn't see any particular reason we shouldn't just abide by the agreement. Barrington was a success largely because of my efforts. I had aggressively sold country club memberships and promoted the gated community in much the same way I had sold soccer tickets—with hard work and persistence. Cash flow at the time was about $500,000, which meant I was owed $4 million. But the membership board didn't quit. At one point it even hired an attorney to intimidate me, but to no avail.

Despite the mounting tension, I was willing to negotiate a reduced purchase price. On the one hand, I thought I deserved the full amount. Yet on the other hand, we had put a lot of hard work into Barrington and my family and friends had spent many happy times there. I felt a connection to it, and I certainly didn't want to see it fail. I met with a group of members and after a few hours of amicable negotiations, we shook hands on a reduced price of $3 million. But a few weeks later, the larger membership committee refused to honor the deal.

At this point I turned the negotiations over to Scott, who had been in charge of Barrington's construction and had worked with the law firm that had drafted the original membership agreement nine years earlier. We had hired a firm in Florida who specialized in setting up equity clubs. I ended up making a number of additional concessions, including another $200,000 reduction in the purchase price. Our original agreement stipulated that I was to be paid for all the unsold $50,000 memberships over a period of nine years, at a minimum of six memberships per year, or $300,000 annually. In return for this further discount, the members also agreed to pay me $10,000 for every social membership they sold until they liquidated the entire debt.

Now that the members own the club, I think they have a better appreciation of how difficult it is to operate a first-class country club within budget. In fact, the membership board had to make a special per member assessment of $3,000 for 2004 and $2,000 for 2005, something we never did during the nine years I owned the club.

One nice part of the agreement is that Scott, John and I retained life memberships at Barrington. John and I also continue to sell lots in the residential development that surrounds the golf course. About two-thirds of them have been sold so far.

Glenmoor: A Labor of Love

While Diversified Equities was building Barrington, I had also become involved with building another country club, which turned out to be a labor of love for both Iris and me. It was one of the most difficult projects we ever undertook, which no doubt helps explain why, to this day, we consider it one of our proudest achievements.

It started with a phone call in the winter of 1989 from a broker asking me to take a look at a 415-acre site in Jackson Township near Canton. As I drove toward the property, I realized why the terrain looked so familiar to me. I remembered the Sundays as a boy when my family would drive to Canton to visit my uncle, Sam Berkman. I never forgot those trips, and I wished my Uncle Sam could see me now as I contemplated what I could do with this magnificent property in his hometown. Once grazed by cattle and planted with corn, the rolling hills were lush and beautiful.

But what really drew my interest was a truly spectacular 169,000-square-foot, five-story gothic structure built in 1931 as the Brunnerdale Seminary. It reminded me of a wonderful restaurant in the heart of Old San Juan, Puerto Rico, called El Convento. Iris and I enjoyed dining there because it is housed in a 300-year-old convent, which has been completely renovated, with special attention given to the preservation of the original structure. It is also a hotel, with each of its 58 rooms and suites recreating Spain's golden age. Modern amenities have been added to make it one of the finest restaurant/hotels in old San Juan.

For whatever reason, I immediately envisioned the spectacular Brunnerdale Chapel being turned into an equally spectacular restaurant as the centerpiece of a country club clubhouse. But if I were going to build a clubhouse, didn't I also have to build a golf course? I didn't know anything at that time about building one, of course. Barrington had not yet been started. But I did know a thing or two about golf. Iris and I had been members of a series of country clubs during the previous forty-five years, beginning with Lakeshore Country Club. Its golf course was little more than a freshly mowed pasture, but it was affordable and a good place to learn. A group of eight of us played together on Sundays, which was the only day I didn't work. We took turns arriving at 3:30 in the morning to put our clubs in the rack in order to secure a 6:00 a.m. tee time, so that I could be home by 10:30 to spend time with the family. The only other opportunity I had to play was when Sol occasionally included me in a weekday afternoon round of golf with a couple of his friends. I always got a kick out of that millionaire playing on a public course.

Lakeshore was one of Cleveland's first golf courses, built in the late 19th Century. At one time its members included Cleveland's elite, most of whom lived in nearby mansions in Bratenahl, Ohio. It had a pool for the kids and a dining room where the four of us would sometimes splurge on a dinner of hamburgers and hot dogs. As we moved from our first house in South Euclid, to a second in Beachwood, to our current home in Pepper Pike, other equally modest clubs followed, like Riviera, Pebble Brook, and Hawthorne. I particularly liked Hawthorne because by that time I was working for myself and could take the time to play golf on Saturdays and Sundays. I developed a routine whereby I worked Saturday mornings and dashed to the golf course by noon. Hawthorne was the only club where Iris and I socialized. Once we moved to Pepper Pike, we joined Beachmont because it is just two miles from our house. But the people there never seemed as real as they had at Hawthorne Valley, and we never have participated in any of its social functions. The one time I did go to a social event, I invited a guest and everyone thought he was the member. Iris and I were never really country club people anyway.

Jack Nicklaus: The Brand, the Man

As we began to formulate plans to build country clubs in both Aurora and Jackson Township, one of our first tasks was to choose an architect to design both golf courses. We interviewed all the top architects, including Tom Fazio, Arthur Hills & Associates, and companies headed by famous golfers like Fuzzy Zoeller, Raymond Floyd, and Jack Nicklaus. We held a competition, giving each of them a topographical map of Barrington and asking them to come up with a preliminary design.

I first met Jack Nicklaus when we flew down to North Carolina to interview him just after his company had opened a new course there. As was his custom, he was opening the course by playing a round of golf with the owners. I felt an immediate rapport with Jack, and I was certain that no name on our courses could possibly be a better draw when it came to selling the homes that would surround them than Jack Nicklaus, the Golden Bear. His company certainly wasn't the least expensive; I figured it would cost us about $1,500 extra per lot, but we could easily recoup that with the panache of the Nicklaus name. We also got a slight discount by having him design both Glenmoor and Barrington simultaneously.

A visit to some of Nicklaus' other courses in Atlanta and Fort Wayne, Indiana convinced me that his was a quality operation. The one we visited just outside of Chicago, in North Barrington, Illinois, even gave me the idea for the name of our club in Aurora. For Jackson Township, we were looking for something that would conjure up the hills of Scotland, and Iris chose "Glenmoor."

As we got started on both Glenmoor and Barrington, I was immediately impressed with Nicklaus' personal involvement. He visited each site at least a dozen times. Using a topographic map as a guide, he and his designers worked with our people to lay out the boundaries of the course, allowing for the residential streets and lots. At Barrington, which was almost completely wooded, they cut a 50-foot swath through the center of each proposed fairway. Then a group of us, including Scott, Iris, Jack, and I, and members of his team, walked the path as Jack laid out his thoughts about the course. Each time more trees were cleared, Jack would repeat the process from hole to hole as he and his team located and designed bunkers and greens. His people worked closely with our land planner so that we could include as many quality residential lots on the property as possible. During construction someone from his organization moved to the Cleveland area so that he would be on the job every day to monitor both Barrington and Glenmoor. Jack played a round of golf with us to open both courses, Glenmoor in July 1992 and Barrington late the following summer.

I now consider Jack Nicklaus a personal friend. Just recently he and his wife Barbara accepted an invitation from Iris to a birthday party for me on Lady Iris in Palm Beach. They were supposed to just stop by on their way to a wedding, but they stayed for two hours. He asked me if I wanted to play golf with him the following day. Well, you don't say no when Jack Nicklaus asks if you want to play golf. We teamed together against two of his friends and won $10! Jack plays to win no matter what the stakes. We have that in common.

Afterwards he drove me back to his office where I was to be picked up. Jack is such a gentleman. He carried my clubs from the car to his office and then back down again once my ride had arrived. How many people can say Jack Nicklaus has been their caddy, even if it was just from the elevator to the street!

I had actually played golf with Jack a few years earlier when I was asked to donate $12,000 to participate in a fundraiser for the Ohio State University golf program. In return, I'd be able to play a round of golf with him. When we arrived at the course Jack asked Iris if she would drive his mother around in a golf cart. I was told by his staff not to be disappointed, but he was on a tight schedule and would have to leave immediately following the tournament. As we were walking toward the clubhouse he invited Iris and me for a drink, at which time he suggested we go with him and his wife Barbara to dinner at his club, Muirfield in Dublin, Ohio. First he drove us back to his house and ushered us into his bedroom so we could shower and change for dinner. In his closet were a half-dozen green jackets. It must have been midnight by the time we finished dinner, but he still insisted on driving us back to the airport himself so he could show us his airplane.

Glenmoor, Not Less

Glenmoor was a challenge from the start, and the local folks did nothing to boost my confidence. Almost immediately after it was announced we had paid $5.6 million for the 415 acres and seminary building, Canton's political establishment, the other country clubs in the area, and the local media weren't shy about ridiculing our ambitious plans. In the first place, the area already had its share of top-flight golf courses, including Brookside in Canton, Congress Lake in Hartville, and Firestone in nearby Akron (where PGA-sanctioned tournaments are regularly played). In the second place, the local real estate establishment doubted whether the Canton area could support the kind of upscale, gated community we envisioned.

I wasn't worried about what other people had to say. I intended to build something unique to Northern Ohio, something incomparable to any other country club. At its centerpiece would be the seminary building, which included the spectacular chapel.

It didn't take long, however, to realize I had underestimated the task that lay in front of us. I soon found myself wondering whether this might just be the dumbest thing I had ever gotten myself into. The seminary building was cut up into many small sleeping rooms, and to adapt them to our purposes would prove to be a monumental task. We were faced with tearing down most of the walls and some of the supporting beams, then rebuilding them. For the first time in my career I became afraid of a job. We went through three architects before finding one who seemed to know how we could pull it off.

The seminary had been closed for years, and the building was in terrible shape. It had been painted in a horrendous fuchsia and orange. Iris' job of bringing back its grandeur was further complicated by the fact that much of the original interior had been replaced, removed, or neglected over the years. It would have been easier, and cheaper, to start from scratch, but we knew we had something unique that we wanted to retain and build upon.

Eventually we began to make headway. We converted the gymnasium into locker rooms, and a large room in the basement into a storage area for the golf carts. Another, low-ceiling room in the lower level became the pro shop.

But the centerpiece of the building remained the stunning chapel near the main entrance. It is the only room in the building that today retains most of its original architecture, particularly the floor and ceiling with most of the inlaid wood on the striking beams. Iris had a giant fireplace built to hide where we had removed some large religious artifacts. Others she replaced with her own handpicked tapestries. She was able to preserve the building's gothic appeal with such expertise that visitors often don't understand or appreciate how much time, energy, and creativity were involved in the renovation. I'm never sure if Iris is beaming or grimacing when people walk in and tell us how lucky we were that the brothers left us such magnificent decorative pieces on the walls.

The chapel, with its size and grace, retains an awe-inspiring solemnity. It is now a formal dining room that can seat 300 people. There are also two private rooms on either side of the fireplace, called the Chisholm and the Chelsea after Scottish golf courses. Cocktails are served overhead in what used to be a choir loft. The main restaurant is called, of course, The Chapel, which hosts events virtually every weekend, everything from weddings and bar mitzvahs, to fundraising parties and corporate board meetings.

Something Unique to Boost Interest and Sales

Yet even with our spectacular clubhouse and an outstanding golf course, I knew we had to do something else to make Glenmoor stand out from the crowd. There was just too much competition in the immediate area, and Canton/Akron was a small market anyway.

As we were building the clubhouse, I decided that a world-class spa would make us unique among other courses and would be the perfect 'hook' for Glenmoor. We incorporated elements from some of the finest spas in the world. In addition to a year-round Olympic-size swimming pool and racquetball, squash, and tennis courts, the Spa at Glenmoor includes everything from weight rooms and personal trainers to oxygen treatments, four-layer facials, and algae and mud wraps.

We also had the idea to build two condominiums to test the market to determine whether we should convert the five floors entirely into residential units. Scott and Jim Schoff were never much interested in taking on the challenge of Glenmoor, and it was exclusively a W&M project, unrelated to Diversified Equities. I was glad to have John McGill involved in this monumental effort, although almost immediately we both began to have second thoughts about the condos when the first two remained unsold. We then decided that rather than build more condos, we'd try the hotel business. With Iris' help, we promptly converted the two condos into luxurious two-bedroom hotel suites and built another 14 hotel rooms, which Iris designed so that no two were alike. But business remained slow; we didn't have much economy of scale, and we were too small to attract large corporate functions. Our solution was to build a state of the art boardroom and convert some unused areas into meeting rooms. We also turned all the unused space on the upper floors into more hotel rooms, for a total of fifty-seven.

A breakthrough of sorts occurred when a woman from Canton fell in love with the club and decided to build her own condominium on the upper floor of the seminary building. We were further encouraged after a well-known jeweler did the same. Meanwhile, we were having success in selling the lots that surrounded the golf course, and several homes valued in excess of $1 million were under construction. Club memberships were also selling, although slowly, but at least it gave us some revenue. Well before Glenmoor opened, we hired a specialist from Texas to help us market our equity memberships. During her first presentation she told us that her review of the marketplace determined that we should sell the memberships for $12,000 each. I quickly did the math in my head, and realized that at that price, even if we sold out all 375 memberships, we would go broke.

I fired the consultant on the spot, and we began selling memberships for $18,000 each. We sold a dozen or so, and when sales seemed to be tapering off, I used a technique I had often used in the past when sales were slow. We raised the price to $22,500, but we also announced that for one week, memberships could still be bought for $18,000. That generated another flurry of sales, as those sitting on the fence jumped at the chance to get in at the $18,000 price. We subsequently used that same strategy before raising the price to $25,000, and then again to $30,000, where it remains today. We now have a total of 325 golf memberships and approximately 450 social and dining memberships.

Another turning point was marketing the spa and opening it to the public. At the advice of all the experts, it had been built as members-only exclusive, making it off-limits to outsiders, even hotel guests. Although we were having some success selling country club memberships, the spa was still largely empty except for peak times. Once we opened to the public, we started marketing it and the hotel together in neighboring cities such as Detroit, Indianapolis, and Pittsburgh and in *Spa Magazine*. We were constantly thinking of creative ways to promote the club, offering various weight-loss program and weekend packages. We even created a daycare center where parents could send their kids while they used the spa or played golf. With a full-scale hotel, supported by a world-class spa and a Jack Nicklaus golf course, business began to improve.

Just as with the Force, I took it upon myself to do everything I could to attract corporate and group clients. We also never stopped trying to generate additional revenue. There was an old structure on the property that had been used as a power house downstairs and nun's quarters upstairs. We gutted the upstairs and installed thirteen dormitory-style rooms, with a living room and bar on the first floor and a barbecue and cocktail area on the roof. Construction costs were modest, and it immediately began generating business for the restaurant and golf and spa facilities. It's a popular destination for bachelor parties, weddings, and family reunions.

As the hotel business grew, the spa and golf course became busier, and the entire project, much to my relief, began to work. By any measure, Glenmoor can now be considered a success. It is considered the premier hotel and spa in northern Ohio. It's been voted the Best Retreat in Ohio by *Inside Business* magazine and a top-ten American Golf and Spa Resort by the American Airline's first class in-flight magazine. Many of the athletes connected to the National Football League's annual Hall of Fame ceremonies stay there every August. The Commissioner's Dinner is held there each year, as well as at least one of the special dinners hosted by the honorees for their guests. At last year's PGA Tournament at the nearby Firestone Country Club, we had thirty-eight of the top players staying with us, including Tiger Woods, Greg Norman, Davis Love III, Ernie Els, and Vijay Singh, who can regularly be seen hitting from Glenmoor's practice range.

A few years ago I put a $5 million mortgage on the club, mainly so that my management team would have the psychological incentive to generate enough revenue to make the monthly payments. The Glenmoor Spa and Country Club now produces enough cash flow to pay its operating costs, including the mortgage, and for ongoing capital improvements such as our current $300,000 modernization of the spa. About 75 percent of the lots that surround the golf course have been sold.

Why did I decide to build a resort hotel, a four star restaurant, a world class spa and country club, and a par 72 championship golf course designed by Jack Nicklaus, all surrounded by almost 500 lots on which would be built multimillion dollar homes? Perhaps folding the soccer team had left a void. Maybe I needed a new challenge, or maybe I was looking to make another statement of success, to once again show the world what I could do with a little hard work. Perhaps I just couldn't help myself—it's natural for serial entrepreneurs to continue to take on new challenges. Or perhaps I was out to prove that at 62, I wasn't ready to be put out to pasture. For whatever reason, Iris and I had thrown ourselves into the Glenmoor project with as much fervor as we could muster. And we lived to tell about it.

How Much Diversification is Too Much?

While I was spending much of my time with Glenmoor and Barrington, John McGill was taking care of W&M Properties' other projects, mostly a continuation of our shopping center developments, anchored by large retailers like Wal-Mart, Kohl's, and Home Depot. Sometimes W&M and Diversified Equities partnered on projects. For example, Scott was friends with Bruce Carbonari, president of Moen Incorporated, the faucet manufacturer, and learned that he was looking to build a new corporate headquarters in the Cleveland area. About fifteen years earlier I had bought a property in North Olmsted, not far from the Great Northern Shopping Center. I had envisioned building a Kmart there, but had never gotten the site approved. The land had appreciated in value, but I just had never been able to find a buyer. Scott came up with the idea that we could build Moen's headquarters on the property, which allowed me to get fair market value for the land. Scott negotiated a sales agreement with Moen, and made a deal with a contractor to build the building. It was somewhat of a gamble since I guaranteed Moen the building at a set price, but I had confidence in Scott and our ability to come in on budget. Indeed, it worked out very well for all of us.

Meanwhile, Scott and Jim Schoff continued to diversify, but with mixed results. In retrospect I think our biggest problem was that success takes focus, and it's difficult to focus simultaneously on a multitude of very different activities, which at that time included everything from track meets, to steel mills, to country clubs, to barges.

At one point, for example, Diversified Equities invested $4 million for machinery, packed in giant crates, intended to be assembled into a one-million-square-foot steel mill. One million square feet. That's the size of ten Wal-Marts. The CF&I Steel Company had originally intended to use the equipment to erect a seamless tube mill in Colorado, but new management there decided to sell it instead. Scott and Jim Schoff were advised that the book value of the equipment was $90 million, so it seemed like a purchase price of $4 million was a bargain. We all thought we had hit the jackpot. We had visions of coining a quick $20 million profit, at least. But almost immediately we started to get nervous. An offer we thought we had from a Chinese company for $32 million fell through. Then an inventory of the equipment revealed that there were parts missing. We had to invest another $1.5 million to make it whole, so now we were on the hook for $5.5 million.

At one point we tried to find somewhere to assemble the plant, thinking that it would be more valuable as a working steel mill than in boxes packed in storage. Scott, Jim, and I flew to Little Rock, Arkansas, where we spent 45 minutes with Governor Bill Clinton. He talked to us nonstop, mostly about how attractive his state was to investors. At the end of the meeting the three of us just looked at each other and realized that while he had been charming, we had no idea what he had promised us, if anything. Scott said that Clinton was the smoothest talker he had ever encountered and that he could be President someday. The rest of us thought he was being silly.

Now we were all uncertain of what to do with this factory in a box, and nervous that we'd be stuck with a $5.5 million investment. A broker we hired sold a small part of it piecemeal, but that hardly solved our problem. Finally a group of investors from India expressed interest. They spent weeks at the Heritage, setting up shop in our basement. They poured over documents and used our telephones and copy machine nonstop. I can still remember taking them out to dinner. They all dressed alike, always in identical leather jackets. We ultimately sold the equipment to them for almost exactly what we had paid for it, including bank loans and interest charges. Only then did we all breath a sigh of relief. I'm told it is now in operation, producing steel in Bombay.

Diversity is good when managed properly, but diversity for the sake of diversity can be distracting and is rarely good. It seemed like there was almost nothing Diversified Equities wouldn't consider. For example, a vice president at the International Management Group (IMG) talent agency had invested in a few of Diversified Equities' early tax shelters, and Scott and Jim hired him to operate Diversified's sports management company. Its first (and it turned out only) client was Ben Johnson. Signing him seemed like quite a coup because he had just set the world record for 100 meters at the 1987 World Championships. When he won an Olympic Gold medal the following year, we thought we had it made. Then Johnson promptly flunked a drug test, forfeited his gold medal, and never won another meaningful race. That was the end of our sports marketing business.

At least the Ben Johnson fiasco hadn't cost us any real cash. A much bigger disaster was the Hilton Hotel Diversified Equities built adjacent to the Medical College of Ohio in Toledo. On paper it looked like a sweet deal. A contractor with whom I had done business in the past had a $40,000 per year land lease from the state of Ohio. He planned to build a 213-room hotel, with a ballroom and upscale restaurant, and an underground walkway to both the medical college and a 40,000-square-foot meeting center owned by the Dana Corporation.

Jim Schoff handled the negotiations with the contractor, who told us that the hospital had promised to refer patients and their families to the hotel. He also said that the Dana Corporation would guarantee us several thousand rooms annually. We also expected to attract health care professionals taking instruction at the nearby education center that the hospital had opened in 1983. It seemed like we couldn't miss.

We had serious problems from the start, mainly because the contractor with whom Jim had been negotiating turned out to be unscrupulous. The completion bond he had provided turned out to be from an off-shore company with no assets, and he perpetrated a massive fraud by forging many of the subcontractors' lien waivers. When a contractor wants to get paid a draw in order to pay his subcontractors, he has to deliver lien waivers from each subcontractor to whom he owes money. This waives all their lien rights as soon as they receive payment. But our partner was forging these lien waivers, taking the money from us, and pocketing it instead of paying his subcontractors. At the same time, he began writing bad checks to the workers for their weekly salaries. This went on for a few months until all hell broke loose. The police started looking for him, and he fled the county. We were left with a half-completed hotel and plenty of disgruntled, unpaid contractors.

Up until this point, John McGill and I were not heavily involved in the hotel's construction except for accompanying Iris as she designed the banquet room and restaurant, which I insisted on calling The Iris. She also chose all the furnishings, artwork, and draperies. But by this time we were at the mercy of the subcontractors, who had already been mistreated by the original builder. John McGill now stepped in and took over construction.

It was a mess. Unfortunately, the situation didn't improve once the hotel finally opened in July 1988. The hospital reneged on promises to promote the hotel, and the operators of the conference center decided to use another, slightly less expensive hotel down the street. We hired Boykin Management to run the hotel and went through three hotel managers in three years in an effort to make it profitable. Ultimately we did manage to get the business from the Dana Corporation, and that helped a little, but no amount of hard work could offset the losses we suffered at the outset because of the criminal activities of our partner/contractor. Scott ultimately negotiated a workout with the lender, and we sold the hotel to the last group we had hired to manage it. We lost about $7.5 million in the deal, which made it the worst single investment I ever made.

Scott and I learned many valuable lessons while working together on the Flats, the Force, the Renaissance Building, and other Diversified Equities projects. They are summarized below.

Traversing the Road to Entrepreneurship

- Even if you think something "can't lose," there are always conditions under which it can, in fact, fail.
- Don't assume that the person sitting across the table from you during negotiations values a win-win relationship.
- Working with local governments to close a deal can test anyone's patience. Approach negotiations knowing that their first inclination is not in your best interests–it's often not even in the best interests of the community.
- When working with government officials, you have to be able to recognize all political implications for those involved to understand what they are likely to support and what they are likely to squelch.
- Think twice about investing in a project in which its success or failure is dependent on forces beyond your control.
- Becoming emotionally attached to a business can fuel you with the extra energy and passion that might be required to make it succeed, but you have to know when to cut the emotional ties and make an objective business decision.
- Hiring a real expert can buy you a great product, with a highly-credible brand to market, as was the case with hiring Jack Nicklaus's company.
- Diversity in business ventures can spark creativity, but also stretch you too thinly.

The Money Dries Up

By the end of the decade, the capital requirements of the many W&M and Diversified Equities projects had begun to be a serious drain on my finances. To put things in perspective, I started the 1980s with $30 million in the bank, and ended it with no reserves at all. Nevertheless, we continued to pursue investments aggressively, since the banks were more than willing to provide the capital we required through unsecured lines of credit. In fact, the combined unsecured credit lines of W&M and Diversified Equities grew to more than $30 million.

Then in early 1990, just as construction had begun on Glenmoor, I received a call from my lead banker at Ameritrust. "The financial and real estate environment has changed," he told me. "We can't lend you any more money." Developers Diversified, Diversified Equities, W&M Properties, and Bart Wolstein along with them, were suddenly in trouble.

Chapter Nine

Diversified Disappears: How I Let My Company Slip Away

A s the 1990s began, my financial situation was exacerbated by problems within the banking industry much more serious than my own. The savings and loan (S&L) crisis could be traced back to at least 1979, when Federal Reserve Board chairman Paul Volker began restricting the growth of the money supply, causing interest rates to skyrocket. In one nine-month period, between June 1979 and March 1980, short-term rates jumped 9 points, from about 6 percent to more than15 percent.

The solution for Developers Diversified at that time had been simple. I shrunk the company, reigned in our overhead, and we weathered those high interest rate years before returning to a more aggressive growth strategy.

But the rapid jump in rates had a more long-term effect on many banks. Interest rate ceilings prevented them from paying competitive rates, so each time interest rates rose, consumers transferred vast sums to other investments, most notably a growing array of higher in-terest money market funds. During the first two years of the 1980s, S&Ls reported a combined loss of almost $9 billion and a collective negative net worth.

The U.S. Congress and the Reagan administration responded by deregulating the banking industry, which allowed S&Ls to offer higher yielding, but riskier, investments. Suddenly S&Ls were al-lowed to lend up to 40 percent of their assets in commercial real estate loans and without any geographic restrictions. This new system had the effect of actually encouraging risky loans, since every bank was charged the same rates for deposit insurance, regardless of how conservative or risky their portfolio. Deregulation also allowed graft to run rampant, as evidenced by the high profile indictments of bankers like Charles Keating, chairman of Nebraska's Lincoln Savings and Loan. In 1989 Congress finally came up with a $157 billion taxpayer bailout, but by then the price tag topped $200 billion. To make up the difference, the Resolution Trust Corporation was formed to sell off the assets of failed S&Ls, mostly at bargain basement prices.

By 1990, banks were under much stricter control of federal regulators. They were under tremendous pressure to reduce their exposure, particularly in their commercial real estate portfolio. They were being told to recategorize their unsecured real estate loans as non-performing and were expected to do whatever it took to move them into the performing loan category or remove them from their books altogether.

Doing Business in Tough Financial Times

In this hostile environment, Ameritrust, with whom I had $70 million drawn against a $100 million line of credit, called to tell me that it wouldn't be lending me any additional funds. In particular, I was informed that the bank would be halting any further loans for Glenmoor, despite the fact that it had lent me the money to buy the land in the first place and to start construction. Without additional cash, I would have a major problem meeting my commitments there. With Scott's help, I scrambled to put together collateral to borrow enough to allow me to finish construction.

Almost immediately after delivering all this good news, Ameritrust called again, informing me that the interest rate on our existing loans would be jumping to 12 percent.

Was this the bank's idea of good business? To me it all seemed so ridiculous. You would think Ameritrust's goal would be to restructure my loans in order to get the bank examiners off its back, not to do everything possible to put me in default. Chalk it up to limited vision, but the bank didn't see that if I defaulted, it would have a much bigger mess on its hands.

This was a far cry from the good old days when a blind banker in Twinsburg put his faith in me and all but offered me a blank check. Now, thirty years later, my banks suffered from a different kind of blindness. I never was in any danger of defaulting on my loans, but that didn't matter to the guys with pocket calculators and a glazed look in their eyes. It didn't help that the different banks that held my loans were constantly being merged or acquired. Over the years, I had built valuable banking relationships; I considered them an important business asset. But the bankers with whom I had done business for years had all been replaced.

I tried to stay calm. I was accustomed to being surrounded by frenzy. I had to believe that my passion and drive would help me overcome this latest adversity.

I also knew that at the end of the day I could not be put into bankruptcy. I was admittedly stretched pretty thin, but the more than 100 properties owned by Developers Diversified, W & M Properties, and Diversified Equities were throwing off more than enough cash flow to service our debt. We were not in default on any of our loans, and I didn't anticipate any problems servicing our debt. A much bigger problem was that we couldn't draw additional funds to finish the projects we already had underway, not to mention begin new ones.

My first order of business was to reverse Ameritrust's decision to increase my interest rate. I asked for a meeting with the chairman of the board; he was an interim chairman, due to the bank's constant state of reorganization. (Ameritrust was about to be acquired by Society National, which soon would be acquired by KeyCorp.) As I looked around his beautiful office, I remembered what a banker friend of mine had recently told me about lender's liability. It dictates that a lender has a responsibility not to take unjustified actions that would doom a project that the lender had encouraged in the first place.

"I'm going to enjoy owning this office," I told the Ameritrust chairman. He looked startled. "Haven't you ever heard of lender's liability?" I asked him.

When a bank gives you a $100 million loan commitment, it has an obligation not to slam on the brakes and refuse to loan you any further funds. In this case, Ameritrust had encouraged me to start Glenmoor. Stopping the flow of money at this point would almost be guaranteeing the project's failure.

Workout

Ameritrust never did raise my interest rate to 12 percent, but I had other problems. I was into Ameritrust for about $70 million and Society

National for about \$40 million. When Society National absorbed Ameritrust, I was suddenly the combined bank's second largest debtor, and that made me a prime target for its bank examiners.

Almost immediately Society National, and later its new parent, KeyCorp, put us in 'workout.' Workout, I learned, meant a complete restructuring of my assets. They had us jumping through all sorts of hoops. Their first suggestion was for me to sell Lady Iris, and the next day Glenmoor. There was no way I was going to sell either. No banker was going to tell me how to live my life.

Scott soon was negotiating full time with the bank's workout department. For weeks, which turned into months, the conference room at the bank's law firm was filled with dozens of piles of paper, each stack representing a shopping center or other asset. Each loan had to be cross collateralized so that it could be recategorized on the books as a performing loan. It was an extremely complicated process because we had to rework the documentation on dozens of mortgages and lines of credit. It took me hours just to sign all the documents. Then the bank decided it was dissatisfied with the job the law firm had done and hired a second firm to restart the process. A few weeks later I had to sign all the documents again.

Our Decision to Take Developers Diversified Public

By this time, however, Scott and I had begun to investigate another strategy. We knew that even once our loans were cross collateralized, we wouldn't have the freedom to operate and to grow as we had in the past. Commercial banks had largely stopped loaning money to private commercial real estate developers, and we'd be fortunate if our loans were renewed when they came due. The days of easy credit were over. We needed to find another source of capital.

In 1960 Congress had created Real Estate Investment Trusts (REITs) as a way for the average person to invest in commercial real estate. Just as individuals can invest in public companies by buying shares of stock, now they could do the same with commercial real estate. Congress tried to make these new corporate entities particularly attractive to investors by requiring REITs to return 90 percent of their taxable income to their shareholders in the form of dividends. Yet except for a few groups of healthcare facilities and one office REIT in 1988, REITs were largely ignored until the early 1990s.

Ironically, the same Tax Reform Act of 1986 that had eliminated Diversified Equities' original line of business also laid the groundwork for us to become one of the very first private real estate companies to take advantage of the possibilities of a REIT. The 1986 law changed the real estate investment landscape in two important ways. Firstly, by limiting the deductibility of interest, lengthening depreciation periods, and restricting the use of "passive losses," it virtually eliminated the potential for real estate investment to create tax shelter opportunities. Secondly, it empowered REITs by permitting them not only to own, but also to operate and manage, most types of income-producing commercial properties. Previously, REITs could only own property, severely limiting their appeal to investors.

Even with these changes, REITs were still not immediately popular. Real estate entrepreneurs didn't particularly lend themselves too well to a corporate structure with shareholders and a board of directors, and companies like Developers Diversified and Diversified Equities had no trouble getting financing from local banks. There was no compelling reason to go public. Foreign investment, particularly from Japan, also helped buoy the overall marketplace.

By 1992, however, the combined forces of the banking crisis, the 1986 Tax Reform Act, and the overbuilding during the 1980s had substantially depressed the commercial real estate industry. Although the value of Developers Diversified's portfolio remained relatively stable, in some areas of the country commercial property values dropped by as much as fifty percent. Credit and capital for commercial real estate became largely unavailable.

Against this backdrop, it was clear that the best and most efficient way to access capital was through the public marketplace. In our case, that meant going public and transforming ourselves into a real estate investment trust. Scott began interviewing securities firms, and it quickly became apparent that a leader in the field was Dean Witter. It had participated as an underwriter in virtually every major REIT IPO completed to date, including the two major commercial REITs that preceded ours, the Kimco Realty Corporation in 1991 and Taubman Centers in 1992. Dean Witter did a good job for us.

The decision to go public was relatively easy because it was the best way to obtain the capital we needed to continue to do business. Infusion of financial resources is really the only reason I recommend going public. Don't go public because you want to, do it because you have to. There are a lot of extra pressures today on public corporations, especially in the area of corporate governance and reporting regulations. When you run a public company, analysts and shareholders second-guess every decisions you make. But when you own your own company, you answer only to yourself.

Workout Continues

As our efforts to go public went forward, the workout became increasingly nasty. While we were willing to cooperate in order to reorganize our loans to the bank examiner's satisfaction, we were not about to be forced into selling assets. I kept telling the bankers that we were not in default and that we had the assets to cover our debt, but they seemed to have another agenda. We were dealing with people who seemed intent on putting us out of business. One member of the workout staff actually had "4-close" on his car's license plate. At one point he asked Scott for the keys to the Renaissance office building, on which Ameritrust held a $35 million mortgage. Instead, we politely asked him to leave the office.

Although the "4-close" guy disappeared, his attitude remained. Society National's workout department was particularly concerned with the Glenmoor development, which admittedly was a more risky proposition than the hundred or so properties already generating cash flow. The bank seemed willing to do almost anything to get Glenmoor off its books. One senior officer instructed the workout department to offer me a 25 percent discount if I would retire the loans on Glenmoor as soon as the IPO closed. That seemed like a good deal to me, but I must have agreed too quickly because as a quid pro quo I also had to agree to use the public offering to pay off the mortgages with the lowest interest rate first. But that was fine with me too, although not for Society National, which by this time had been absorbed by KeyCorp. I agreed to forego the 25 percent discount, but only after we negotiated a $3.5 million nine-year interest free loan. Less than two years later the bank asked me to pay it off in full, which I did but at a steep discount.

The nutty thing was that even when it was clear that the IPO was inevitable and only weeks away, the bank continued to breathe down our necks. I guess they just never believed we would pull off the public offering. It was a complicated deal, that's true. Most real estate companies, and Developers Diversified, W&M Properties, and Diversified Equities were no exception, are parent to a number of business entities. Each asset, in turn, has its own different ownership or partnership structure. To clean all that up into a simple corporate form that would appeal to investors was no easy task.

Or maybe it was just that Society National was loathe to admit that it had unnecessarily spent more than $3 million in legal fees to twice document a restructured collateralization that as soon as the IPO closed would immediately be irrelevant, since we'd then have plenty of cash to retire all our non recourse debt. We even went so far as to have the senior people at Dean Witter meet with KeyCorp's management to explain that the IPO was on target. But none of this made any difference to the workout group. Even after the IPO was priced and all the shares were sold, during the week before we actually received the money, the bank was still asking us to come down to sign documents for the alternate restructuring. The stock was already trading on the New York Stock Exchange, and the workout managers continued working overtime. It was just crazy.

Road Show

As the offering date approached, Scott and I, along with Blake Baird from Dean Witter and his assistant, Paul Donahue, went on "road shows" to present the details of the new company—Developers Diversified Realty Corporation, also known as DDR—to the analysts and underwriters who would be selling the public shares to their clients. We went from office to office, using flip charts to provide a detailed description of the assets that would be part of the new public company, the management team that would run it, and our plans for future growth. The goal, of course, was to persuade these people to buy shares in the IPO. During road shows when we and the underwriters actually visited the shopping centers that would be owned by the new DDR.

The final road show included visits to 25 cities in six weeks. It was exhilarating. We would leave the office of an institutional investor and minutes later receive a call in the limousine confirming an order for $20 million in equity. We were giddy. After months of having banks slam doors in our faces, sophisticated investors were literally throwing money at us. It was extremely gratifying.

IPO Solves All My Problems

The IPO worked like a charm, and for a few weeks I was on top of the world. Overnight, the banks were off my back—it was wonderful.

In February 1993 Developers Diversified Realty Corporation, a company I had built from nothing twenty-five years earlier, raised $202 million in the second largest public offering of any REIT ever. The 9.2 million shares of stock were oversubscribed five to one, a much better performance than either Kimco or Taubman, and the stock price almost immediately jumped twenty percent. Eight months later a secondary offering would generate another $111 million.

There was a lot for investors to like about the new DDR, including diversification, a positive industry outlook, and dividends. We owned shopping centers in twenty-five states, with tenants that included virtually every major U.S. retailer. Many investors had decided that a recovery of the commercial real estate markets was just over the horizon, and that it was a good time to invest in commercial real estate. They also liked the high dividends that were made possible because REITs pay no corporate taxes. Our investors would soon be rewarded for their prescience.

Wall Street also liked that I had insisted we not create what was called an UPREIT, a tax saving structure that Taubman Centers had used. The tax consequences of an UPREIT would have been much better for me personally, but I felt strongly that my shares should be fully aligned with the interests of the shareholders.

The success of our IPO marked the birth of the modern REIT. At the time we went public, in February 1993, there were three significant commercial REITs in the United States. Today there are 180, with assets totaling more than $300 billion.

On Top of the World

For me personally, my money problems were over. The public offering paid off $165 million in debt, including $37 million for which I was personally liable. After working hard for forty years, I was ready for some security for Iris and me. And I was definitely ready for my day in the sun.

I was excited about what lay ahead. I envisioned myself sitting on top of the world, running a large public company with powerful assets and the wherewithal to become one of the leading real estate players not only in Ohio but in the entire country. I'd be the most powerful person in a $500 million corporation, soon to top $1 billion. I'd finally be a player in the local community. Civic leaders would ask for my advice and support. Then after a few years, I'd step down and turn the company over to the new generation. Maybe they'd give me a gold watch. My lifelong dream would have come true—Bart Wolstein from the wrong side of Taylor Road would have finally made something of himself.

How I Let My Company Get Away

It took me a couple of months to realize something had gone seriously awry. The first inkling I had was when I heard people talk about stock options, and I asked Scott how many I had. I didn't have any, he told me. I also had no health insurance. While Scott was running DDR as president and CEO, it turned out that I wasn't even an employee. As chairman of the board, I received $100,000 per year, a small fraction of what Scott or even Jim Schoff was earning. I was chairman of the new company, that's true. I also owned almost 20 percent of the outstanding shares and was the largest single shareholder. But I had nothing to do. I had no responsibilities. No one called seeking my advice. No one asked me anything. I had no stock options, no health insurance, virtually no salary. I was a nobody. A rich nobody, but a nobody nevertheless.

What the hell had happened?

I had gone along with the division of the titles as prescribed in the IPO, with Scott taking the role of president and CEO and me as chairman. Frankly, I never gave it much thought. The company we were taking public was my own, the result of forty years of hard labor. I had always been the boss. It never occurred to me I wouldn't remain the boss. What a painful mistake. I should have been more thorough.

Maybe Scott and I should have discussed our respective roles more thoroughly before we proceeded with the IPO. Maybe we could have come up with a better transition plan where I could have become more involved in the company in ways that would have been more stimulating for me. Maybe I should have tried to perform the role as CEO for a few years to see if I liked it.

How can I explain it? I, of all people—the guy who makes sure the coffee is fresh at the Bertram, the towels are thick at Glenmoor, the potholes are repaired at Macedonia—let my company slip out of my control. No detail has ever been too small for me, yet when it came to the biggest deal of my life I was asleep at the wheel.

I have no one to blame but myself. I should have asked more questions. I should have had my own attorney looking out only for my interests. And I certainly should have insisted that the underwriters and my lawyer sit down and explain exactly what they envisioned my role would be in the new company. I guess, in retrospect, I realize that I should have taken more control of the situation when I actually had it. And I learned a painful lesson that regardless of who is sitting on the other side of the table, you can't assume that your interests are their paramount concern.

After a few months, when the euphoria had subsided, I was miserable. Being the chairman of the board of a New York Stock Exchange publicly traded company was certainly prestigious, but I was bored. Scott, as president and CEO, was running the company on a day-to-day basis. My role as chairman was to assure that the business plan was sound and that the management team was effectively implementing that plan. My role was also to be a public ambassador for the company, attending industry conferences and joining Scott in meetings with investors.

While I was the "boss" in the sense that Scott reported to the board of directors and I was chairman of the board, this was not what I had envisioned. I was a "roll up your sleeves" type guy who enjoyed working in the trenches. Sitting on the throne watching others execute the business on a daily basis was not for me. Besides, running a public REIT was entirely different than the entrepreneurial firm I had left behind. Scott was not free to act on his instincts without first contemplating what the reaction of the investment community would be. He was dealing with complex issues like optimizing the capital structure, securities compliance, financial disclosure, accretion analyses, and many other matters I never had to deal with before. It seemed that just knowing how to make money for shareholders was not enough. My talents were wasted in this environment.

But perhaps my dissatisfaction with my role in the public company stemmed from something deeper than just the notion of not being the boss. I realized that all the money and prestige in the world could not satisfy my entrepreneurial desire, my need to build and create new things. Being thrust suddenly into a public company, with shareholders and vice presidents and committees and an encyclopedia full of SEC and banking regulations, was a shock to the system. I've never been very good with committees, or even partnerships. I'm not comfortable making decisions with a show of hands because I'm accustomed to making them myself, taking the heat with the failure and the glory with success. I've never minded being second-guessed by the marketplace, but never very happy when it's by bureaucrats.

The Difficult Years

The next few years were among the most difficult of my career. I only agreed to stay on because Scott and others felt that my abrupt departure would upset Wall Street. I chaired the board meetings, but it was obvious to everyone I wasn't happy, and that was a new experience for me.

I spent most of my time working on those assets that hadn't become part of the public company. These included Glenmoor, Barrington, the Renaissance, my holdings in the Flats, some residential projects, and a variety of undeveloped land scattered throughout dozens of states. Eventually I knew I would have to cut my ties with DDR altogether.

Scott did his best to keep me involved, and I certainly was willing to do anything that was asked of me. After all, I was a major shareholder and wanted to see the company succeed. Scott asked me to go with him to Chicago, for example, to meet with General Growth Properties, a large REIT. I had done a favor for the top people there a number of years earlier. General Growth was in the process of buying the assets of Homart, Sears and Roebuck's real estate arm, and was looking to sell Homart's strip center assets, which Scott wanted to purchase. This was a huge undertaking for DDR at the time, as the purchase price exceeded $500 million. I felt good that I had a hand in this important transaction. Scott also asked me to accompany him on a European road show to attract international investors. We visited three countries in two and a half days, meeting with prospective investors. I also attended an International Council of Shopping Centers conference in Singapore to explore real estate opportunities in Asia.

But these trips weren't nearly enough for me. It didn't help that Jim Schoff kept referring to me as "the old man." Finally, in early 1998 I resigned from the DDR board and opened a new company, Heritage Development. At the suggestion of Dean Witter, I agreed to retain the title of DDR's Chairman Emeritus.

Starting Over

Back on my own, my first few projects were modest. I built a few freestanding Staples office supply stores, one in Akron and another in Arkansas. At the same time, I continued to take care of Glenmoor, Barrington, and the undeveloped land I still owned.

In 2000 I opened the Bertram Inn and Conference Center in Aurora, about fifteen miles from my house.[13] I had acquired the land as a defensive mechanism. It was zoned for industrial use, and I was concerned someone would purchase the property and build within a stone's throw of the expensive homes at Barrington Country Club.

Because it wasn't on a freeway, I knew we'd need some sort of calling card to make the Bertram a success. At Glenmoor I had decided it would be a world-class spa, but that was for a country club. This time I identified a lack of meeting space in the area, so we decided to launch the Bertram as a conference center. Within a year we had opened with 162 rooms, two ballrooms, and a number of meeting rooms. But a year later our research showed that even when our meeting areas were being used to their capacity, we still had empty hotel rooms, and that we didn't have the capacity for some of the larger meetings we were pitching.

As of this writing, Iris and I have just finished a major addition that includes an 82-seat amphitheatre, another ballroom, and a state-of-the-art boardroom. We anticipate that the added space will generate enough overnight guests to pay for the additions within a few years. Rooms are highly profitable, much more so than the low profit margins of the food and beverage part of the hotel business.

We are now in the process of building sixty-one more hotel rooms, including eight midsize meeting rooms with their own lavatories and wet bars in order to free up the larger meeting areas for other events. The Bertram has always been profitable. We think these expansions are a prescription to make it a much larger, more permanent success. One advantage we have is that I've funded the construction myself. Banks don't like to lend money to hotels like the Bertram because they don't fit into a niche they can understand. They prefer motels just off the highway, for example. But where is the fun in that?

Another unique feature of the Bertram is its Leopard Restaurant, which Iris and I made a huge effort to turn into what is now consistently named one of the top dining establishments in northeast Ohio. During the second and third years after it opened it received the Au-

---

[13]After Steve Marton's father died, to honor him, Steve and I did something we had always wanted to do. While his family was sitting shiva, we walked the 15 miles from my house to the Bertram Inn. It was a hot day, but we made it, although at the halfway mark I called the hotel and had two bottles of cold Evian delivered to us.

tomobile Association's Four Diamond award, which has been awarded to only five restaurants in the state. Iris is in charge of everything from the menu to the place settings at both the Leopard and the adjacent Paws bar. The food at the Leopard is truly delicious. Come try it out for yourself and I promise you'll agree. In fact, bring this book and you'll get a 20 percent discount.

Iris is intimately involved in not only the Leopard, but every aspect of the hotel's layout and design. During its original construction, and during the major additions, it is Iris who walks the construction site every day, asking questions and making decisions at every turn. We are always making changes to adapt to the market. Iris decided, for example, to enclose the outdoor eating area, which was receiving very little business, and attach it to the bar to create a more informal restaurant called Paw's, which has been quite successful. Once it was clear that the gift shop wasn't profitable, we turned it into a small meeting room. We did the same with the area that held a bank of public phones and created a boardroom. With the rise of cell phones, people don't use pay telephones much anymore.

First Union

Shortly after we went public, Scott and I became embroiled in a strange controversy that we neither asked for nor deserved, yet we couldn't seem to shake. It all started in late 1994 when Richard Osborne tried to take control, or at least shake up, a Cleveland-based REIT called First Union Real Estate Equity and Mortgage Investments. Osborne was the head of OsAir, his family's industrial and welding gas company. He was also a stockholder in First Union, and had become increasingly frustrated over its continued poor financial performance. But First Union did own a variety of valuable real estate, including office buildings and shopping centers. Osborne figured the company was worth more for its breakup value than its stock valuation, so he started adding to his holdings.

I didn't know any of this at the time. I had barely even heard of First Union. I knew it only vaguely as one of the early, not particularly successful, REITs that had been created before their legal structure had been liberalized.

In early 1995 Richard Merel, a Chicago lawyer working with First Union, ran an anonymous advertisement in the *Wall Street Journal* soliciting investors for an unnamed real estate deal. This kind of blind ad isn't unusual. It's a way to float business ideas without tipping the hand of the principals.

Mark Escaja had been Developers Diversified's in-house accountant, but when we went public, Scott thought we needed someone more experienced to see us through the IPO, so we moved Escaja over to work on my personal projects including Barrington and Glenmoor. Mark saw the ad and wrote to Merel inquiring about the details.

That's when, completely unbeknownst to me, my name first surfaced. Probably to enhance his credibility, Escaja wrote to Merel on the letterhead of one of the companies I owned, Heritage Capital Corporation. Escaja subsequently spoke with Merel by phone several times, apparently implying that he was acting on my behalf. But he was doing no such thing. He had acted completely on his own, without my knowledge or approval. I suppose he thought he'd freelance on the side while working for me.

But I knew nothing of any of these activities by Escaja, Merel, Osborne, or First Union. The first time I heard of any of it was when I was in my driveway, getting into my car one cold Saturday morning. A sheriff's deputy approached me with a huge stack of papers. First Union had filed suit against Osborne, me, Scott, and DDR, claiming we had violated the legal rules under which First Union operated, including the REIT's 9.8 percent limit on share ownership by one person or group.

Somehow First Union chairman and CEO James Mastandrea had gotten the idea that I, in cahoots with Osborne, had accumulated more than ten percent of First Union's outstanding shares. Where they got this notion I'll never know. I didn't own a single share of First Union and had never contemplated owning a single share. I had met Osborne once, when he was seeking investors in his equity fund, curiously named Turkey Vulture. (No wonder Mastandrea was suspicious of him.) Escaja had arranged a brief meeting. Osborne met with Scott and me in my office for fifteen minutes and we declined to invest in his fund. First Union was never mentioned.

No one ever contacted me to ask if I was involved with Osborne. No one asked or bothered to investigate whether I owned a single share of First Union. If they had, I could have avoided more than a year of legal hassles.

After being served in my driveway, I personally called First Union's lawyers at Squire, Sanders & Dempsey, as well as a few members of First Union's board of directors. I tried to explain that there had been some kind of mistake. Scott and I were asked to submit testimony and documentation to prove we had no involvement in the takeover. We were happy to oblige and turned over to them all our records of stock purchases for the previous two years.

Still, Squire, Sanders refused to drop us from the lawsuit. Soon the newspapers were regularly reporting that Scott and I were somehow involved in a nefarious takeover of First Union. It was embarrassing, to say nothing of expensive and time consuming. It seemed like every week we had to read our names in the newspaper linked to some kind of strange conspiracy. The story just snowballed, until I had people in the investment community calling me to complain that First Union's real estate portfolio was a terrible match with DDR's. Barry Greenfield, fund manager at the huge Boston-based Fidelity Real Estate Fund, which owned about $2 million of DDR stock, called to tell me he was so distressed about the news reports that he was considering selling off all his shares. I had to explain to him that we had no interest in First Union, had never had any interest in First Union, and had never owned a share of its stock. It was all a mistake that refused to go away. I knew Barry personally, and after talking to him he understood the situation. But I couldn't very well talk to every analyst, reporter and DDR stockholder in the United States. It would have been comical if it hadn't been so damaging.

Finally, we convinced the court that we had been mistakenly drawn into this mess, and in November 1995, just about a year from the day I had first been served with papers, we were dropped from the suit. In order to put it behind us once and for all, First Union agreed not to pursue an appeal in exchange for us agreeing not to bring claims for defamation and abuse of process. Early the following year, I read in the newspaper that Osborne and Mastandrea had settled their differences, with Osborne selling his shares back to First Union at a slight premium.

In the end, the only winners were the lawyers. What else is new? According to published reports, Osborne said the court case cost him about $1 million in legal fees, and the court battles and share price settlement cost First Union about $1.5 million. I guess we got off easy, since we spent only about $150,000 to defend ourselves.

At least my association with Escaja had a happy ending. I knew that after the First Union fiasco we needed to part ways, but he had worked as my accountant for fifteen years and I didn't feel I could just suddenly terminate his employ. Instead, I offered him a deal too good to refuse. I set him up with a $200,000 line of credit for the first year and $200,000 for the second, and told him we'd be 50-50 partners in any kind of real estate development he was able to initiate. At the end of two years, we'd split the profits, but he wouldn't be responsible for any losses. To his credit, two years later Escaja sent me my money back, plus a profit of $200,000. He ironically had made most of his money by acting as a broker selling one of the early Kmarts I had developed. He then went to work for another developer and we ended our partnership. I've recently had several meetings with Mastandrea, who has been urging me to go into business with him on a number of ventures.

McGill and Wolstein, Together Again

I don't think I knew until I left DDR how constrained I had felt working for a public company, even as chairman. For the first time ever I hadn't looked forward to going to work in the morning. Part of it was that I wasn't in charge, and that still grated on me. Maybe part of it too was that a public company and I were a hopeless mismatch of skills, and starting back up on my own was the ONLY answer for me.

As I got back into the swing of the development business, I started to think about once again partnering with John McGill. I knew John's experience with the public company had been similar to mine. I couldn't imagine he was truly happy there. The initial plan had been for DDR primarily to manage and acquire shopping centers, but not to actually develop them. Wall Street was uncomfortable with the risks associated with finding land and building from scratch, a process called greenfield development. Nearly every investor at the various IPO road shows expressed that concern, believing that it was more risky building from scratch than buying existing developments. But that would have left John totally out in the cold, in the same position he had been ten years earlier prior to us starting W&M Properties when I had scaled back Developers Diversified's development slate because of high interest rates.

This was totally anathema to my philosophy, of course. By building a development myself from the ground up, I had total control and the potential for the greatest reward and the greatest sense of accomplishment. Ultimately, DDR was successful in changing investors' perceptions about greenfield development and it became a major focus of its growth strategy.

Still, inside I believed that John probably felt the same itch I did. He was never comfortable operating within the constraints of a public company. When I asked him to join me in a new 50-50 partnership, I got the feeling he wondered what had taken me so long to ask, and in June 1999 John and I became equal partners in the Heritage Development Corporation.

Chapter Ten

Giving It Away Without Throwing It Away

W hen I first started in business, I thought I could be both an entrepreneur *and* an insider. I tried, but I was wrong. I thought that since it worked for me in business to take risks, speak my mind, and do what I thought was right no matter what anyone told me, I could do the same in the rest of my life. I thought that I could just be myself, and I'd reach the same stature within the business and political establishment as I had in the real estate business.

I learned that you can't have it both ways. You have to choose. You can either be a maverick or an insider, but not both.

The Outsider

Merriam Webster's dictionary has two definitions for the word, *outsider,* and together they pretty much sum up the first 75 years of my life. The first definition is "a person who does not belong to a particular group." That's me. I've never been invited to join the downtown business group, the Union Club, or been asked to sit on the board of a single public corporation. I've built over 1,000 homes and more than fifty million square feet of commercial space, but I've never been part of the "Cleveland Taliban," as my friend, State Representative Tim Grendell, calls the local establishment. In fact, just recently when I presented the City with an ambitious proposal for a new convention center on the site of the old railroad yard in downtown Cleveland, in walking distance from the Cleveland Indians ballpark and the Gund Arena, the *Cleveland Plain Dealer* pretty much admitted that the project was doomed, not because it wasn't the best site, but because I wasn't a political insider.

Webster's other definition of an outsider is "a contender not expected to win," which accurately defines my career. All my life people have been telling me that this project or that project won't work, or that I'm embarking on an unworkable task. They told me that Twinsburg was an impossible place in which to sell middle class homes, indoor soccer would never catch on, Glenmoor was a bottomless money pit, and the OEPA would never let us build in either Parma *or* Bainbridge Township. If I had a nickel for every time I was told that a real estate development or some other idea I was pursuing was unrealistic or hopeless, well, I'd have a barrel full of nickels.

Ask Me If I Care

I'd like to say that I wouldn't have had it any other way, that I don't care a lick about becoming an insider. But I think it's more accurate to say that I *couldn't* have had it any other way. I believe no true entrepreneur can. On one hand, the restless, anti-establishment personality that characterizes the typical entrepreneur helps create financial success. Yet on the other hand, it keeps us on the outside of the establishment looking in.

Does that mean I think all entrepreneurs are outsiders? Yes, I think it does. Not all entrepreneurs remain outsiders, often because they don't remain entrepreneurs. Bill Gates is one of the most successful entrepreneurs in the history of the planet, but is he still an entrepreneur today?

I've had one unique advantage over the past 55 years, and that's Iris. Walk into any of my most important real estate projects—the Renaissance Building, the Glenmoor Country Club in Canton, the Bertram Inn, even the first basement-less homes I built four decades ago—and you will see Iris's influence at least as much as my own. Being on 'the outside looking in' is a lot easier when you have someone you love, the perfect partner, by your side.

It would be easy to say to hell with the establishment, I don't care about being an insider. But that's not altogether true because for as long as I can remember, ever since I worked so hard at attaching myself to my Uncle Dan, I've tried to become an insider. But over and over again, I've learned that becoming an insider would mean becoming someone I'm not, someone I could never be.

The Jewish Federation

The one time in my life when I crept closest to becoming an insider was in the mid 1970s, when I increased my involvement with the Jewish Community Federation, the umbrella organization responsible for all non-profit giving to Jewish causes. Iris and I always tried to give within our means, and sometimes beyond our means. In Cleveland, if you are Jewish, that has always meant giving to the Federation, which funds various programs, from local food banks, to programs for the elderly, to local hospitals. For many years it actually published each donation in a bound manuscript so that everyone knew what everyone else had donated. Iris and I began contributing to the Federation in the 1960s. We began to step up our contributions once I began having some success on my own, first in Twinsburg and then when I started Developers Diversified in 1965.

By 1976 I had worked my way up to become the general co-chairman of the Federation's fundraising arm, the Jewish Welfare Fund, in line to become chairman. You can't get much more inside the Jewish community than to become the fund's Chair. But it all blew up at a meeting at the home of the Federation's chairman, when the personality traits of an entrepreneurial outsider confronted the compromises necessary to become part of the establishment.

I think the Federation's annual operating budget at the time was about $20 million. As the meeting came to order, the chairman announced that we had a shortfall of $800,000 from that year's fundraising campaign and that everyone in the room, about two dozen of us, would be expected to take out our checkbooks to make up the deficit.

I immediately didn't like the idea, and I knew Iris would like it even less. We had just given $70,000 to the Federation, and that was a lot of money to us in 1976. Under the Federation's unwritten rules, we would have to increase our gift in 1977 and each year thereafter. That was the price of being an insider. I may have been on my way to becoming one of the nation's leading builders of Kmart stores, but I was still a small private developer, stretched pretty thin.

The Cleveland Jewish community generally allows a few people within the Federation to set the agenda. The rest are expected to keep their opinions to themselves. So far, I had gone along with that, throwing my money in with everyone else's to fund the Federation's various worthwhile programs.

Going along with the crowd is not my style, however. As we went around the room, person after person made additional pledges just as the chairman had requested. I watched this, and thought to myself that this was no way to run an organization. When it was my turn to speak, I stood up and proposed a different plan of how to make up the shortfall.

The first thing I suggested we do was collect money that had already been promised. I knew from the real estate business that bills aren't paid by pledges, but by cash received. The Federation was receiving thousands of pledges every year, but without follow-up, many were never collected. Compounding the problem was the fact that most people weren't about to make an additional financial commitment if they hadn't even fulfilled a previous pledge. It was a relatively simple idea to create a system whereby people were regularly reminded of their pledges and if necessary encouraged to send in a weekly or monthly check, as small as it might be, until the pledged was fulfilled.

My second suggestion was that rather than asking for additional contributions from a select group of board members, we should encourage participation from the broader Jewish community. This would also have the added benefit of encouraging more people to become involved with the Federation's other activities.

I thought these were perfectly reasonable suggestions, but suddenly the chairman interrupted me, saying "we don't want to hear from you." There was a noticeable gasp throughout the room, but after an uncomfortable silence I responded by saying, "You'll never hear from me again." The meeting then continued just the way the chairman wanted. I kept quiet, with tears in my eyes. It still hurts today, when I think about that moment.

The chairman at the time happened to be a billionaire, while the rest of us were only millionaires at best. I guess that meant he deserved a level of respect beyond his position as chairman. He ran his company with an iron fist, but I didn't think it was appropriate to lead a philanthropic organization that way. He needed to show respect to others and acknowledge their ideas. It was then that I decided it was better to accept the scorn of the inner circle than be treated as poorly as he treated me during that meeting.

My big opportunity to become an insider, at least in the local Jewish community, had just gone up in smoke. I received six calls that night apologizing for the chairman's rudeness. The full-time Federation president showed up at my home to apologize in person. But I never heard from the chairman. The damage was done. I resigned my co-chairmanship a few weeks later.

For years afterwards, I was ostracized by a select group within the Cleveland Jewish community. In fact, in 1978 when Iris and I threw a big black tie party to celebrate the opening of the Heritage, many of them boycotted the event. But in the end, the chairman did the Federation an injustice. I've become a leader in the philanthropic community, raising and donating many millions of dollars to a variety of organizations. Had the Federation treated me differently, it would have benefited as well. Interestingly enough, over the years people have periodically come up to me to offer their congratulations on my convictions, telling me that they too always believed that the Federation should be operated more democratically.

My experiences with the Federation marked a turning point for me. In my younger days I was always willing to yield to people's demands, whether it was a request for money, a dinner invitation, or a "great deal" someone was offering me in business. But Iris and experiences such as this one taught me how to take control of my life and make independent decisions. Rather than yield to other people's demands, I try to decide for myself the right thing to do when faced with either a business or personal decision.

Israel Bonds

My rift with the Federation in no way diminished the responsibility Iris and I felt to contribute to Jewish causes. Shortly after I ended my relationship with the Federation, we made a $125,000 contribution to the Jewish National Fund for a tree planting center in the American Centennial Forest in Israel just outside of Jerusalem. I also became extremely active in Israel bonds.

Israel bonds have been around since the formation of the State of Israel in 1948, when the new national government needed a way to raise the capital necessary for its very survival. In 1951, on the third anniversary of Israel's statehood at a rally in Madison Square Garden, David Ben-Gurion officially launched the Israel Bond Organization. Since 1951, $18.5 billion has been raised through sales of the bonds.

I'm proud of the small role Iris and I played in this effort. During the two years I was chairman of the Cleveland chapter we sold well over $10 million worth of bonds through various fundraising efforts. Former Israeli prime minister Yitzhak Rabin spoke at the dinner when I was installed as president. I had already been to Israel on Federation business. Now I returned several times to work with the international organization of Israel Bonds. I had the opportunity to meet Golda Meir, and when General Moshe Dayan came to Cleveland I picked him up at the airport. He was a tough guy who traveled with a gun on his hip, but he pleaded with me not to make him give a speech. He only wanted to answer questions. But we had a full house at the Beachmont Country Club and I insisted he do both, and he reluctantly agreed.

In 1999 Scott and I were presented with the Star of David Award by the State of Israel Bonds at a fundraiser in the ballroom at the Renaissance Hotel. My friend, former Senator Bob Dole, was nice enough to come to present it to me. I still probably have more Israel bonds in my portfolio than anyone in Cleveland.

Cleveland Magazine

Another turning point occurred when I was asked by *Cleveland Magazine* to be profiled in an upcoming issue. I still owned the Force, and the idea as presented to me was that the magazine was interested in a story about what we had done to turn the team around. I was always ready to do anything that might generate ticket sales, so I readily agreed.

The article, published in the February 1982 issue, turned out to be a personal attack on me. It barely even mentioned the Force. It was clear where most of the anonymous quotes had come from, since many of them were thinly veiled references to my split with the Jewish Federation.

Particularly galling were the passages that were so blatantly untrue. I didn't mind so much when the author wrote that the "tight knit clan of corporate movers and shakers" had "so far turned its back" on me, or that my casual dress "set (me) apart from the rest of the conservatively dressed men," or that my speech was "blunter than would be expected of a man of his wealth." These charges didn't bother me because I couldn't debate their veracity. That was me—I did speak my mind, and my business did not demand that I wear $1,000 suits.

But the personal attacks from unnamed "friends" and "associates" accusing me of being hardnosed and always having strings attached to any favor I might do or any charitable contribution I might make wounded Iris and me because the accusations were so clearly false. The ironic part was that half the article was a positive rags-to-riches story of a poor Cleveland boy who made good. In fact, many people subsequently told me what a positive story they thought it was. But the other half of the profile was filled with unnamed people saying unkind things about me. It would have been funny if it hadn't been so personally hurtful.

Yet what could I do? What's the old saying? Don't pick a fight with anyone who buys ink by the barrel. I couldn't very well publish another article listing the many times I had made an anonymous donation or bailed out a friend or acquaintance from financial trouble. Just recently, for example, I bought a house for a young man who manages my restaurant at the Bertram Inn. He got himself into some severe credit card debt, and asked me to go look at a condominium he was about to buy. I took one look at it and didn't like what I saw. It was in a ghetto, with no parks or playground where he and his wife and two children could feel safe. I bought him a house in Twinsburg. As soon as he has enough equity and can get a mortgage, I'll pass ownership on to him. I feel like I've saved the lives of a couple of kids, and it's a great feeling. I don't need any other reward than that.

Iris was particularly devastated by the *Cleveland Magazine* article. At least I could throw myself into my work. She didn't feel like leaving the house for weeks. It frankly took us both several years to get over the sting completely.

The hurt was partially soothed, however, when the magazine was inundated with so many letters from people who knew me that the managing editor was compelled to devote a full page in a subsequent issue defending the article's author against an onslaught of criticism. In the next few issues the magazine printed more than a dozen letters that disputed most of the magazine's accusations. While I couldn't defend *myself*, people who knew me could more easily write about my various acts of volunteerism that the article had ignored, like my work as a Grand Jury Foreman and Cuyahoga Community College trustee, my participation with Israel bonds, or the many times during the process of developing a shopping center that Developers Diversified had made a donation to the community for a ball park or civic center that went far beyond our agreement. In 1979 Iris and I had become the first husband and wife to be given the B'nai B'rith gold medallion for humanitarianism. But all this came out only in the letters to the editor, after the article had been published. I think my favorite line in any of the letters was by my friend Richard Livingston, who wrote that the author "must have learned his journalism style from Lizzie Borden."

I subsequently became friendly with the publisher of *Cleveland Magazine,* Lute Harmon. He has admitted to me more than once that he wished the article had been edited quite differently. I'd have to agree, but I did learn a valuable lesson from the experience. If a negative story is released, hold your head up high. I found that many fewer people focused on the negative things written about me than focused on my accomplishments.

Scott tried to make Iris and me feel better by pointing out that we shouldn't pay any attention to an article written by a total stranger, but rather to the letters written by people who had known me for years, in some cases all my life. That did make us feel a little better. It also made me realize that the break with the Federation was probably a permanent one. It was obvious where the most hurtful quotes had come from. Subsequent leaderships at the Federation have made several attempts to bring me back into the fold, and frankly I always assumed they would eventually be successful. I think they saw the contribution I was making to other organizations and they missed the energy I brought to the work. But each time they approached me I told them the same thing, that they'd have to make the first move to restore my reputation, and they never did.

Deciding How to Give It Away

Some of Iris's and my greatest pleasures in life have come from getting personally involved with the charities we support. I don't think someone is a real person unless he or she has feelings for and a commitment to others. Iris and I have focused our dollars and efforts on areas that interest us the most—children, medical research, and education. Rather than just throw our money into a big pot, Iris and I like to see for ourselves what our dollars are accomplishing. Through our experiences with organizations like United Cerebral Palsy, University Hospitals, Case Western Reserve University, Hebrew University, and Ohio State University, we've found that there are many ways to make charitable giving rewarding.

Giving It Away: How to Make It Rewarding

- Identify your general areas of interest
- Learn about the organization and the specific programs it offers so you can speak about it to others
- Make more significant contributions to fewer organizations rather than spreading yourself too thinly
- Support organizations to which you have an emotional connection and evangelize them to others
- Don't just write a check without having a say in what your money will accomplish and how it will be used
- Make the organization responsible and responsive to you so you know how it is doing and what it is accomplishing
- Become involved with the organization by contributing time, not just money, by either being on the board or volunteering
- Develop an ongoing relationship with the organization rather than making a one-time donation
- Don't expect anything in return for your contributions
- Recognize and appreciate what you do get in return, particularly that warm and fuzzy feeling inside that you have done something worthwhile

---

Iris and I don't really believe in leaving all our assets to our children and grandchildren so they never have to earn a living. They'll be much better off having to exercise their mind and going out in the world to make a success in their own right. So for Iris and I, our challenge is to enjoy giving our money away in our lifetime. It's not an unpleasant situation. I'm much more comfortable writing a $50,000 check to a good cause than I am spending $2,000 on myself.

Jogging for Dollars

One of my earliest charitable commitments was to the local chapter of the American Heart Association. I got involved with them after Iris remarked to me one day that I was getting a little paunchy. I looked in the mirror and couldn't blame Iris for her honesty. I weighed 205 pounds, and had become somewhat of a professional eater. I loved to eat, and was very good at it.

Iris's remark really hurt my ego, and on my 40th birthday I started jogging. I quickly became a jogging nut. I kept thinking of my father, who used to walk everywhere very fast. Maybe that was just because he had no choice since he didn't own a car.

The first time out I could barely run a quarter of a mile. Gradually I increased my stamina until I was regularly running ten, thirteen, seventeen miles before breakfast. I didn't care if it was ten degrees below zero. I'd put on my mask and gloves and run every day. I dropped my weight to 172 pounds with a 34 waist and was in fantastic shape.

One day in 1972 I agreed to promote a half marathon charity run sponsored by the Cleveland chapter of the American Heart Association. A camera crew from one of the local television stations filmed me eating breakfast, jogging, and talking about my efforts to raise money for the association. They even filmed me at a local restaurant eating lunch, profiling the ingredients of a hearty but healthy meal. The report was scheduled to air on the evening news on Wednesday, three days before the Saturday event. I came home from a jog and walked down the circular stairs to take a shower before watching myself on television. I tripped and broke two toes and couldn't run again for two months. I never got back into jogging in the same way again. In fact, in 2003, more than thirty years after the original injury, I had an operation to straighten both toes and was on crutches for six weeks.

For a while I switched to the bicycle, but I was never as fanatical about it as I had been about running. In 1995 Scott, Jim Schoff, and I were invited to Israel on a bicycle trip. After a stopover in Tel Aviv, where we changed into our biking clothes, we flew to the Lebanese border. There we were met by one hundred bicycles, with our names on them. We cycled 500 miles in eight days, from northern Israel, through the Golan Heights and Jerusalem, ending in the Negev Desert near the Red Sea. At 68 years old, I was one of the oldest riders, but I kept up with the pack, never lagging behind.

Politics, Fooey

It was also during these years when I began to contribute in a serious way to political campaigns. I actually started contributing well before I had any money. My first efforts were passing out flyers for my Uncle Dan, who was a close confidante and advisor to Congressman George Bender. These were the days when U.S. Congressmen played a much more important role in their local communities than they do today. While I was in law school, Uncle Dan also put me on a committee for the presidential candidate, Wendell Wilkie. I was in the audience when Wilkie came to Cleveland to make a speech, which was my introduction to national politics.

In 1951 I ran for office myself for the first and only time, for councilman in South Euclid, the Cleveland suburb where Iris and I lived. I was a Republican, like my Uncle Dan. (You had to be if you were going to hang out with him.) I was studying to be a lawyer, and I figured I would follow in his footsteps. I campaigned hard, and wrote an elaborate speech, talking about all the wonderful things I was going to do once I was elected. Three of my law school classmates came to the house several times to help me draft it. I must have practiced it a hundred times in front of a mirror, and two hundred times in front of Iris. I can still see Iris, extremely pregnant, standing on a street corner passing out flyers. She also designed my posters and bumper stickers. Iris knew the speech by heart. I thought I did too, until I got up in front of an audience of a few hundred people and my mind went completely blank. I had forgotten every word. That was the last time I ever wrote a speech. I've found that speaking from the heart without notes is more effective anyway. I did fool my mother, however, who though I was reading from a prepared text.

I can proudly say I came in second in the council election. True, there were only two candidates.

Once I opened an office in Twinsburg, I contributed to the campaigns of a number of local politicians, including Congressmen James Stanton and Charles Vanik. Vanik served in Congress for twenty-five years, until 1981. One day he called to tell me about a piece of land a friend of his had for sale in Twinsburg. Michael Miller and I bought it and are only now developing it, thirty years later. I also opened an office in Twinsburg for Scoop Jackson when he was running for the democratic presidential nomination in 1972, and I supported him again in 1976. Jackson was a Democrat, but a conservative, and a great friend of Israel's. I raised a considerable sum for his political action committee and frequently went to New York for fundraising meetings. I had visions of him being President of the United States and Iris and I being invited to the White House for dinner. In my greatest fantasy, I'd receive a U.S. Ambassadorship.

The first Ohio Governor I got to know well was James Rhodes, who in my mind was the state's last great governor. While Governor Rhodes was in office the state of Ohio flourished. He had a dynamic personality and used it to encourage businesses to move to Ohio. He'd go to every major groundbreaking in the state, and would always mark the occasion by saying "profit is not a dirty word in Ohio." That resonated throughout the country and encouraged many companies to walk through the doors he had opened.

I contributed to every one of Governor Rhodes' three gubernatorial campaigns. To his dying day he would call me, the last time about investing in an invention that filtered air through office buildings.

In 1975 Rhodes named me as a trustee of the Cuyahoga Community College. The board was lead by Robert Lewis, whom I had known for years. He had been my law school contracts professor and was a hell of a guy. He tutored me and a few other law students many times at my house and never charged us a nickel. The president of Cuyahoga Community College, Nolan Ellison, was a big muscular former basketball player at the University of Kansas. He was also brilliant. We became great friends, and the three of us accomplished a lot for the college. We helped streamline its bloated workforce by setting up a school-wide computer system, well before there was a personal computer on every desk.

But our most important accomplishment while I was chairman of Cuyahoga Community College was the opening of a new campus on the east side of Cleveland. By the time my term was over, the college had almost 25,000 students.

In a very peripheral way I've been involved in every Cleveland mayoral campaign since Anthony Celebrezze left office in 1962. Michael White came to me for advice as a state senator, well before he decided to run for mayor. I contributed to his campaign because I thought he had the moxie to be a great mayor. He ran against City Council President George Forbes, whom I thought would be a *fantastic* mayor, so I contributed to his campaign too, even though they were running against each other. White won the election, but I was very disappointed with his performance as mayor. The city really declined during his twelve years in office.

Candidates aren't at all shy about coming around to ask for money. Once they're elected, however, you typically don't see them until their next campaign. I tried to establish a relationship with George Voinovich, for example. He was pleasant enough whenever I met him, but we never were able to accomplish anything together. I spoke with him many times about various proposals to improve downtown Cleveland, but nothing ever came from it. When he first ran for governor in 1991, I often introduced him at rallies as the next governor of Ohio. Iris and I sponsored a gala fundraiser for him at a downtown hotel, and his campaign encouraged us to attend his victory party in Columbus. But we were sorry we did. No one gave us the time of day. I was sitting next to someone in the hotel lobby who had personally written his campaign a check for $100,000, and he was ignored too. Voinovich, who has now become a U.S. Senator, still surfaces asking for money, but I'm done with politics.

As I grew older, I became more confident and less concerned about whether politicians, or anyone else for that matter, listened to me. Iris helped me with this. I realized that it's better to do what you think is correct, give away money only when it feels right to you, and let the chips fall where they may. As a real estate developer, this may not always be the most effective strategy. It certainly didn't help me with Governor Taft's administration when it came to my battles with the OEPA in the 1990s, as discussed in chapter six.

Years ago I decided I was no longer willing to take out my checkbook unless a candidate was interested enough to meet with me one-on-one and listen to what I had to say. I supported George Bush senior, but when they asked me to support his son and invited me to a meeting in Texas, I told them I wasn't interested in being one of seventy-five guys to watch him enter the room for ten minutes, after which everyone would be expected to leave a check for $25,000. That's not for me. I'm looking for a dialogue, not for being used as an ATM machine.

I always tell politicians that I'm also not expecting them to do me any favors, only to listen to what I have to say and determine for themselves whether it's the right thing for the city, state, or country. I think I have something to contribute to the political discourse that can be measured by more than just dollars and cents.

Bob Dole

Supporters, like customers, want to feel appreciated, but most politicians are too arrogant to recognize that. When I was first approached about getting involved in Bob Dole's 1996 U. S. Presidential campaign, I made it clear that I wasn't interested unless I met with him alone and developed some kind of personal rapport with him. A visit was arranged in his Senate office in Washington, and we talked for the better part of an hour. He and I immediately hit it off. I held a $1,000 per plate dinner for him during the presidential campaign that raised $400,000, then raised another $250,000 in direct solicitations at a $25,000 per plate luncheon where he was the featured speaker.

As one of the top ten people on Bob Dole's finance committee, I attended a meeting of his supporters in Washington, D.C. I listened to several people talk about campaign strategy, but never once did someone come up to talk to me. After a while, I left. No one even missed me.

That evening at a cocktail reception I buttonholed one of Bob Dole's young aides and reprimanded him for not being respectful and virtually ignoring the campaign's top contributors. Just then the Senator entered the room and walked up to Iris and me and gave her a big hug and a kiss on the cheek. He stood there for a few minutes talking to us, joking with us, and making us feel special. "See what I mean?" I said to his young aide when Dole finally left us. "That's what you should have done."

I've always tried to acknowledge people myself. If I host a dinner to celebrate the completion of a job or an anniversary of one of our larger projects, or if I'm sponsoring a fundraising event, I try to go around the room and say something special to every person in attendance. It makes people work harder because they feel appreciated, and it's easy to do because I genuinely appreciate the work people do for me.

In my mind, Bob Dole lost the election because he wasn't allowed to be himself. He's a warm, intelligent, very humorous guy, but none of that came through during the campaign. If he had ignored his consultants and rejected the boilerplate speeches that were written for him and instead used his own wit and genuineness, he would have been much better off.

United Cerebral Palsy

Iris and I gradually began to approach our philanthropic efforts, particularly once we were in a position to make more sizable donations, similar to the way we approached our political giving. My experience with the Federation, and then with subsequent donations to numerous other organizations, is that you write a check and then have no say in what your money is accomplishing. Once Developers Diversified went public and we were in a position to step up our giving, Iris and I wanted to see firsthand the good things that could be accomplished with our contributions, and not just leave it to others to spend it as they wished. If we were going to get serious about giving away our money, we wanted to do it in a serious way.

Our first major gift was to United Cerebral Palsy (UCP) of Greater Cleveland. Scott had been president of the board, and he introduced us to its director, Susan Dean, who was in the midst of a capital campaign for the construction of a new $6.5 million building at East 101st Street and Euclid Avenue.

Iris and I were immediately interested, as the organization combined two of our philanthropic interests, children and medical research. As Susan introduced us to the kind of services the UCP offered, their efforts on behalf of local children touched our hearts. Cerebral palsy is actually a broad term used to describe a group of chronic conditions affecting body movement caused by injury to specific areas of the brain. The damage usually occurs in the fetus, or shortly after birth. "Cerebral" refers to the brain, and "palsy" to weakness resulting in poor muscle control. Although cerebral palsy is not curable in the accepted sense, the kind of training and therapy emphasized by the UCP of Greater Cleveland has produced dramatic improvements in thousands of individuals.

The capital campaign for the new building was made up of three equal parts of about $2 million each. The State of Ohio was contributing about $2 million, revenue bonds were being floated for another $2 million, and the organization was seeking to raise the final $2 million through its own fundraising efforts. As the largest part of that final piece, Iris and I wrote a check for $750,000 for the naming rights to what became the Iris S. and Bert L. Wolstein Center.

Our involvement, however, went beyond writing a big check. Over the years I've learned that there are two, equally important, parts to philanthropy. One is making financial contributions; the other is contributing your time and encouraging others to contribute.

In the first place, Iris immediately participated in the design of the building, adding her usual special touches, including upgrading the floor coverings and tiling, choosing the doors and windows, and even the color of the brick. We also agreed to head up several fundraising events, beginning with a June 1999 black tie gala to mark the opening of the new building. The highlight of the event, which drew a thousand people, was when my friend Michael Bolton made a surprise appearance.

Without telling anyone, I had made arrangements to fly Michael into Cleveland for the evening. Toward the end of the event I walked up on stage and announced that a good friend of mine would like to sing a few songs. The lights went down, the spotlight up, and Michael walked in to great fanfare. I heard people gasp. Some insisted he must be a look-alike rather than the real Michael Bolton. It was a special evening, and we raised more than $500,000 for the UCP. Two years later Iris came up with the idea of renting the entire Sea World park for a fundraiser. Initially everyone thought the idea was unorthodox, if not a little crazy, but she pulled it off. Together we organized the event, which netted the charity another $1 million. To this day, we're proud to still be the organization's largest annual donor.

I had always been a big Michael Bolton fan. Iris and I had seen him several times in concert at the Blossom, an outdoor amphitheatre just outside of Cleveland. When I noticed him in the pro shop at Barrington Country Club one day in 1997, I immediately introduced myself. We got to talking, and he invited Iris and me to his concert the following night. Afterwards we visited him in his dressing room, where we must have talked for two hours, about everything from family to careers to Judaism. He's much younger than I am, of course, but we just hit it off. Every time Michael comes to Cleveland we play golf and have dinner together. We've reciprocated each other's invitations to participate in various philanthropic efforts. Michael has incorporated an organization called The Michael Bolton Charities, aimed at helping children and women at risk. Iris and I attended one of his fundraisers in the Hamptons a few years ago and sat at his table. Just recently Iris was thrilled when we happened to see him on the *Today Show* and he was wearing the black Armani t-shirt she had sent him as a birthday present.

Iris and I have continued our close involvement with the UCP. The organization looks to us each year to provide a sizable matching grant, and we are happy to oblige. Susan then uses the grant as the basis of her fundraising campaign, since our donation is ostensibly dependent on it being matched dollar for dollar by others in the Cleveland community.

The Ohio State University

I've always been a Buckeye fan, so the Ohio State University football program was another natural candidate for receiving a donation once Iris and I started giving away significant money. The first time we made a contribution to the school was actually through the $12,000 gift to Jack Nicklaus' charity golf tournament. It gave me the opportunity to play a round of golf with the Golden Bear, but also, to my surprise, to have the opportunity to purchase football tickets each year. I was happy about that, because Iris and I had become huge Buckeye fans and were not always able to buy good seats.

All of a sudden we started attending every game. At that point the school's development staff obviously had its eye on us because during the renovation of the stadium in 1999 I was approached about making a sizable contribution. I suggested that I designate $5 million, or even $10 million, of a $20 million life insurance policy to Ohio State, but they couldn't quite understand how that sort of gift would work. No one lives forever, and if universities and other charitable organizations were more creative about their pursuit of legacy gifts, in a few years they would begin to experience a continuous windfall. But Ohio State rejected my proposal out of hand. I think it was worried I might stop paying the life insurance premiums, although after a few years they could have just paid it themselves and still come out way ahead.

Next Iris and I began talking with the university about the naming rights to the elevator and lobby area of the stadium, but in the middle of the negotiations they sold those rights to the Huntington Bank. In 2000, Iris and I agreed to give the school $1.5 million toward renovating the stadium's bell tower, and the recruiting area, press room, and locker rooms inside. They named the tower the Iris S. and Bert L. Wolstein Football Center, and the large lettering spelling out our names, which is very visible from inside the stadium, makes a lot of people think that the stadium is named after us. Iris and I were introduced to the crowd between quarters at the opening home game of the 2001 season. After every Buckeye victory the bell in the tower is rung. This time they allowed Iris and me to have that honor, which we gave to our grandson, Harrison. That was a real thrill for him, and for me too.

But the best thing about my association with the school is that we now have a loge suite for every game at the 40-yard line. Each year the coach sends me field passes, which I use to take a friend or business associate on the field before game time when I introduce them to Coach Jim Tressel and some of the other coaches and players.

The Buckeyes have given Iris and me a lot of pleasure over the years, culminating in our trip to Tempe, Arizona in January 2003 to watch them win the national championship. I envy Coach Tressel. It's wonderful to be around such talented, dedicated kids. In 1999 his predecessor, John Cooper, asked me to talk to the team before a game against Purdue. I gave the players a pep talk not about football, but about the importance of staying focused and doing the best they could every day, every play, every week, every month, and every year. Anything less will be quickly apparent and they won't be able get to where they want to go. Goals are accomplished by performing at a higher level than anyone else, and the only way to do that is to make that extra effort. You can't cheat in effort, in training, in life, I told them. I went the long way, with no shortcuts. I tried to convey that pathway to these kids. By the way, they won the game.

Case Western Reserve University

Iris and I liked the idea of supporting educational institutions. In 2000 we started talking with the Weatherhead School of Management of Case Western Reserve University (CWRU) about a donation. About twenty years earlier, just before the credit crunch, I had proposed building a museum on campus to teach about the Holocaust and other genocides. It was my own idea, and I presented the school with a detailed proposal. The centerpiece of the museum would have been rotating exhibits to highlight both historical and contemporary genocide. We would design our own exhibits, and partner with other holocaust museums from around the world to create programs aimed at high school and college students and the adult public.

I made it known that I was prepared to step up with a large donation and be responsible for raising the rest. All the University would have had to do was endorse the project and provide the location. The president and the provost of the University both liked the idea, but when it was presented to the board, they turned it down with no real explanation.

By 2002, however, the Weatherhead School had a new Dean, Mohsen Anvari, and he and I immediately hit it off. I was looking for somewhere to house my archives, and Mohsen and I quickly settled on a $2.5 million gift, split between a $1 million renovation of Sycamore Hall and the creation of an endowed chair. Sycamore Hall was renamed Iris S. and Bert L. Wolstein Hall (Wolstein Hall for short) and turned it into a four-story student center and a place to hold my archives. The chair, a Professorship in Management Design, was named after Iris.

Iris and I subsequently also agreed to chair a committee established to raise $172 million for the Weathered School's endowment. I'm ready to work hard, just as I did for the Federation, Israel Bonds, and United Cerebral Palsy, to help turn Weatherhead into one of the top business schools in the country.

University Hospitals

One day just before Christmas 2002 I awoke to read in the *Cleveland Plain Dealer* about a 50-year partnership that had finally been signed between the boards of University Hospitals (UH) and Case Western Reserve University. For years UH and CWRU had been unsuccessfully trying to agree on how to share research dollars and to continue their historically close ties. Only after a change at the top of both organizations did the new president of CWRU, Dr. Edward Hundert, and the new acting chief executive of UHHS, Dr. Fred Rothstein, settle their differences and sign the partnership agreement.

As part of that agreement, the operations of UH's existing research institute was folded into the joint venture, and the university agreed to buy half of the $110 million biomedical research facility under construction on Cornell Road. According to the *Plain Dealer*, the new building was to be named the UHHS-CWRU Partnership Research Building until a benefactor could be found to give it a permanent name.

As I read the article a bell went off in my head that Iris and I might become that benefactor. This would be a way to make a significant contribution that wasn't tied to anything except helping people of all religions, races, and income brackets.

Iris and I had had a checkered history with University Hospitals, but we didn't let that stand in our way. Back in 2000, when I was having my own health problems, I wanted to establish a relationship with a hospital. I had almost $6 million in a philanthropic fund that I had to allocate during the next few years if I wanted any say in where the money would go. I suggested that we give $3 million to the hospital, split equally between the trauma center and the orthopedic department. In return, I wanted Iris on the board of directors at Babies and Children Hospital, a member of the University Hospital system. I also suggested that I be named to board of University Hospitals. If I was going to establish a relationship with the hospital, I wanted to be in a position to make sure that my gifts were being put to good use. Iris was elected to the Babies and Children Hospital board, but the University Hospitals board never did name me a director. I withdrew my financial offer, and after her initial term expired, Iris was not encouraged to remain.

By the end of 2002 there was fresh leadership at both UH and CWRU. As soon as I arrived at the Heritage after reading the report in the *Cleveland Plain Dealer,* I called Mohsen Anvari. He told me he was having lunch that same day with Ed Hundert. That afternoon Hundert called me, and we decided to get together for breakfast the following morning.

I made President Hundert an offer, and the broad smile on his face signaled to me that it met his expectations. He told me he'd just have to run it by his board of directors, and I told him I'd have to do the same, although mine was a board of one–Iris.

Over the years every time I talked money with Iris she would ask me, "Well, how much is that per week?" But in this case I was confident that she would be as enthusiastic about this gift as I was. Indeed, we both thought that together, UH and CWRU had the wherewithal to create one of the top research medical centers in the world. We liked the idea that we might play a small role in making that happen. The following day, just like that, Iris and I agreed to donate $25 million for the naming rights to the new center.

Fundraising 101

I was amazed to learn that in 2002 there were only thirty philanthropic gifts in the United States larger than $25 million. I guess I shouldn't have been surprised that our gift to the research center made the front pages in Cleveland and elsewhere. It also opened a Pandora's box. Not a day goes by now that I don't get a request for donations, large and small, although mostly large. I respect the fact that nonprofit organizations are in need of donations, and I want to help those that meet our criteria. But leaders of some organizations think nothing of arranging a lunch to ask for $2 million, $5 million, $50 million, $200 million. I'm not exaggerating. I wonder what's in their heads.

I was asked recently by Case Western to give a speech to a group of fundraisers and estate planners—professionals working with potential donors to give legacy gifts. I told them that fundraising is very simple, so simple in fact, that I didn't even quite know how to explain it to them. Most importantly, potential donors have to be cultivated. The role of a development person is to interest a potential donor in the cause and show them how they can fit in. Eventually, they have to be made to feel like a part of the family. "Hi, how are you, can I have $50 million?" is just not going to work, I told them.

To be a successful fundraiser you have to put your money where your mouth is. If you ask people to donate money, you have to be donating serious money yourself. If you ask people to buy bonds, you have to buy bonds. That's why I don't think people without assets can be effective as large ticket fundraisers.

It's also important for development people to do their homework so they don't make requests that have no chance of being successful, put the potential donor in an awkward position, or are insulting. In 1990, for example, I agreed to serve on the board of a local college. I knew I'd be expected to make an annual contribution and that was fine. The college was doing worthwhile work that I supported. It was soon suggested that I purchase its naming rights for $5 million. In the first place, I was in no position at that time to make a $5 million donation. And in the second place, in my opinion this was an inflated figure. The naming rights I think were recently sold for less than $1.5 million, so that hunch has since been borne out.

More recently, another non-profit cultural institution in Cleveland asked Iris and me to come in for lunch so they could explain their expansion plans to us. Several weeks later the president invited me to lunch again, at which time he suggested I make a contribution of $50 million! That's one expensive lunch, and I wasn't even that hungry. It seemed to me, at our second meeting there was little justification for requesting such a large donation without trying to understand Iris's and my interests or concerns. After all, the largest gift they had ever received for that project was $14 million. So what made them think I would suddenly become their largest benefactor without ever having been part of the organization?

Fundraisers need to do a much better job of merging the organization's needs with the interests and capabilities of prospective donors, rather than just asking for an amount seemingly plucked out of thin air. From a nonprofit's point of view, fundraising should be considered an art, not unlike establishing relationships within the real estate community or within any other business environment. From the donor's point of view, however, it is a business. We want to buy quality, and to pay what that quality is worth so we can stretch our dollars and use them to have the greatest possible impact on a variety of organizations.

Chapter Eleven

Rx For Cleveland: Taking Pride In My Hometown

The nitty gritty of Heritage Development is still building shopping centers, but there is another, less lucrative part of our business that I take as seriously as any other. We want to make a difference in the City in which I have lived all of my life. It's not as if these projects have a huge financial upside for us personally. From a financial stand-point, we'd be much better off spending our time building more shopping centers, or investing our money in treasury bills for that matter. But we'd like nothing better than to use our knowledge and experience to help revitalize Cleveland.

Unfortunately, Cleveland has rarely made it easy for us or any other developer, especially on the bigger, more ambitious projects. I speak from experience. Despite the successful Renaissance office building that we built on Playhouse Square in 1988, my record for getting things done in Cleveland is not particularly stellar. Remember the Playhouse Square hotel debacle? Or our unsuccessful effort to stop the convocation center and build a downtown arena instead? There have been other lost opportunities along the way as well.

Yet I remain optimistic. I believe there are many ways to increase the vitality of Cleveland. There are a variety of projects, from building a new sports stadium to revitalizing the Flats, that could definitely help Cleveland boost its standing among the list of great American cities. But just as with any business, it takes vision and leadership to accomplish long-term goals.

249

Sports Stadium

We are currently negotiating with the City of Cleveland and Cuya-hoga County to build a 25,000-seat soccer specific stadium in downtown Cleveland. I've already been offered the Cleveland franchise of the MSL (Major Soccer League), and will accept it if I have a new stadium for the franchise to occupy. It would not only accommodate soccer, but also high school and college football and soccer games, and summer concerts. It would provide a major boost to downtown Cleveland. But a project of this sort requires a variety of government incentives in order to make it viable. The City and County seem serious about wanting to work with us. We'll see if they can show the inclination and imagination to make it happen. If the desire is there, the deal could be done in two hours. Everyone knows what needs to be done. The City has done it before with Jacobs Field, Gund Arena, and Browns Stadium.

In this case, Cleveland has a rival, as Summit County has expressed serious interest in helping to build the stadium in the City of Akron. Currently the County is working to identify the best location.

Revitalizing The Flats

Until a few years ago, the Flats was a popular tourist destination along the river. I regularly run into people who haven't been to Cleveland in a few years and still assume it has the same vibrant night life they remember.

There's no reason why the Flats can't return to or exceed its glory years. This time around, we could avoid some of our earlier problems by having control over the types of tenants so that they would share a vision for the entire development rather than just their own businesses.

Something that was once successful can often be successful again, but rebuilding a failure requires examining the reasons for its demise, as well as identifying the changes that have occurred in the intervening years. During the past fifteen years Scott and I have made at least four separate attempts to have the City participate in revitalizing the Flats, but successive city administrations never had the vision to make it happen. In virtually every other city where there has been an opportunity to develop its waterfront, the local government has worked with developers to make it a reality. Just look at Baltimore.

Look around the country and you'll see that progressive cities take control of land, declare it a blighted area, buy it, bulldoze it, and ask developers for proposals for its revitalization. All it would take in Cleveland is a little focus and recognition that each side of the Flats needs a single owner who can control his own destiny. Just as a mall has one owner in charge of security, maintenance, and attracting a certain class of tenants with synergies, the Flats, and any other waterfront property, needs a master plan with a single owner intent on and responsible for its success.

At the moment, the Flats continues to deteriorate, producing no tax revenue or any other benefit to Cleveland. Scott has assumed the responsibility to try to work with Mayor Jane Campbell's administration to move our latest proposal forward. I'll keep my fingers crossed because with the proper cooperation from the City, this prime waterfront property could be transformed from eyesore into destination. It could again become a vibrant downtown attraction that would provide substantial tax revenue to Cleveland.

Just recently, Scott, who has become much more of a Cleveland insider than I'll ever be, started from scratch, presenting the City Council with a detailed master plan for an ambitious $165 million project. It includes 250 residential units and 250,000-square-feet of retail and entertainment space, including a state of the art movie theater. The City will have to use eminent domain to purchase the land Scott and I don't already control. It would then sell the properties to the highest bidder with the best plan, so the purchase wouldn't cost the City anything. The City will also have to agree to some tax increment financing, and to make some infrastructure improvements. Except for a parking garage we hope the Port Authority or Cuyahoga County will build, our proposal has us financing the rest of the $165 million project ourselves.

Collision Bend

Yet another time I ran into deaf ears at City Hall was in the mid 1980s when I became interested in a 55-acre property on the Cuyahoga River called Collision Bend, so called because iron ore freighters have to navigate the sharp turn, sometimes not so successfully. I started negotiating with the majority owner of the property, while at the same time I had plans drawn up for an ambitious project to include more than a hundred residential units and an upscale marina. The project would have been good for the city, totally changing the waterfront area in Cleveland and acting as an important catalyst for other major projects along the river. But I never could get anyone from the City to even take a serious look at it.

Meanwhile, Forest City, another Cleveland developer, stepped in and took control of most of the land around Collision Bend. As an almost knee jerk reaction, I paid $2.5 million for five prime acres along the water in front of their property. I didn't even take an option; I just bought it outright. I thought I could leverage it once Forest City began developing the rest of the area, or perhaps joint venture with them and develop it together. Instead, I paid dearly for breaking my own rule of never buying a piece of property that can't be sold the next day for a higher price. To date, Collision Bend has still not been developed. I've been sitting on my five acres for almost twenty years, making it probably the second worst real estate investment I ever made, after the Hilton Hotel in Toledo.

However, the sun may yet shine on our five acres along Collision Bend. John and I are working on a new plan to build condominiums there. We are presently negotiating with an adjacent property owner to do a joint venture, which ultimately could include 500 residential units and a significant marina. We have hired an architect to prepare some conceptual ideas for the development of residential units along with a marina, and hopefully my foolish investment may yet turn out to be profitable.

Rock and Roll Hall of Fame and Museum

In my opinion, the Rock and Roll Hall of Fame represents another significant missed opportunity by the City, despite the fact that it is a wonderful museum and it's great that it's located in Cleveland. In 1983 Atlantic Records founder and chairman Ahmet Ertegun approached the heads of various record companies with the idea of creating a Rock and Roll Hall of Fame and Museum. Officials from Cleveland and the State of Ohio lobbied Ertegun hard to locate it in Cleveland. They argued that the late disk jockey Alan Freed had coined the term "rock and roll" in 1951 on a Cleveland radio station, and that the Hall of Fame should be located in rock and roll's birthplace. They put an impressive financial package together, as well as an aggressive public relations campaign. It resulted in 660,000 people signing a petition in support of bringing the Museum to Cleveland. In fact, in a *USA Today* poll Cleveland got more than 100,000 votes, far more than its nearest rival. In 1986 the new Rock and Roll Hall of Fame Foundation awarded Cleveland the site, and following an extensive search, world-renowned architect I.M. Pei was chosen to design it.

So far so good. But then City officials dropped the ball. In the first place, they negotiated themselves out of holding the annual induction ceremonies in Cleveland, ceding that right to New York City. That eliminated an extremely valuable publicity and revenue opportunity. An even bigger mistake was their decision to build the museum on a postage stamp size parcel of land along the lake, on the other side of the freeway, isolated from the rest of downtown. I spoke with Ahmet Ertegun by phone and tried to convince him it made absolutely no sense to locate the museum in such an inaccessible spot, far from the hotels, restaurants and retail shops downtown. On a visit to New York I telephoned him again to try to schedule a meeting. I wanted to try one last time to convince him to reconsider his position, but he refused to see me. He told me he had no interest in being part of a large commercial development, and didn't feel they needed the ancillary revenue it would bring.

That turned out to be a big mistake, since through the years the Rock and Roll Hall of Fame and Museum has often had trouble meeting its budget. Instead, try to imagine, for example, the museum as the centerpiece of a thriving commercial development on fifty acres of Collision Bend, along the river. It would have been fantastic for the City and the museum.

But that would have taken entrepreneurial vision. I've never seen a business that would refuse a revenue stream, but city governments don't function like businesses. That's part of the problem. I envisioned a gondola that in the nice weather would take tourists from Tower City across the river to the museum. Since Tower City already attracts tourists because it is the city's transportation nucleus and is filled with hotels, it is the logical feeder of customers to the museum. But I lost that fight too, and the Hall of Fame, while a wonderful idea and opportunity, has in my opinion never fulfilled its promise.

The Need for a Convention Center

Ironically, Collision Bend is currently playing a role in Cleveland's latest demonstration of ineptitude. Every professional city planner says Cleveland desperately needs a convention center, but the City just can't seem to get behind a plan to build one.

In early 2002 Mayor Campbell asked the Cleveland Tomorrow organization, made up of Cleveland area CEOs, to evaluate proposals and recommend a convention center site. The idea was to put a bond issue on the November 2003 ballot. That was the City's first mistake. Cleveland Tomorrow is a fine organization, but in my opinion it is not qualified to choose the ideal site on which to build a huge, complicated project like the kind of convention center Cleveland needs. Comparing the benefits and drawbacks of different convention center sites is an extremely complex task, requiring expertise in a wide range of financial and engineering areas. The City of Cleveland needed to hire an independent consultant–a national expert in this area–rather than rely on a group of businessmen, no matter how well meaning.

So it was no wonder that the competition became a circus and that the entire process was stymied. Part of the problem was that each of the initial four sites were fatally flawed. The site on Lake Erie, for example, just west of Cleveland Browns stadium, would have meant dismantling and moving an active port complex. This would have been an astronomically expensive undertaking that couldn't be accomplished in any reasonable period of time. Besides, why would the City want to build a big box building that would block off prime waterfront property? It's not as if people go to a convention center for the view.

Another proposal was to build adjacent to the existing convention center. Because of a deed restriction that restricts building a structure on top of the mall, the structure would have had to have been buried under ground, cross under Lakeside Avenue, and be cantilevered over the railroad tracks. The roof would have had to be built to withstand the tremendous stress of the weight of the soil and trees on top, as well as the hydrostatic pressure from water pressing against the walls and roof. This would have made construction wildly expensive. It also would have required tearing down several existing office buildings, including the County administration building. Others would have to have been seized under eminent domain, followed by the relocation and compensation of tenants. Even after all this effort and expense, there would still have been no room for parking or staging (the loading and unloading large trucks).

Another proposal was to tie a new convention center into the old Erieview Tower and Galleria on 13th Street. This site was considered unrealistic by most everyone because the developers didn't even own the land that would be needed, and a complicated eminent domain process would have been required to make it work. The road pattern in and out of the center would also have created a mess.

Then there was the site spanning West Third and Sixth Street, near Public Square, running west into the warehouse district. This is the plan that was favored by both Forest City and former Indians owner Richard Jacobs because it would connect directly to their other down-town projects—Forest City's Tower City Center complex and Jacobs' Marriott at Key Center. But this was probably the most unrealistic proposal of them all, since it would have placed a huge box between the fast developing warehouse district and the rest of downtown.

Once it was clear this proposal was going nowhere, Forest City came up with another plan to build the convention center at the back of Tower City. It would have meant building a 75-foot tower of park-ing garages and ramps, on top of which would be perched the con-vention center, leaving no room for staging, very limited parking, and no possibility for expansion. Traffic would have been a nightmare, and the huge trucks would have had to wind around narrow ramps to make deliveries.

To make this plan more appealing, Forest City sweetened it to include residential apartments to be built on fifty or so acres across the river, along Collision Bend. Their proposal, however, included the giant escape clause, "if market conditions so warrant." Ironically, in order to put this development on the waterfront, Forest City would have to buy the five acres of water front exposure owned by one Bart Wolstein.

Norfolk Southern

As John and I became increasingly convinced that all the convention center proposals were unrealistic, destined never to get chosen, we op-tioned a 50-acre site from the Norfolk Southern Railroad Company just across the highway from Jacobs Field, where the Cleveland Indi-ans baseball team plays. The Westin chain agreed to participate with us in a 650-room hotel to be connected to the convention center by a glass-enclosed atrium that would include restaurants and shops.

Ours was the only site, nestled between two freeways, which would not have created chaos downtown, either during construction or during staging. It was also the only site large enough to allow for future expansion. Unlike the other proposals, we would have built the center ourselves and leased it back to the city. We made it clear that

all the details, including the amount of the annual lease, were nego-
tiable. We were even willing to consider a plan whereby the City
would own the center after twenty-five years. The last time a private
developer offered to build such a major public project in the Cleveland area was thirty years ago, when Nick Miletti built the Richfield
Coliseum in the suburbs after his downtown proposal was rejected.

John and I spent more than $300,000 to put together our pro-
posal, including commissioning detailed architectural plans by Gino
Rossetti, the same architect we had used a decade earlier to design
our proposal for a downtown arena. But once again we never got a
serious airing from the City.

In June 2003 Cleveland Tomorrow recommended putting the
convention center behind Tower City, and as a fall back on the site of
the existing convention center. Almost immediately the Cuyahoga
County Commissioners and the City of Cleveland began feuding
about the amount of the tax levy and how it would be divided. The
issue was never put to a public referendum as required before any
proposal can move forward, and it does not seem likely that convention center will be built in Cleveland any time soon.

Dealmakers Needed

The paralysis concerning choosing a convention center site is just the
latest example of political paralysis in Cleveland. In my experience
over the last fifty years, each of the eight City administrations has
lacked the leadership and vision to take the actions necessary to revitalize downtown and make it competitive with other cities. In my
mind, the biggest problem is that there's no single person in either
the business community or the political arena who everyone looks up
to as someone who can make things happen. There's no forum to
even have an interesting discussion. Politicians are too eager to pass
the buck by trying to make decisions by polling numbers or public
referendum. Leaders are elected to lead, not to take a survey before
making every tough decision.

Cleveland needs to be run as a business. If the City were run like
a public company, it would be a booming success story, because every
day its employees would come to work and make things happen. The
City certainly owns valuable assets, but our political leaders don't
seem to know how to exploit them. The naysayers who say tourists
will never come to Cleveland are wrong. Cleveland has more to offer

than most cities its size. We don't need to compete with New York, Chicago, Las Vegas, or Miami. Our competition is the likes of Nashville, Columbus, Cincinnati, Minneapolis, Pittsburgh and Detroit. In addition to both the lake and river waterfronts, Cleveland has first class art museums, the Rock and Roll Hall of Fame, the Playhouse Square theatres, and one of the world's most renown orchestras playing in a remodeled, state-of-the-art symphony hall. We also have professional football, basketball, and baseball teams.

What Cleveland needs is a heavy dose of entrepreneurial leadership and vision. City leaders and managers need to have the same drive and focus as they would if they were running a for-profit company. The Mayor of Cleveland needs to be a dealmaker. I like the way Raymond Pierce, whom I supported for Mayor in 2001, puts it: "People should be making deals in every room in City Hall. If you're not making deals, you shouldn't work there." But not only does there seem to be a lack of dealmakers in City Hall, it's not even clear who we should talk to about a creative project. Mayors and City planners from various suburbs call John and I regularly, inviting us to meet with them to discuss how to boost development in their towns and cities. But never have we received a similar call from anyone in Cleveland.

If I were running Cleveland as a business, I wouldn't sit and wait for the phone to ring. I would organize a sales team and develop plans to revitalize individual streets and communities, using tax credits or abatements or federal funding or whatever it takes to create economic activity. Cleveland's politicians always talk about having to do things in the neighborhoods, rather than downtown. But before you can improve people's environments, you have to find them jobs. Only then can they buy homes and build communities. Only then can the City, with federal help, make deals to build parks and playgrounds so that the residents in neighborhoods have a place to raise their children, and modern shopping centers so they aren't being gouged by independent grocers.

Cleveland needs creative ideas, and creative leaders to carry them out. As a one-newspaper town, the *Cleveland Plain Dealer* should also be a much more forceful voice for change, Much too often it is simply satisfied with the status quo. Take Cleveland's lakefront, another area for which the City has never developed a plan. So many times, from so many different politicians, I've heard, "Oh, we can't move Burke Lakefront Airport, the FAA would never allow it." But that's nonsense. There's just never been the will to look at the big picture and focus on getting it done. The Lakefront Airport takes up more than

200 acres right downtown along the waterfront that could be used for condominiums, parks, or establishing an entirely new community.

We need to think out of the box. Just recently, for example, there was a proposal in the legislature to put slot machines in the race-tracks, a terrible idea because it would take money from those people who can least afford it. Instead, why can't the City and State think bigger and bolder? If they believe that legalized gambling is a way to create economic development and additional tax revenue for education, why not instead invite one of the large Las Vegas casino operators to build an upscale casino in downtown Cleveland? It could be an entertainment Mecca with restaurants, hotels and shops along the river that would generate substantial tax revenue and many thousands of jobs. And as part of the price of doing business, why couldn't Cleveland insist that the casino operator build an adjoining hotel and convention center? That would be another way to get a convention center built using private funds. Some people argue that legalized casinos would only encourage people of modest means to gamble, but that's just what putting slot machines at race tracks would do. Besides, there are casinos in virtually every adjoining state to Ohio and also in Canada. If people want to gamble, they can get in their car and drive to a casino.

Attracting Companies to Cleveland

When Iris and I were married in 1948 Cleveland's population topped 900,000. Today it's less than 500,000. Cleveland has fewer hotel rooms today than it did in 1940, and has experienced a similar exodus of corporate headquarters. In my fifty years of observation, there has never been a solid master plan for the revitalization of downtown Cleveland. We've just sat and watched as one corporation after another has fled to the suburbs or, more often, other states. I'm not saying Fortune 500 companies are going to move back to Cleveland, but we could set our sights on mid size companies, or regional offices.

Cleveland needs an entrepreneurial leader who will create an aggressive master plan to attract people and businesses. Bringing companies back to Cleveland is no different than getting people to a soccer game or to a hotel or to join country club. The Force, Glenmoor, and the Bertram Inn are successful because Iris and I made it our business to make them successful. We had a plan, and are continuously focused on coming up with ways to implement and supplement that plan. Corporate executives don't wake up in the morning and say they are going to move to Cleveland. They have to be courted aggressively. The City could *give away* land for corporate headquarters and still come out way ahead. There's never been the necessary effort on the part of politicians to make it happen, and maybe that's because they don't know how.

It's not brain surgery; it's just common sense. You don't have to reinvent the wheel. If you want to have a successful downtown, just look at what other cities have done. Chicago didn't put their stadium or a new museum on the water, inaccessible to hotels and restaurants. They put residential units on the water so that people would move in and then the restaurants and hotels would follow. There must be more undeveloped waterfront property in downtown Cleveland than in any other city in the United States. It doesn't have to be that way.

Changing the Face of Downtown and Building a New Airport

In order to attract commerce to Cleveland, most everyone agrees that the City is missing at least two important ingredients—a first class airport and a convention center. Without these two entities, revitalization will always be hampered.

We used to have the best airport in the region, but sixty years later we have the same airport with a few Band-Aids. The last six City administrations have responded to the need for expansion and modernization with patchwork remedies, smoothing over problems rather than creating long-term solutions. Instead, we should have followed the example of so many other cities like Tampa, Orlando, Pittsburgh, Detroit, and Cincinnati and rebuilt the airport from scratch. If Continental Airlines were ever to pull its hub out of Cleveland, Cleveland Hopkins Airport would become little more than a commuter airport, serving a major blow to the City's efforts to compete with comparable cities. Without a first class airport serving every major U.S. city with nonstop flights, it will be very difficult to encourage companies to move to Cleveland or to encourage those already here to stay.

The City needs to think creatively about its airport *and* a new convention center. To do that, it needs to invite innovative proposals from all sectors of the community. For example, I recently suggested an idea that would have combined the building of a new convention center with the expansion or rebuilding of the airport. But again, we never could get anyone from the City to focus on it.

The IX Center, with more than a million square feet of exhibit space, is the ninth largest convention/trade show center in North America. It held more than 30 multiple-day events in 2003. It is located fourteen miles from downtown Cleveland, near the airport. The City recently bought the IX Center from Ray Park, but gave him a long-term lease to operate it. Cleveland now wants to break Park's lease early so it can tear down the building and expand the airport. But Park isn't willing to shut down a successful exhibit hall. He feels an obligation to the hundreds of employees who work there.

Park also owns a company that dismantles steels mills. The International Steel Group (ISG), in turn, owns the steel mills that still line the Cuyahoga River in downtown Cleveland. The City could have asked Park, in concert with Heritage Development or some other developer, to buy the 125-acre site that ISG has put up for sale. Park's company could have dismantled the mills, and a developer could have built a multiuse facility on the ISG site, combining the IX Center and a convention center into one large building. Park could have joint ventured to design and build the new facility, which could have been leased to the City, which in turn could have leased it back to Park. The 1.6 million-square-foot building would have been about four times the size of any of the existing convention center proposals, and flexible enough to accommodate both large trade shows and more intimate conventions.

This would have solved everyone's problem. Park will eventually lose his lease on the IX Center anyway, and it would have guaranteed the jobs of his employees. He would have turned the existing IX center over to the City like they wanted, which would have solved the City's two-fold problem of how to expand or build a new airport or expand their runways, and how best to build a convention center.

This is just one example of how just a little creativity in Cleveland could go a long way toward solving its most important problems. But it would take an entrepreneurial attitude on the part of City Hall, something I haven't yet seen.

Postscript:
Self Employed and Loving It

W hen I left the public company, I went back to being on my own again. I actually had a physical response to being free of the shackles of working at a giant public company. A weight had been lifted from my shoulders; a bounce had returned to my step. Clichés, I know, but that's how I felt.

In retrospect, the real loss was not what could have been, but the four years I had spent unable to do my own thing. Not being in charge of the new Developers Diversified Realty Corporation may have been a blow to my ego, but was it the worst thing in the world? It may have seemed like it at the time, but of course it wasn't. Perhaps starting up again on my own was inevitable. Maybe I never would have been happy at the public company no matter what my title or authority. I am, after all, an entrepreneur at heart.

In this case, being "on my own again" meant being back in partnership with John McGill. I think John and I share the same hunger. Growing up poor, we are both driven by the desire to succeed. For us, success has resulted from working hard, and has been fueled by the knowledge that we have no fall back strategy if we fail.

We also feed on each other's enthusiasm, which means never putting down the other's ideas, no matter how far out they might seem at first. Together we try to explore reasons why a project *can* work, not why it *won't* work. We also allow each other to take a proposal as far as it can go until it reaches its own natural conclusion. Over the years I think I've convinced John that given time, decisions have a way of taking a natural course toward an inevitable conclusion.

We also don't let our egos get involved in the decision making process, so we've never had a dispute over authorship. I don't even care about being right; I want my company's decisions to be right. I've always told the people who work with me that I'd rather be the publisher than the author. You can have fifty authors, but as the publisher you reap the benefit of all of them. You can only write one book at a time (which is difficult enough, as I've now experienced firsthand), but you can *publish* many books simultaneously.

A New Niche

In June 1999, once John and I had become equal partners in the Heritage Development Corporation, we began to take advantage of our relationships among the nation's top retailers to jump right back into the shopping center business, building centers in Maryland, Pennsylvania, Florida, Ohio, and several other states. We also created a new niche for ourselves by purchasing under performing malls around the country, tearing them down, and starting over with new tenants.

Our first turnaround was a mall in Baltimore that we bought from Simon Properties. I go way back with Mel and Herb Simon, who took their real estate company public a few months after DDR. Since then Simon Properties has become the largest owner of malls in the United States. The Simons also own the Indiana Pacers basketball team.

Simon Properties was divesting itself of some of its poorer performing developments, and we took the Golden Ring mall off their hands. It had deteriorated badly after a new mall had been built just a few miles away. But John and I liked the location, at the intersection of Interstate 695 and the Pulaski Highway. We tore it and the adjoining parking deck down, and developed a new Sam's Club, Wal-Mart, and Home Depot, as well as a number of out lots which we leased to smaller retailers. We purchased an empty building next door, a former Montgomery Ward store, from Kimco, which we gutted and then subdivided and filled with more than twenty national retailers, including Office Depot and Petco. The Golden Ring is now a thriving 400,000-square-foot retail complex. We're just finishing a similar turnaround at another property we purchased from Simon, also outside of Baltimore, and one in Johnstown, Pennsylvania that we bought from Lehman Brothers.

John and I are back in business, working with some of the largest real estate companies in the United States and taking on a number of new challenges. In Garfield Heights, Ohio, for example, we've been asked to build a shopping center on a landfill. It's a complicated job, but John and the engineers we've hired have figured out a way to do it, and the project is moving forward. This is a $70 million, 750,000-square-foot retail project, expected to also include almost a million square feet of office space.

Opening Up Our Books

John and I have a number of other proposals on the drawing board. The president of CWRU, for example, asked us to develop a project it has been trying to get off the ground for years, to turn a parking lot owned by the non-profit group, University Circle Inc. (UCI), into a multiuse facility. It turned out that UCI, charged with implementing a master plan for Cleveland's University Circle area, was being unrealistic about the value of its real estate. It had been trying to ground lease the land at annual rates that bore no relation to what the market warranted, which is why developers had been walking away from the project.

Working the numbers backwards, we showed UCI that the long-term lease it was asking for was about three times what could be supported by the projected revenue from the residential and retail space being planned. The key to persuading UCI to reduce its price was opening up our books to present them with the numbers that made our case. We showed them exactly how we had backed into what we considered a fair land lease, based on the current market rents for both residential and commercial properties in the area, as well as a reasonable return on our investment.

This has always been an important part of our business strategy. We're not afraid to open our books to property owners or potential joint venture partners because we're not trying to pull anything over on anyone.

We expect to begin construction in the Fall of 2004 on a ten-story complex on the campus of CWRU that will include 200 apartments, an underground garage, and 6,000 square feet of ground floor retail space that will include the college bookstore.

Won't Be Stretched Too Thinly Again

From experience, John and I have learned that big is not necessarily best. In the old days, we had our own leasing department and a staff of in-house attorneys and accountants. At one point in the 1970s and early 1980s I had almost one hundred people working for me, including more than a dozen people just looking for land. That worked well during the boom years, when almost any development proved profitable. But I learned that it's easy to get big; it's much more difficult to get small. During the commercial credit crisis of 1988, and then again in the early 1990s, our high overhead was one of the factors that contributed to our financial difficulties. I wasn't going to go through that again.

This time, John and I have vowed to keep Heritage Development lean and our overhead low, no matter how busy we get. Including John and I and our two secretaries, Heritage Development employs only sixteen people, including four project managers and four people in the accounting department. We outsource services as we need them. Instead of hiring our own attorneys or real estate personnel, we now have outside firms at our beck and call. We may pay slightly more than we would if these people were on our staff, or if we managed the centers we own ourselves, but we also only pay for what we need. We never have to worry about being forced to carry underutilized personnel. No more bloated payroll structure, dependant on a never-ending growth curve to survive. Our new strategy also eliminates reporting levels, so decisions get made by either me or John immediately. And we have found no drop-off in quality. Quite the contrary, in fact. We give the accountants, lawyers and real estate brokers with whom we work a lot of business over the course of a year. They know that in return we expect them to do whatever it takes to meet deadlines and to perform up to a certain standard.

Finally Florida

At the same time we keep a lean operation in Ohio, we also recently opened an office in Florida. Florida has been a chief bugaboo of mine because I've always regretted abandoning the state. In fact, I reluctantly stopped doing business in Florida on two separate occasions. In both cases we had stuck around only long enough to see that it was ripe with opportunities, particularly compared to the slow growth in Ohio and other Midwestern states.

The first time I left Florida was when I was developing sites for Kmart. I had just gotten my feet wet there when my contacts at Kmart encouraged me instead to move into the Midwest to pursue the company's strategy of building smaller stores in midsize markets. I reluctantly agreed because at the time Kmart was pretty much Developer Diversified's only client. We hadn't yet figured out that there were other retailers interested in expanding their presence into a fast-growing state like Florida.

John and I returned to Florida in the mid 1980s and developed a number of sites into substantial shopping centers. But then we abandoned Florida again when we went public because DDR wanted to focus only on major metropolitan markets.

Of all the growth areas, Florida is the one we know best and the one close enough for us to easily monitor. Arizona, Nevada, and California are simply too far away. Besides, Lady Iris is docked in Palm Beach, so I'm in Florida frequently in the winter anyway.

Some of the properties we are now looking at in Florida include large areas for office buildings and residential units, both single family homes and apartments. Our strategy is to stick with what we know by building the shopping centers ourselves and, after building the roads and infrastructure, sell the improved land to other builders who will construct residential units and office space. On the largest sites, we may even seek to partner with a major residential developer. These days most sellers are insisting on 100 percent cash up front, which limits the number of parcels Heritage Development can acquire at one time.

I don't think we can miss in Florida, and we've already begun amassing inventory there. We currently have letters of intent on a half dozen significant properties with a total land cost of about $350 million, on which we are proposing developments costing well over $2 billion.

Back on the DDR Board

Although I will always have some regrets and even some hard feelings about my exit from DDR, I rejoined its board of directors in 2002. The company has done very well during the eleven years since it went public, and that's a credit to Scott and the management team. Its earnings per share have quadrupled, and its stock price has more than tripled, dramatically outperforming the overall stock market. DDR's assets have grown fifteen times, to well over $8 billion. It has clearly established itself as the nation's leading developer, owner, and manager of large market dominant community shopping centers. It recently completed a $350 million IPO in Australia, creating a company on the Australian Stock exchange to co-invest with DDR in the United States.

I take great personal pride in DDR's performance and accomplishments, both as a founder and as a father. As a member of its board, I will try to assure that the company never loses sight of where it came from and never fully abandons the entrepreneurial spirit that made it great. While I am well aware of the complexities of running a large public company, many of the simple rules still apply. If you can create value by developing great properties whose investment returns exceed your cost of capital, that can't be bad.

Never Slowing Down

At 76, I haven't slowed down. I guess I don't know how to slow down. I wake up every morning before 6:00 a.m. to do an hour of exercise, and arrive in the office around 8:30 a.m. I run Glenmoor and the Bertram Inn, and John and I review together every investment before Heritage Development Company moves forward on it. I also spend a lot of time evaluating proposals by charitable organizations.

By delegating authority, I have plenty of time to enjoy myself. Iris and I are certainly enjoying our six grandchildren–Kimberly, Tiffany, Harrison, Ilana, Shelby, and Merrick. We were at the hospital when each one of them was born, and we take advantage of being able to spend time with them.

After all these years, I find myself in a state of limbo of sorts, neither an outsider nor an insider. On one hand, I still don't serve on any public company boards except for DDR, or on any important municipal business committees. On the other hand, I see my name in the paper more than I ever did. I am constantly called for advice by not only nonprofit organizations and business people, but also mayors and other city officials from around the Cleveland area. Perhaps I've settled into a third category of my own making, neither insider nor an outsider, but one who hovers mysteriously between the two.

All of this is certainly keeping Iris and me busy. I don't have time to look backwards. But if I did, I would remember the events that changed my life. I'd remember growing up on the wrong side of Taylor Road, and learning in the Navy that hard work is rewarded. I'd be thankful for my legal education, which gave me confidence that I knew things others did not, and for the real education I received from Uncle Sol. I'd recall my refusal to fail in Twinsburg, and the lesson that the fear of failure is a great motivator. I'd recognize my good fortune in hooking up with Kmart and the Young brothers. I would also remember the thrill of working with my son, and the wonderful ride he, Iris, and I had with the Cleveland Force. I'd reflect on the difficult times too, when employees I believed were loyal betrayed me, or the jolt I received after going public. I would also remember doing things as a family, both blood and business, and of the pleasure of doing great things with them and becoming a philanthropist.

Mostly, I would think of Iris, the partner who has been by my side every day as I've crossed over to the other side of Taylor Road.

Index

page numbers in bold indicate photographs